MW00812957

TRANSFORMATIVE SCHOOLING

Discussions of achievement gaps are commonplace in education reform, but they are rarely interrogated as a symptom of white supremacy. As an act of disruption, award-winning scholar Vajra Watson pierces through the rhetoric and provides a provocative analysis of the ways schools can become more racially inclusive. Her research is grounded in Oakland where longitudinal data demonstrated that Black families were sending their children to school, but the ideals of an oasis of learning were being met with the realities of racism, low expectations, and marginalization. As a response to this intergenerational crisis of miseducation, in 2010, the school district joined forces with community organizers, religious leaders, neighborhood elders, teachers, parents, and students to address institutionalized racism.

Seven years later, Watson shares findings from her investigation into the school district's journey towards justice. What she creates is a wholly original work, filled with penetrating portraits that illuminate the intense and intimate complexities of working towards racial equity in education. As a formidable case study, this research scrutinizes how to reconfigure organizational ecosystems as spaces that humanize, heal, and harmonize. Emerging from her scholarship is a bold, timely, and hopeful vision that paves the way for transformative schooling.

Vajra M. Watson is the Director of Research and Policy for Equity at UC Davis and the founder of Sacramento Area Youth Speaks (SAYS). As a scholar-activist, Dr. Watson seeks innovative ways to align people and systems that advance social justice. Watson received her B.A. from UC Berkeley, and holds her doctorate from the Graduate School of Education at Harvard University.

TRANSFORMATIVE SCHOOLING

Towards Racial Equity in Education

Vajra M. Watson

Routledge
Taylor & Francis Group

NEW YORK AND LONDON

First published 2018
by Routledge
711 Third Avenue, New York, NY 10017

and by Routledge
2 Park Square, Milton Park, Abingdon, Oxon, OX14 4RN

Routledge is an imprint of the Taylor & Francis Group, an informa business

© 2018 Taylor & Francis

The right of Vajra M. Watson to be identified as author of this work has been
asserted by her in accordance with sections 77 and 78 of the Copyright,
Designs and Patents Act 1988.

All rights reserved. No part of this book may be reprinted or reproduced or
utilised in any form or by any electronic, mechanical, or other means, now
known or hereafter invented, including photocopying and recording, or in any
information storage or retrieval system, without permission in writing from
the publishers.

Trademark notice: Product or corporate names may be trademarks or registered
trademarks, and are used only for identification and explanation without intent
to infringe.

Library of Congress Cataloging-in-Publication Data
Names: Watson, Vajra, author.
Title: Transformative schooling towards racial equity in education /
Vajra M. Watson.
Description: New York, NY: Routledge, 2018. | Includes bibliographical
references and index.
Identifiers: LCCN 2017035671 | ISBN 9781138106987 (hbk: alk. paper) |
ISBN 9781138107007 (pbk: alk. paper) | ISBN 9781315101309 (ebk)
Subjects: LCSH: Educational equalization—California—Oakland. | Educational
change—California—Oakland. | Education, Urban—California—Oakland |
Discrimination in education—California—Oakland. |
Community and school—California—Oakland.
Classification: LCC LC213.23.O34 W37 2018 | DDC 379.2/60979466—dc23
LC record available at https://lccn.loc.gov/2017035671

ISBN: 978-1-138-10698-7 (hbk)
ISBN: 978-1-138-10700-7 (pbk)
ISBN: 978-1-315-10130-9 (ebk)

Typeset in Bembo
by Deanta Global Publishing Services, Chennai, India

Even with all the words imaginable, I cannot piece together a sentence that expresses my eternal love for the both of you. Tsadiku and Adiyah, I give thanks and praise to The Most High for the gift of being your mother.

CONTENTS

FOREWORD

The vulnerability of Black males and the risks they face as a result have been particularly evident in education for many years. On all of the indicators of academic achievement, educational attainment, and school success, African American males are distinguished from other segments of the American population by their consistent clustering in categories associated with failure and marginalization. They are overrepresented among students who are disciplined, suspended, and expelled, and underrepresented among those in honors and advanced placement courses or labeled as gifted. These are not new patterns. In fact, these patterns have been in place in schools throughout the United States for so long that in most places the problem has been normalized and accepted as an unfortunate aspect of the status quo.

This was the case in Oakland when I began teaching there in 1981. As a young Black man who was available twice a week to be hired as a substitute teacher (I was also a full-time graduate student at UC Berkeley), I was frequently assigned to work in some of the toughest middle schools in the City: King Estates, Frick, Havens Court, Elmhurst, Madison Park, and Lowell. I learned early on that because I was a Black man it was assumed that I would have more success in working with Black male students who were almost always framed as a "problem." I also learned that I could not count on an absent teacher leaving me a lesson plan or expect the principal to be effective in leading the school.

Despite the challenges I faced as a sub, I learned to love the job. Traveling by bus across Oakland in search of the school where I had been assigned for the day turned out to be a great way to learn about the community. As a native New Yorker, I was struck by the fact that much of Oakland, particularly the East and West sections, were nothing like the neighborhoods where I grew up in

Brownsville, Brooklyn, Harlem, and the South Bronx. Instead of large housing projects there were neat, middle-class homes with yards. The styles worn by my students were different (there were lots of boys and girls with geri curls and hairnets in the 1980s), but in many ways, they were not unlike kids I'd grown up with: tough exteriors, but warm, funny and friendly once you got to know them. Having taught previously in tough schools such as Providence, R. I., I quickly learned how to concoct lesson plans that would engage my students, allow me to get to know them a bit, and get me through the day without too much stress.

During the two years I worked as a substitute teacher, and later as a researcher for three years at Lowell Middle School in West Oakland, I gained firsthand insights into the challenges confronting Black male students in Oakland Public Schools. I broke up numerous fights, I took over classrooms where beleaguered teachers cried out for help because they didn't know what to do, and I worked with community members to counsel students whom we thought were at greatest risk. On several occasions, I met with superintendents, school board members, and principals about what should be done, but despite what seemed like genuine concern over discipline problems and subpar academic performance that plagued Black male students, nothing creative or effective was done to address the dire situation.

Finally, the dismal status quo facing Black males in Oakland became a priority when Dr. Tony Smith was appointed superintendent in 2010. Shortly after arriving, Smith launched the Office of African American Male Achievement (AAMA), and appointed Christopher Chatmon to serve as its director. I met with Chris shortly after his appointment and we discussed the immensity of the challenges he would face in this new role. I let him know that I was skeptical about what could be accomplished by a single person with few resources and no real authority over principals or teachers. Still, I was happy to see that something was being done and impressed by the enthusiasm and vision that Chris brought to the new job.

Over the years, I heard reports about the work being done by AAMA in Oakland under Chris's leadership but my doubts about what could be accomplished remained. Tony Smith left as superintendent after four years, and while the new replacement seemed to embrace AAMA, the district as a whole seemed rudderless. In beset by numerous challenges, I wondered what Chris and his colleagues could accomplish to prioritize the needs of Black male students.

A few years later, I learned that Dr. Vajra Watson, a friend and former student, had been hired to evaluate the AAMA program and to document its impact. I was delighted by the news. For several years, Vajra had earned a reputation as a leading "equity warrior" because of the powerful work she has done through Sacramento Area Youth Speaks (SAYS). Vajra brought a laser-like focus on equity and her vast array of skills as a researcher to the project and to this important new book. Unlike typical evaluators who attempt to utilize an objective scholarly stance to conduct a dispassionate assessment of a project or program, Vajra made her commitments to the goals of AAMA clear from the outset. Like Chris Chatmon and the others who carry out this work in Oakland, Vajra Watson was motivated to undertake the research on the AAMA because she understands the critical need to make a difference for the young men served by this initiative. As the reader will see, her commitments to equity do not prevent her from drawing attention to findings that help the reader to understand why this program has been so successful. Through the use of portraiture, a methodological practice she honed to great effect in her first book – *Learning to Liberate* (Routledge 2012), Watson is able to capture the details that make it possible for AAMA to have a positive impact on the lives and the education of the young people it serves.

For those who have grown tired of hearing about the problems facing Black males, who are no longer interested in hearing the litany of failures in urban public schools, and who long to hear about solutions to these and other complex social and educational issues, this book will be a breath of fresh air. Written with passion and intelligence, Dr. Vajra Watson has presented her readers with a book that will be an invaluable resource for educators, parents, and policymakers who seek to use education as a means to solve and address some of the challenges facing Black males in America today.

During my years as a teacher in Oakland, I and other educators would have benefited from having access to a book like this one and the insights it contains. I recall, on one occasion in particular, meeting with the principal at a West Oakland middle school about how to address the needs of her most "at-risk" students. During our conversation she noted with a sense of resignation that all of her most troubled students were Black and male. Drawing upon her experience as an educator for several decades, she shared her belief that what these students needed was guidance from caring adults. She also acknowledged that her teachers needed guidance in how to forge caring relationships with her Black male students because too many of them were antagonistic or felt threatened and afraid of the students they were supposed to help.

Now that *Transformative Schooling* has been published and released that principal and many others may find some comfort in knowing that this book can serve as a resource for tackling the complex issues facing Black males and the schools they attend. As Vajra shows us, there are no easy or simple answers to the challenges facing African American males, but there are strategies and approaches that can indeed make a difference. Vajra identifies these and illuminates why they work as she documents the impact they have upon Black male students. In so doing, she helps us all to move beyond blame and critique to begin thinking creatively and constructively about what can be done. For that reason I think of this book as a gift and, as one of the many who will benefit from it, I thank Vajra Watson for the labor of love that produced it.

Pedro Noguera
Distinguished Professor, Graduate School of Education
and Information Studies, UCLA

PREFACE

The Person behind the Pen

Research is not a stand-alone mirror of reality, but a kaleidoscope that is comprised of tiny fragments of mirrors and shards of colored glass that, when pointed towards the light, reflect off of one another forming magical patterns. The person who holds the kaleidoscope is meaningful because what gets included is as important as what gets omitted. And with the slightest turn of the wrist, the final image can change altogether. Irrespective of methodology, researchers make significant decisions that inevitably inform the hue of colors that take shape to inform the findings. As a process of scientific inquiry, I used each person's frame of reference, including my own, to shape—but not solely reflect—the final picture that composes this book, *Transformative Schooling: Towards Racial Equity in Education*.

Before delving into the heart of the work, I offer myself up for scrutiny. Even though I am not the focus of the research, I am, like all scholars, a part of the investigation. Even when my voice is not pronounced, I am here, inside the study, navigating the terrain. To deny my positionality throughout the process would be a misnomer, disingenuous, and invalid. As a white female researcher my identity is inextricably linked to this investigation into Black male achievement. As with all studies—qualitative and quantitative alike—it is vital to ask: w*ho is the person behind the pen*?

We all have pivotal steppingstones which, brought together, comprise the journey of our lives. For me, a significant number of these moments took place at school. In the first grade, my father became enraged that Mrs. Slider tried to claim that Christopher Columbus "discovered" a land that was fully inhabited and civilized. I remember him explaining to me that my teacher was an ignorant liar. This same teacher then told me I was slow and might be held back because I could not read. I learned to sound out letters just to spite her and everything she stood for. Then there were those first weeks of the second grade when I announced I wanted everyone to call me Jennifer so that I would fit in. Thankfully, I just couldn't deal with the façade and went back to being Vajra. In the seventh grade when my friends were doing I-Search papers in social studies class about dolphins and other topics I found obscure, I was desperate to know, *why does racism exist?* I remember going to the Berkeley Public Library on a quest and the librarian handed me an array of books, from Gandhi's memoir to James Banks' *Multiethnic Education*. At this stage, I continued to examine racism as a phenomenon of marginalization (the colonized), without a critical understanding of the ways it interlocks with privilege (the colonizer). Although I benefited from structural racism, I did not see it.

I began explicitly examining whiteness when my classmate in eighth grade, Lydell Wilson, wanted me to comprehend that the white man is the devil. I listened to his claim and then I told him he was not a real Muslim. So he told me to go read *The Autobiography of Malcolm X* and *The Fire Next Time*. I did go read these books and, with a bratty, pale-skinned-privilege, spent lunchtimes and school dances debating Lydell about the oneness of humanity and his misdirected perspective.

Then, in the ninth grade, a life-altering moment changed my course. In 1992, I was in the first de-tracked English class at Berkeley High School. My teacher was a gay white male in his late forties who reveled in European literature and the canon. When Mr. B would insist on the inherent value of Eurocentric texts, my classmate, Lance X, would grunt and speak things under his breath about the insidiousness of the readings. One day, Lance was absent. And on that particular day, another student, Eva, took it upon herself to raise her hand right in the middle of the lesson to broadcast the following question: "What's wrong with that boy who sits over there?" With a sour expression spewed across her face, she pointed at Lance's empty chair. I found her indignation rather appalling and I assumed the teacher would quickly curtail the conversation. But that is not what happened. For the rest of the class period, everyone was talking recklessly about Lance. Mr. B was fueling the discussion with his own hurtful comments; he also called on students who were ridiculing Lance because he was in the Nation of Islam. Mr. B was quick to call on me the second my hand went up to speak. "What I will not do," I chimed, "is talk about someone behind their back. How dare you disrespect someone who is not present to defend himself? You're all weak for that, especially you, Mr. B! I can see now what Lance is talking about. White people are evil. And everyone else is just lost. I'm outta here!" I got up and walked out. Up until that point, I never understood whiteness as wickedness; my perspective transformed on that school day.

From that moment onward, I changed my schedule around and enrolled in the Black Studies and Xicana/o Studies Departments. At that time, Berkeley High School had the only such departments in the nation. All of my A-G courses (except math and science) were fulfilled inside the walls of these spaces.

I entered these classrooms with a little trepidation and a lot of curiosity; I devoured the readings, did all my homework, and was determined to learn. In my Xicana/o literature class, like all my classes that semester, I was the only white student. This, however, did not stop me from owning the space and filling the classroom with my voice and presence. Mr. Melgoza would ask a question and like a rocket, my hand would shoot into the air. It was a pattern—one that I was completely unaware of at that time. One day, Mr. Melgoza asked me if I spoke Spanish. I told him I did not. The next day and for the rest of the school year, all of our readings and class discussions would be in Spanish. Mr. Melgoza called on me to read a passage from the text. I was reluctant, but he encouraged me to make the effort. It was extremely painful; I incorrectly sounded out words and some of the students laughed at me. When Mr. Melgoza asked us to discuss a topic, I was made speechless.

Many things transpired in that space that fundamentally shaped my experience with my self, my skin, and the world around me. In my silence, I began to learn what it means to be white. I began to see that even before my birth, I was bred to embody my race and own space. Mr. Melgoza showed this to me when he shifted the power dynamic. I watched as my classmates literally came alive; the classroom finally belonged to them. I had assumed they did not know the answers or care about the texts we were reading; I soon discovered that was not the issue. The root cause, in many respects, was my bravado. While whiteness was making me invincible in school it was making others invisible.

These realizations led me into the following school year with a bit more common sense, self-awareness, and collective consciousness. Although I had a long way to go—and still do—I was becoming more awake to the ways I perpetuate white supremacy.

After a month of never speaking a word in Mr. Davis' African American History class, it was my turn to present. I walked to the podium holding *The Nigger Bible* (de Coy, 1967). I read a radical excerpt and gave a short presentation on the evils and fallacies of whiteness and the making of "the Negro." I talked about one of my sweet aunties who called walnuts "nigger nuts." I shared every racist moment I could muster from memory to unveil the manipulative nature of white supremacy. I laid it all out on the line. I gave my most sincere modern-day testimony that slavery did not end, but only shape-shifted like a ghost: still ever-present, undeniable, yet hard to pinpoint. Mr. Davis started jumping up and down; he even ran out of the room and back again. He said he did not know it, but he had been waiting for a student like me. The feeling was mutual and, after I graduated from Berkeley High (1996), I returned to work in the Black Studies Department. Altogether, I spent nearly every weekday for seven years under the tutelage of Hodari B. Davis.

Inside the Black Studies Department, I discovered a home for social justice education. I was pushed, challenged, and given a mind-blowing education. While my peers in other parts of the school were reading *To Kill a Mockingbird* and *Romeo and Juliet*, I was devouring *The Destruction of Black Civilization*, *The Isis Papers*,

Iceman Inheritance, *They Came before Columbus*, and countless other texts that still adorn my bookshelf and inform my studies. My mom always tells people that when I turned sixteen I begged for books. This was ironic to her since she barely read anything. But I had fallen in love with learning. My curiosity and quest carried me forth academically in ways that neither I, nor anyone in my family, could have ever imagined.

During this time at Berkeley High School, white teachers and students told me, quite frequently, that I was being brainwashed by Black people. One day I was cornered on the third floor of the C-Building by two heads of the History Department. They were so angry that I crossed the unspoken divide at B-High and did not know my place. They said that I was not learning anything but hate-speech and venom—the same nonsense spewed by Malcolm X years ago. These older white male teachers proceeded to try to chastise and shun me. I remember looking up at them as their pale faces turned red with anger and contempt. At first I felt intimidated, and then I got frustrated, found my composure, and looked up at them—straight into their eyes. I said point blank: *I am not in these classes learning what it means to be Black. I am learning what it means to be white!* As soon as I made this statement, they took a step back. I then took a step forward, out of the corner they had me in, tightened the straps on my backpack, and walked away. None of the white teachers ever bothered me again.

I offer this glimpse into my education because it shapes the way I understand and respond to diversity and multiculturalism. By no means do my courses of study give me some kind of pass—I am a white woman doing research on/with Black people—and this fact does not escape me, nor should it evade the reader. As Malcolm X so eloquently pronounced: "If the present generation of whites would study their own race in the light of their true history, they would be anti-white themselves."

I have been grappling for solutions to racism long before I stepped foot inside Oakland Unified School District. Up until this point, however, my research has been on small beacons of hope and pockets of resistance (Watson, 2012; 2013; 2014; 2016). The Office of African American Male Achievement (AAMA) offers something different: institutional transformation wedded to racial justice. As a holistic intervention, a systematic radical Black love wrapped around students inside the schoolhouse and raised them up as kings.

As a case study, Oakland helps elevate the conversation about equity in education. According to a wide range of critical theorists (e.g., Apple, Freire, Giroux), schooling is political. While this is true, it is not entirely accurate. The politics of education cannot be detangled from the Gordian knot of white supremacy. This is more complicated than a racial achievement gap, for white supremacy is a learned ideology.

What happens when we ask students to inadvertently choose between who they are as human beings and who we expect them to be as students? The question is like a loaded gun, especially in most low-income schools where disconnections between educators and children are vast, even detrimental. To put it another way, if your education teaches you to internalize your own oppression, it is injurious.

Grounded in an African philosophy of learning (Ladson-Billings, 1994; Perry, Steele, & Hilliard, 2003), my study of Oakland illuminates an education that is embedded to a praxis of empowerment. Throughout this journey to uncover seeds of the solution, I discovered that the opposite of racism is not equality; it is empowerment. Empowerment releases us from the entrapment of the social reproduction of racism. What unfolds in the subsequent chapters is the ways racial justice unlocks human justice.

As will be demonstrated throughout this book, the Office of African American Male Achievement re-centered the narrative and created *rituals of resistance* that reverberated throughout the ecosystem. Altogether, a school district *and* a community joined forces to resurrect possibility. As a beacon of hope, AAMA forged new educational pathways for Black families. Along the way, they built upon legacies and traditional lessons from Africa and throughout the African Diaspora, including America. Teachers and students looked back into the libraries of Timbuktu; fathomed galaxies mapped by the Dogon people of Mali; swam into the harshest depths of the Atlantic to mourn ocean-floor gravesites; and smiled, laughed, and relished in the beauty of Black power. It continues to be a glorious day. And the future is still led by the children.

ACKNOWLEDGMENT

This research project was partially funded by Open Society Foundations, The Institute for Black Male Achievement (IBMA), and the W.K. Kellogg Foundation. I am grateful to these sponsors and Oakland Unified School District's Office of Equity for the opportunity to leverage research in service of social change.

1

THE RESEARCH JOURNEY

My relatively small study in Oakland (*The Black Sonrise*, 2014) turned into a larger and longer project than I originally anticipated; such is the nature of qualitative research. Fortunately, I have been able to spend the last five years (2012–2017) documenting the slow and intricate ways a school district shifts toward more equitable policies and practices. Utilizing a framework of *targeted universalism*,[1] Oakland Unified School District has strategically moved its most marginalized students and families into the center of school reform. Nowhere else is this more evident than within the Office of African American Male Achievement (AAMA). What began as a piecemeal one-man operation in 2010 has turned into a national model of systems change for social justice. Toward this end, I have the immense honor and privilege of helping tell the story of AAMA. I am not alone in doing so. Prior to joining the team in 2012, Professor Na'ilah Suad Nasir at UC Berkeley and her graduate students were already immersed in the work going on in Oakland. Their studies are pivotal to this larger examination (e.g., Nasir, Ross, Mckinney de Royston, Givens, & Bryant, 2013).

By way of introduction, I want to provide some context for AAMA. In the K–12 system, the urban school crisis affects African American males unlike any other ethnic or gender group (Ferguson, 2001; Ginwright, 2010; Noguera, 2008). Consistent with national trends, Oakland Unified School District (OUSD) was facing major challenges with successfully educating this demographic. While African American males and females lagged behind their white counterparts academically, when considering race and gender together, the disparities were even more extreme. In 2009–2010, Black male students comprised 17 percent of the population, but accounted for 42 percent of the suspensions annually and their graduation rate was only 41 percent.

As a response to the endemic failures, OUSD joined forces with community organizers, religious leaders, neighborhood elders, teachers, parents, and students to launch the Office of African American Male Achievement. These pioneers made the formal commitment that, "African American male students are extraordinary and deserve a school system that meets their unique and dynamic needs." To accomplish this goal, Oakland dared to name institutionalized racism—and not the children—as the problem. Various listening campaigns and initiatives were launched to disrupt underachievement by elevating a counter-narrative of Black educational excellence.

It is also important to acknowledge that there were people inside schools already doing "the work" long before AAMA existed. Among them was a school principal who called Black boys *king* on a daily basis, a math teacher who became a school leader to better advocate for African American students, a technology teacher who spent years trying to align his purpose with his radical pedagogy. These individual actors tended to work independently, some even antagonistically, with the larger institution. Even though their impact on students was real, it was piecemeal. AAMA became a tool of alignment; it became the house that would hold Black male students and Black male educators together—differently, intentionally, and holistically.

In naming Christopher P. Chatmon as the first Executive Director of African American Male Achievement and launching an AAMA Task Force under Chatmon's leadership back in 2010, Superintendent Smith and OUSD were collectively committing to interrupt the disenfranchisement and failure of African American male students.

When AAMA first opened its doors, there was a flood of interest from families. For the first time in generations, they had an office, *inside* the district, which was built to be on their side. Chatmon introduced himself through a district-wide robocall[2] and parents called him back, in droves. AAMA had to buy voice transcription software just to keep up with the messages. Between 2010 and 2013, they responded to over 1,800 concerned families. The need for AAMA was actually overwhelming; Chatmon could have spent all of his time responding to individual needs. He had to create larger initiatives to address the underlying problems. If there are root causes, then naturally, there are root solutions. Over the course of the last seven years, Chatmon and his colleagues have been relentlessly pursuing an education model that elevates students of color. They have discovered answers in spite of the constant upheaval in leadership (five superintendents since AAMA began), inconsistent funding and political battles.

My research into educational equity strives to contextualize and bring empirical evidence to bear on the pedagogies and educational philosophies of people at multiple tiers of a school system who are striving for institutional transformation. Although the findings from my research are overwhelmingly positive, I also want to be explicit in stating that there is no such thing as a flawless organization, and AAMA does not strive for perfection. I have been amazed by the ways the team is open to criticism and critique in a manner that fuels reflection as part of their practice. This form of praxis is commendable. Each year, distant onlookers and close stakeholders witness the continuous refinement and development of the AAMA model. As a result, with each passing cohort of students, AAMA changes a little, grows a lot, and expands in some unpredictable ways as the youth continue to take the lead. There are young people in Oakland Unified School District whose entire middle school and high school experience has been embedded within the milieu of AAMA. For them, having classroom assignments about internalized racism or institutional oppression during the school day has become *normal*.

A Quest for Answers

The transformation of an inner-city school district is a colossal challenge. Oakland Unified School District is the fourteenth-largest school system in California. Improving an institution of this magnitude takes vision and tenacity, patience and perseverance. While policies shape institutional culture, it is people who are the drivers of social change. These equity warriors exist in all parts of the Oakland ecosystem—from the boardroom to the classroom, from the district office to the schoolyard.

Based upon the premise that we embody our narratives, I illuminate individuals who are on the frontlines battling, grappling, succeeding, and struggling with how to navigate a bureaucracy to better serve the needs of all children. Toward this end, my overarching research question scrutinizes racial equity as a daily practice inside classrooms (micro-level) as well as at the institutional level (macro-structural), giving particular attention to the people at all tiers of the hierarchy who are striving to reconfigure education in the twenty-first century.

Along this journey, I sought to answer three specific questions: First, I take up a query posed over a decade ago by Asa G. Hilliard and his colleagues (2003): *What are we asking African American children to do, not just once, but over time, again and again, when we tell them to commit themselves to achieve in school?* Building on this idea and recognizing that the school system itself is sick from the injustices of racism, my second question is: *In what ways does the Office of African American Male Achievement shift the ecosystem of the institution to better serve the needs of African American children and youth?* And third: *How does Oakland Unified School District—charged with the care and education of all children—become a catalyst for district-wide healing, equity, and achievement?*

Methodology

As a qualitative scholar activist, I recognize that far too often, the process of data collection and analysis—objectifying subjects, renaming participants and places, the coding and categorizing, and then taking credit for someone else's stories—replicate patterns of oppression and misrepresentation. Thus, research in not devoid of racist tendencies, often it is a perpetuator. Our research epistemology is an important piece of the puzzle. So to answer my questions, I sought a qualitative methodology that would guide a rigorous, in-depth investigation. Portraiture was a natural fit. Since it is "common to social scientists ... to focus on what is wrong rather than search for what is right, to describe pathology rather than health"

(Lawrence-Lightfoot, 1983, p. 10), I chose a methodology that is rooted in a search for solutions. I relied on the methodological principles of portraiture to help me understand the people who are struggling to improve a large urban school district.

As a qualitative tool, portraiture shares commonalities with ethnography, but is distinct in five particular ways:

1.   The portraitist does not simply listen to the story; she/he listens for the story.
2.   The portraitist utilizes the entirety of her/his being to unearth answers to complex questions told through the lives of individuals who embody some semblance of the answers.
3.   The portraitist explicitly guards against fatalistic, pessimistic inquiries into problems but searches for solutions by examining nuances of goodness.
4.   The portraitist does not make participants anonymous, nameless factors but seeks to acknowledge, honor, and validate their stories by using the real names of people and places.
5.   The portraitist is committed to sharing findings that are accessible to audiences beyond the academy as an explicit act of community building.

Altogether, the methods of portraiture entail observational work, thematic in-depth interviews, and document analysis (Lawrence-Lightfoot & Davis, 1997), all of which I employed to create a viable and accurate account.

Portraiture grants a descriptive narrative to communicate essential findings. However, this does not imply subjectivism. Drawing mainly from grounded theory (Miles & Huberman, 1994; Strauss & Corbin, 1998; Tuckman, 1999) to construct each piece, I systematically analyzed the data collected through field notes, questionnaires, surveys, and interviews. This combination of various types of data combined with particular analytic strategies allowed me to conduct my research.

I am indebted to an array of stakeholders for trusting me with their narratives and opening up the doors of their life's work to an external study. I conducted interviews with the former superintendent, Antwan Wilson; Dr. Jean Wing, who is the head of Research Assessment and Data; Charles Wilson, deputy superintendent; Maria Santos, former deputy superintendent; and Kim Shipp, the parent organizer for OUSD. I spent years watching, listening, and interviewing Christopher Chatmon and his staff, among them Jerome Gourdine, Matin Abdel-Qawi, Baayan Bakari, Kevin Jennings, and Jahi Torman. I attended countless AAMA events and conferences at school sites and in the community. In the tradition of participant observation, I spent time inside classrooms and in deep dialogue with various middle and high school students as well as with the AAMA Student Leadership Council. All of these encounters provided me with the subtle clarifications and nagging complexities that comprise reality—even in empirical studies. I struggled with new ideas and juggled multiple truths.

Each of the participants holds a unique perspective on AAMA, and they are all valid (Maxwell, 1992). Particular opinions and idiosyncrasies might seem disjointed or even polarizing to some, but it is the diversity of views that layer the narrative. In other words, discrepancies can add depth. As a social scientist, part of the legitimacy of research is measured in our ability to toil, sift and sort through multiple data sources until we unearth answers.

As I have written elsewhere (Watson, 2014), many studies focus on the leaves—that is, the facts and figures that are the by-products of certain kinds of programs. Then there is research that emphasizes the branches, those correlations of how, why, and where the leaves connect. And there are plenty of examinations that simultaneously consider the historical context: the roots. My focus, however, was to dig (literally and figuratively) through years of information and layers of discoveries, constantly triangulating among multiple sources, to uncover the seed of the story. For it is the seed that holds the soul of the work—the essence.

Extending this metaphor of a tree, neither policymakers nor practitioners can plant a tree with leaves, limbs, or even roots. To authentically sustain and replicate this work in Oakland and beyond, the seeds of social justice need to be identified and planted abundantly, for this is how a single tree can sprout into a forest.

After years of investigation, this book serves as a culminating analysis wherein I present insights from people who took time out of their horrendously busy schedules to sit with me and reflect on the AAMA journey. These individuals had to feel an enormous sense of trust in order to allow me to mine them for answers, in what Lawrence-Lightfoot and Davis (1997) call human archaeology. And they did trust me with their voices and experiences so that I could share the waters of their wisdom, which—when poured—moistens the ground, nourishes the seeds, and spurs growth. On every level, this is serious, intense, and provocative work. I made every attempt to depict effectiveness in a way that is nuanced, accurate, and authentic. If I fail to accomplish this, I take full responsibility. The change agents who you will meet in the subsequent chapters became vulnerable to me in order that they might become real to you, and inspire you to consider your own areas of expertise and spheres of influence so that the dissonant voices of discontent across the world become harmonious chords in the choir of liberation.

Notes

1 Targeted universalism sees marginalized populations in American society as the canary in the coal mine. In other words, the problems of society are likely to spill over into the lives of everyone, just as the lower Ninth Ward was not the only part of New Orleans to suffer in the wake of Katrina or the subprime credit crisis did not end in poor, urban communities, but spread throughout the global economy (Powell, 2010; Powell & Watt, 2009). Applying Powell's framework to the school district, a plan was devised to elevate African American male students and, in the process, improve the educational ecosystem for all children. For more details on targeted universalism in Oakland, see Chatmon, C., & Watson, V. (2018). "Decolonizing School Systems: Racial Justice, Radical Healing, and Educational Equity inside Oakland Unified School District," *Voices in Urban Education*, 48.
2 An automated telephone call that delivers a pre-recorded message or announcement.

2

REMEMBER, RECLAIM, REIMAGINE

Today is in the low 70s with bright blue skies and sunshine that brings a glisten to the waters of the Bay Area. Although it is fall, for me it's a windows-down music-bumping kind of day. I almost do not mind that I am stuck in bumper-to-bumper traffic along I-80. As I crawl along the freeway on my way to Laney Community College for the annual AAMA GradNation community symposium, I inhale the brisk cold salty air and absorb the view: on one side I see the Bay Bridge and on the other the Golden Gate. Against the city landscapes, the water seems endless and timeless.

My thoughts wander to a history before the freeway, the concrete, the traffic, and the bridge tolls. Perhaps it was an era of greater freedom and deeper peace. Amidst this nostalgia, I also ponder the history of this land, in particular. I think about the Ohlones (also called Costanoans) and the Coast Miwoks who were robbed of their homeland.

The histories of Natives and African Americans in this country are similarly haunting. As the two distinct involuntary immigrants (Ogbu, 1991), neither group sought to come to the United States in search of riches and opportunity. Rather, the altruistic American Dream was harnessed from their massacres and enslavement, intergenerational disenfranchisement, and attempted annihilation.

Now, hundreds of years later, Natives and African Americans remain the most marginalized on all major indices of health, wealth, and education.[1] This is not coincidental; it is the by-product of methodical, historical, and institutional oppression.

I take a second look at the horizon and peer toward Alcatraz Island. Alcatraz is part of this story about the liberation from miseducation. But why? This small area in the center of the Bay has a fascinating and tumultuous history that relates to the interlocking tapestry between Americanization, criminalization, and self-determination, all of which are key concepts to understanding the struggle to reclaim schools.

In the fight for sovereignty, on November 20, 1969, a group of Natives from various nations (tribes) who were mostly California college students attempted to reclaim territory and send a message to the world demanding an end to colonial rule. They chose Alcatraz,[2] a small island off the coast of San Francisco, to wage their war against imperialism. They declared the land "by right of discovery" and demanded the U.S. government provide funding to turn it into a Native American cultural center and university.[3]

Place matters; it is not accidental that AAMA was born here. The land holds its own story.

The Bay Area has a rich heritage of community and cultural organizing. As just two examples, the American Indian Movement (AIM) and the Black Panther Party are two powerful local organizations that used their political platforms to demand new modes of education. Building upon these traditions of activism in Oakland, the Office of African American Male Achievement has picked up the baton and carried it into the school district. While their campaign is unique to the history of Black people, it is connected, like patches in a quilt, to patterns of displacement. Occupation cannot last forever.

Rituals of resistance are omnipresent. In many ways, settler colonialism is the catalyst for an ongoing, intergenerational quest for justice (Bonds & Inwood, 2016; Patel, 2016; Rowe & Tuck, 2017). While opposition to domination is instinctive, a reactionary stance can be its own form of entrapment. hooks (2009) shares that:

> Our theory was far more progressive and inclusive it its vision than our everyday life practice … Many of us found that it was easier to name the problem and deconstruct it, and yet it was hard to create theories that would help us build community, help us border cross with the intention of truly remaining connected in a space of difference long enough to be transformed.
>
> *(p. 2)*

Building on hooks' commentary, how do we shift some of the focus from critiquing to building, from dismantling to creating, from deconstructing to reclaiming?

The work of AAMA is more than counter-hegemonic, it is grounded by a worldview that predates borders, walls, and ownership. There was life before colonialism and vast civilizations prior to European imperialism. This is not a matter of opinion; it is chronological fact (Browder, 1992; Clarke, 1993; Diop, 1974; Jackson, 1970; Rogers, 1972; Sertima, 1976, 1992). When analyzed within a historical context, the mythology of white supremacy is a relatively young idea (Bradley, 1978; Coates, 2015; Lopez, 1997; hooks, 2013). This is not to diminish the pervasiveness or destructive power of racism, but to disrupt its monolithic hold.

Making Race/ism

In *The Isis Papers*, psychiatrist Frances Cress Welsing presents her theory of color-confrontation. Her work builds upon a tradition of scholarship that focuses on racism as the preeminent disease of our time. In the opening of this seminal text, she explains the ways racism has done more to promote non-justice than any other socio-material system. She cites a precise message from Neely Fuller (1971): "If you do not understand White Supremacy (Racism)—what it is, and how it works—everything else that you understand, will only confuse you." This provocative statement grounds my analysis of racial equity inside schools today. I also rely upon the work of critical race theorists who demonstrate that because white supremacy is so deep-rooted, it is embedded into our daily lives and institutions. Although the dominant narrative explains the plight of young Black male students as disproportionately failing within a post-racial colormute system (Pollock, 2004), critical race theory holds that their situation is actually a manifestation of the racial politics that are intrinsic, even vital, to the day-to-day functions of society at large and schools in particular (Crenshaw, 1995; Ladson-Billings & Tate, 1995).

Modern-day school systems are a direct by-product of the capitalistic nation-state that relies on stratification to function. Since its inception, these divisions and tracking systems have been racialized (Beckert & Rockman, 2016). And many scholars argue that times have not significantly changed (Dumas, 2014; Lewis & Diamond, 2015; Oakes, 1985). Just recently (2017), a national survey was conducted of 1,200 Black and Latino families who are raising children between the ages of five and eighteen. They report that prejudice against their children is getting worse. And for those families whose children have white teachers, they explicitly stated that schools are "not really trying" to even educate their children.[4] Racial inequality is a pandemic, like a virus that reemerges from one generation to the next.

In 1848 Horace Mann claimed that schools would be the great equalizer and over 150 years later, in 2011, the U.S. Secretary of Education, Arne Duncan, said that, "In America, education is still the great equalizer." This mirage of meritocracy alongside the master-narrative of opportunity supports and sustains the inequities. According to the data, equality is more mythology then reality, more prophecy then reliable probability. What if we boldly and unapologetically decipher the differences between an education that engages, encourages, and empowers all students from one that divides, deceives, and destroys the vast majority of them? Where would our answers take us? And how would they shape the way we teach, learn, and lead?

A burgeoning body of qualitative and quantitative research demonstrates that diversity in schools, including racial diversity among teachers and ethnic studies courses, can provide significant academic and developmental benefits to students (Cherng & Halpin, 2016; Dee & Penner, 2017; Picower & Kohli, 2017).

Compared with their peers, teachers of color are more likely to have higher expectations of students of color; confront and challenge issues of racism; serve as advocates and cultural brokers; and develop more trusting relationships with students, particularly those with whom they share a cultural background (Boser, 2014; Villegas & Irvine, 2010). While the data is promising, the teaching force still does not reflect the study body.

According to Hancock and Warren (2017), white women, in particular, have a tremendous influence on the ideological, political, and cultural scaffold of American public schools. Even though children of color are expected to comprise 56 percent of the student population by 2024, the elementary and secondary school workforce continues to be overwhelmingly white. In fact, the most recent U.S. Department of Education Schools and Staffing Survey (SASS), a nationally representative survey of teachers and principals, showed that 82 percent of public school teachers identified as white. This figure has hardly changed in more than fifteen years.[5] "Without question," explains the former Education Secretary John King, "when the majority of students in public schools are students of color and only 18 percent of our teachers are teachers of color, we have an urgent need to act. …The question for the nation is how do we address this quickly and thoughtfully?"[6] It is here that the work of the Office of African American Male Achievement (AAMA) comes into full view.

Remaking Schools

AAMA operates from a premise that traditional public schools were not designed for the success of African Americans. So as a response to this crisis, inroads have been made and strategic inputs have been developed to protect students from the deleterious impact of racism and the mythology of white supremacy (Nasir et al., 2013). Their approach is bold and unapologetic.

During 2015–2016, OUSD offered seven accredited courses focused on African American male students at twenty school sites, which equates to AAMA working daily with 16 percent (822) of all Black males in the district. Moreover, 100 percent of OUSD schools are required to set specific learning goals for their African American male students. In the area of workforce diversity, AAMA recruited and retained seventeen new African American male teachers, which increased the diversity of the overall teaching pool in Oakland from 7.1 to 10.6 percent. Among these hires, 92 percent have stayed in the classroom for over three years. Since AAMA began in 2010, suspensions for African American males have decreased by 55 percent and student arrest rates have also decreased by 40 percent. Reading scores, as measured on the Scholastic Reading Inventory (SRI) test, has increased by 8.2 percent. The number of African American males on the honor roll has also increased, by 11.3 percent, and graduation rates are now over 60 percent.

As this case study of Oakland seeks to demonstrate, any entity constructed from the hands of human beings can be transformed as well. Institutions greatly impact but do not make individuals; that is to say, human beings make systems, not the other way around. In *Decolonizing Educational Research*, Leigh Patel (2016) challenges us to consider "whether an entity borne of and beholden to coloniality could somehow wrest itself free of this genealogy" (p. 4). Applying this to my own research, I wrestle with the ways education—or more specifically, the school site—is both the doorway into social control and the window out of it. This quandary is multifaceted as individual actors coalesce their efforts and work within and beyond the confines of the institution to recreate possibilities, reconfigure schooling, and envision alternative futurities.

The freedom fighter Steve Biko taught that the greatest weapon in the hands of the oppressor is the minds of the oppressed. If education is a civil right, then an education for liberation is part of a larger civil war because those who control schools have their hand—literally and figuratively—on the future. The struggle over school is real; let's stop asking, *what are we fighting against?*, but rather, *what are we fighting for?* This is a calling to live and work differently in spaces of collective accountability and radical vulnerability. It's about a call to arms; arms that reach out, grab hold, and do not let go.

Notes

1 If given without historical context, statistics on particular groups of people can actually further stereotype, exploit, and victimize (Tuck, 2009; Tuck & Yang, 2014).
2 In the mid-1800s, Alcatraz was a U.S. military prison armed with canons against enemy combatants. By 1934, it was converted to a federal prison and housed criminals like the notorious gangster Al "Scarface" Capone. In 1963, the prison was shut down under the auspices of being too costly.
3 http://www.history.com/news/native-american-activists-occupy-alcatraz-island-45-years-ago.
4 http://civilrightsdocs.info/pdf/education/New-Education-Majority-Poll-2017.pdf.
5 U.S. Department of Education, National Center for Education Statistics. "Table 209.10: Number and percentage distribution of teachers in public and private elementary and secondary schools, by selected teacher characteristics: Selected years, 1987-88 through 2011-12." Digest of Education Statistics, 2013. https://nces.ed.gov/programs/digest/d13/tables/dt13_209.10.asp.
6 Former Education Secretary John B. King, Jr., Speaking at Howard University, March 8, 2016. https://www2.ed.gov/rschstat/eval/highered/racial-diversity/state-racial-diversity-workforce.pdf.

3

RITUALS OF RESISTANCE

I finally find parking and make my way into the GradNation Summit. At 8:30 a.m. on this crisp Saturday morning (November 8, 2014 to be exact), Laney Community College is bustling with children and youth; parents and grandparents; teachers and administrators; community organizers and university scholars. The sun is shining, the wind is blowing gallantly, and the vibe is welcoming. Participants are bundled outside in clusters, greeting one another with warm smiles and friendly hugs. A young man, whom I recognize from one of the student leadership meetings, is wearing a suit and tie, and appears to be surveying the crowd. A few moments later, he makes an announcement: "Please make your way into the presentation hall and get some breakfast because the program will begin momentarily." Following his directive, we shuffle into the large lecture room that has rows of bolted-down chairs and flip-up desks. It definitely feels like we are getting ready for a college lecture, but that approach would not be akin to the Office of African American Male Achievement (AAMA).

Within minutes, nearly every seat is taken. There are approximately 125 people, of all ages, and nearly everyone in the space is African American. Seven-foot-high posters announcing "Engage, Encourage, and Empower" adorn the front of the room. After a light breakfast and some further mingling, Brother Chatmon comes to the podium and asks the crowd to recite through call-and-response:

> It's not about me.
> It's not about you.
> It's about the children.

Throughout Chatmon's opening remarks, he shares with participants that the AAMA has a "structural understanding of how a system needs to work in service of students." Irrespective of district upheavals, AAMA has remained on a steady course to shift the narrative and outcomes for African American male students. Even on this early Saturday morning, there is a consistent show of passion and perseverance. Chatmon's grin radiates with pride as he looks out at the audience and says, "Today marks another important milestone in this victory."

Chatmon introduces various speakers who share wisdom and perspective about the work, including Congresswoman Barbara Lee. She provides an AAMA testimony: "If only I had AAMA when I was a single mom on welfare with two sons," and she pauses to make eye contact with the folks in the room. She resumes her speech, pleading with the parents to get even more involved: "I know how important this is! I'm from the Town!" Congresswoman Lee chokes up between her words and shakes her head. "This is not just my job," she continues, "but my mission to help save our sons." She explains the layers of institutionalized racism that starts as young as preschool and provides the audience with data on expulsion and suspension rates for "mere babies ... Black babies."

Another guest speaker comes to the front: Professor Tyrone Howard from UCLA. Dr. Howard is the founder and director of the Black Male Institute and has written extensively on African American achievement (2010, 2013, 2014, 2016). Without using the podium, he walks through the crowd and proclaims: "I stand as a testimony of what happens when adults invest in children. I grew up in Compton and people did not expect us to go far but I had adults who never stopped believing in me." He explains that "the folks doing wrong by our children come in all colors," and that the core issue is to fight for excellent teaching as the standard. Brother Howard shares a little data and proclaims: "One year of a bad teacher will undo two years of progress." As a community, he concludes, "we have to affirm our children and tell them that they matter because they are living in a society that villainizes them." The families are clapping and cheering. He then underscores that "AAMA shows the love" and that he is an ally, advocate, and brother of the program.

Following the featured speakers, eight African American male high school students make their way to the front of the room. They quietly take a seat in the row of plush red-and-yellow chairs. Each student is well dressed in button-down shirts and khakis; it appears the attire was predetermined.

Even though each student on the panel has unique testimonies and personal idiosyncrasies, there are echoes in their stories that resound in a proclamation to change schools. When asked to provide suggestions to improve the education system for students of color, they discuss three core ideas:

1. Change the way educators teach the curriculum. A student asks rhetorically, "What are you doing as a teacher to make it relatable?"
2. Students need mentors before, after, and during school; "just people in our lives we can really relate to."
3. Stop criminalizing troubled students with punishments, labels, and lowered expectations. "Right now," a student shares, "school is trying to bring us down."

These voices fall into the ears and hearts of the larger AAMA family who sit raptured and applaud their children for taking a stand. As I look around the room, it is a bit disheartening that there are not more school leaders and teachers present who would also take the time on a Saturday to build alongside the community. Nevertheless, the work carries on in struggle and celebration.

Before the students leave their seats, Brother Daniel Mora, the facilitator, shares a story. "Buenos días. Good morning," he begins with a smile. Mora opens up that his mom has a fifth-grade education and that when they left Mexico they simply traded "one area of poverty for another." Mora grew up in the West Oakland Acorn Projects until they were torn down and he got relocated to East Oakland. He tells the youth and audience that "probation mandated me to go to school," but he did not care and dropped out in the sixth grade. "I hated school," he quips. During one of his stints in juvenile hall, Mora was given a mentor. He reflects, "I finally saw myself as a thirty-year-old man." When Mora got out, his mentor, who had also survived the streets, took him to the DMV to get an ID, got him a job as a janitor, and helped him enroll in school. Mora's personal testimony brings claps of agreement and outbursts of support from the crowd. A mom who is trying to keep her restless toddler appeased on her lap shouts out: "You tell it, keep talking."

Mora is an Oakland success story. Even though he spent time in the hall, he eventually went to community college and transferred to UC Berkeley. In college, his life began to really turn around. He received the UC Berkeley Chancellor's Award for Public Service given to students "who have distinguished themselves through their public service and have improved their neighborhoods." Mora shares these accolades to demonstrate what is possible; as he facilitates the panel, he sprinkles the youth with that "school game."

Brother Mora asks the eight young men to take a stand before the audience of children, parents, and elders. He tells them, "Repeat after me." In unison, the voices in the room reverberate with strength, solidarity, and purpose:

> I am deserving of a decent education.
> I understand that bettering myself is not all about me.
> I understand that bettering myself will also impact my family and
>   community.
> People before me fought hard so that I could benefit from the opportunity
>   of life's gifts such as an education, be able to have my own identity, to
>   speak up if treated unfairly, and pursue any career that I choose.
> I have the power to improve my schools.
> We have the power to improve our community.

As the program comes to a close, Chatmon thanks Brother Mora and the student panelists for their insights. He exclaims, "This right here is the counter-narrative. These are the stories we need to lift up and perpetuate in order to carry the torch of change forward." Brother Chatmon closes:

We love you.
We appreciate you.
We thank you.

Chatmon leaves the podium to go down the aisle and hug each student. On the right side of the room a visual artist, aptly named Picasso, is putting finishing touches on a mural he has been painting while the students were speaking. As a collective, we pause, and watch the grace of his hands visually translate the summit. Chatmon jumps back on the mic: "Truth is told through the arts," he shouts. "It is our artists that are making sense of what we are doing on a whole other level. Give it up for Picasso!" We applaud for the muralist, the students, and the hope.

***

The GradNation community symposium is a wonderful introduction to the ethos of AAMA. As a community, we *broke bread* by sharing in breakfast together. And in just a couple of hours, African American families heard from a congresswoman, college professor from UCLA, and the students themselves. The young people advocated for schools to become uplifting spaces and emphasized that they need people in their lives they can authentically trust, connect with, and relate to. Also, participants were given information on their parental rights and ways to insure their children's classes reflect a college track (having an A-G course sequence for UC and CSU eligibility).

As the GradNation event exemplifies, AAMA has created its own rituals, networks, and rites of passages that support African American boys on their journey to becoming healthy and successful men. Amidst the wails of the world, failure rates, nihilism, and persistent state-sanctioned murders of Black people by the police, AAMA events are incredibly uplifting, celebratory, and inspiring.

Butch Wing, executive director of the Rainbow Push Coalition in the Bay Area, recently attended an AAMA community report-out at the Fox Theatre in downtown Oakland. He attests:

> Here was a room full of young Black men, brimming with self-confidence, self-pride and love. Focused. Disciplined and determined to make a future for themselves, their peers, their community. This was a room of young Black men—Kings—who, true to Reverend Jesse Jackson's mantra, knew *they were somebody. Young, gifted and Black*. But even more impressively, this sense of values seemed to permeate the collective group, the whole AAMA community of youth, teachers, mentors and elders.

At seven years old, AAMA is an organizational entity with its own personality and power. AAMA lives in the eyes of Black boys in Oakland on their first day of school. These children come face-to-face with educators that explicitly love and value Black life. AAMA also lives inside the minds and hearts of the staff who spend countless hours planning together, debating curriculum, and designing intervention strategies—this has become their own space for building, bonding, and brotherhood. Simultaneously, AAMA lives in the soul of the student's families, those mothers, fathers, siblings, cousins, aunts, uncles, and grandparents who have embraced AAMA as a necessary extension of their village—a continuum of care that helps guard against the malicious forces of inhumanity. Their advocacy gives AAMA legitimacy and longevity. AAMA lives in the hands of the Black women: administrative assistants handling the daily operations, grandmothers volunteering to cook for an event, a mom helping set up chairs or getting off work early to get her son to a speaking engagement. It is these queens who are often the unsung sheroes in a movement to engage, encourage, and empower African American male students to reach their fullest potential. In unison, these individuals are the bloodline and body of an academic revolution.

4

AN ONTOLOGICAL FIGHT
FOR FREEDOM

Social justice does not just live in our heads, but also in our hearts—and most definitely in our hands and feet. In other words, it is not merely what is conceived that is revolutionary, but what is achieved. The successes of the Office of African American Male Achievement are numerous. In order to fully grasp the significance of their day-to-day operations and accomplishments, it is important to consider the historical and theoretical underpinnings of their work. A framework is needed to contextualize this larger struggle for racial equity.

The literature on African American male achievement is disjointed. In education, a vast number of studies focus on what is happening currently, as an a-historical phenomenon. While this empirical work is informative, it fails to recognize the ways legacies shape our current landscape. Building on the work of Asa G. Hilliard (1998) and others (Perry, Steele, & Hilliard, 2003), I will, in the tradition of *sankofa*,[1] look backwards in order to move the analysis forward. For this to happen, a foundational understanding of Black history is necessary.

Curriculum is not neutral; it is political (Apple, 2004, 2013). Unfortunately, many students and teachers alike have been intellectually misled by an ideology that reifies and worships whiteness. Classroom textbooks and pedagogical practices continue to reinforce a white, European narrative (Loewen, 1995). In most schools, students learn about Black history through lessons that begin in slavery and then focus on the Civil Rights Movement (Watson & Wiggan, 2016). As a form of disruption and intervention to this curriculum, Afrocentricity became a paradigm to turn learning back to Africa. In the 1960s and 1970s, Afrocentric schools were formed across the county to provide alternative forms of education (Pollard & Ajirotutu, 2000).

According to various scholars (Dei, 1994, 1996, 2012; King, Swartz, Campbell, Lemons-Smith, & López, 2014; Pollard & Ajirotutu, 2000), Afrocentric schools tend to be standards-based, but re-frame history with Africa at the beginning of the human timeline, not centuries later after the arrival of European invaders: "Although Afrocentricity is a world-view embraced in opposition to the subjugation of non-White peoples by Eurocentrism," explains Dei (1996), "it is not an attempt to replace one form of hegemony with another" (Dei, 1996, p. 181). An African-centered curriculum embraces world history—for indeed, the concept of race was not invented until the fifteenth century. Blackness preludes a Western worldview and predates the United States of America.

Human History

Africa is the birthplace of humanity with a history that is rich and diverse. Various scholars have documented the vastness of African civilizations that existed prior to European invasion and colonialism (Browder, 1992; Clarke, 1993; Diop, 1974; Jackson, 1970; Rogers, 1972; Sertima, 1976, 1992). Ancient Abyssinia, the dynasties of KMT (Egypt), the Zulu nation, and the Ashanti empire are just some examples. In fact, there is evidence that many Greeks, including Plato and Pythagoras, studied in Northern Africa (James, 1954). One of the first international universities in the world was constructed in the early 1400s in the capital of Mali. Sankore University had a student body of 25,000 and an advanced degree system that higher education still mimics (Windsor, 1969).[2]

African people have made tremendous contributions to science, mathematics, and government. This is an important point. Examinations into ancient civilizations can broaden our horizons about what is possible. Simultaneously, history exposes the layers of fallacy and cover-up, and can dispel the manufactured lies about an entire continent. In actuality, deceitful misinformation was used to justify the enslavement of African people.

The transatlantic African holocaust (or Maafa, KiSwahili for disaster) describes the slave system established by the Portuguese that was soon thereafter dominated by the English from the fifteenth to nineteenth centuries (Figure 4.1). Most historians estimate that between nine and eleven million people survived the middle passage. However, this does not account for the overall death toll: between twenty-five and forty million African people died during the Maafa.[3]

During this time, West and Central Africa were destabilized from the loss of their populations. Consider for a moment that by the end of the 1800s, in the central African regions of the Kongo,[4] one-third of the countries' population had been sold. The severity of the trauma on these societies is almost unfathomable. It is haunting to consider that during this time, the art of the Kongo drastically changed. The faces of figurines were marked with red pouring from the eyes to depict grief; nails adorned the body to demarcate constant, perpetual pain. The color choices were also significant and ritualistic: black for life, white for death, and red for states of transition.[5] The enslavement of Africans was not just about the body; it brought atrocious amounts of pain to the human soul.

FIGURE 4.1 Diagram of the packing of people; a slave ship from the House of Commons of Great Britain in 1790

Illegal to Learn

The rationalization for slavery had repercussions around the world. In the United States from 1619 to 1865, laws justified slavery, stating that Africans were not human beings. During slavery, learning was forbidden, and teaching slaves to read or write was considered a crime. Below are two examples of policies related to the education of African Americans:[6]

South Carolina Act of 1740

Whereas, the having slaves taught to write, or suffering them to be employed in writing, may be attended with great inconveniences; Be it enacted, that all and every person and persons whatsoever, who shall hereafter teach or cause any slave or slaves to be taught to write, or shall use or employ any slave as a scribe, in any manner of writing whatsoever, hereafter taught to write, every such person or persons shall, for every such offense, forfeit the sum of one hundred pounds, current money.[7]

Virginia Revised Code of 1819

That all meetings or assemblages of slaves, or free negroes or mulattoes mixing and associating with such slaves at any meeting house or houses, in the night; or at any SCHOOL OR SCHOOLS for teaching them READING OR WRITING, either in the day or night, under whatsoever pretext, shall be deemed and considered an UNLAWFUL ASSEMBLY ... either from his own knowledge or the information of others, of such unlawful assemblage, may issue his warrant, directed to any sworn officer or officers, authorizing him or them to enter the house or houses where such unlawful assemblages may be, for the purpose of apprehending or dispersing such slaves, and to inflict corporal punishment on the offender or offenders, at the discretion of any justice of the peace.

Even though it was outlawed, enslaved Africans persevered with the understanding that education and liberation are symbiotic. In *Self-Taught: African American Education in Slavery and Freedom*, Heather Williams (2005) analyzes primary documents and critical secondary sources to meticulously decipher acts of resistance. Even under the most severe limitations, Black people developed ingenious strategies to become literate. "In South Carolina," she writes, "Edmund Carlisle cut blocks from pine bark and smoothed them into slates. He dropped oak into water to make ink, and he used a stick as his pen" (p. 20).[8]

When physical slavery was outlawed, it was still dangerous to learn. But even amidst the oppression, African Americans constructed and operated their own schools. Williams discusses how students would ask for longer class days in order to maximize their instructional time. She demonstrates that education, for African Americans in particular, became an extension of emancipation. Figure 4.2 provides an important snapshot of the timeline toward freedom.

In the seminal study, *The Education of Blacks in the South*, James Anderson (1988) analyzes the history of southern Black education from 1860 to 1935. From Reconstruction to the Great Depression, schoolhouses for Black people literally popped up in every corner of the South; they were spontaneous, grassroots, and emerged with no government funding or support. These independent educational centers served as the beacons of personal and communal empowerment.

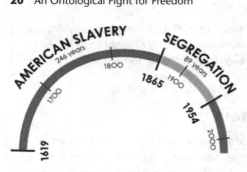

FIGURE 4.2 From the American slave system until today

Forbidden to Teach

Since education is esteemed in the African American community, it is not surprising there was a plethora of Black educators throughout the nineteenth and twentieth centuries (Tillman, 2004). In many cases, they were the original teachers for social justice. By 1954, there were 82,000 Black teachers in the South. In the eleven years following the *Brown v. Board of Education* decision, however, the number of Black educators plummeted: more than 38,000 African American teachers and administrators in seventeen Southern states were fired because all-Black schools were forced to shut down.[9]

Charles Bolton (2005) in *The Hardest Deal of All: The Battle Over School Integration in Mississippi, 1870–1980* documents the systematic firing of Black teachers in one of the last states to desegregate after the Brown decision. Between 1970 and 1973, the number of white public school teachers in Mississippi increased by almost 9 percent, while Black teachers fell by 12 percent. White administrators categorized African Americans with impeccable credentials as poorly qualified, thus dismantling a career in education for entire generations of Black people.

Instead of attending local schools, African American children were forced to participate in mandatory integration programs throughout the country. This meant leaving their neighborhoods in order to take bus rides to predominately white institutions that were, in some cases, hours away.

Michael Dumas, a leading scholar on Black Critical Theory, is one such student. He grew up in Seattle in the late 1970s and he was part of the social experiment to desegregate education. His experiences impact his research trajectory and scholarly focus. In a compelling article, "'Losing an arm': Schooling as a site of black suffering" (2014), he conducted an ethnographic study of four Black leaders who were involved in the struggle for educational opportunity decades ago. The elders he interviewed reflected, reminisced, and cried through their own haunting pursuits to transform schools.

The longitudinal arc of their stories is compelling, especially because none of them believes substantial progress has been made. One of Dumas' participants is a retired administrator. At seventy-six years old, she reflects on the struggle for equal schools disparagingly: "We were fighting for integration and forgot about education, thinking they were one and the same, that if our kids got into schools with White kids, that is was gonna be alright" (p. 13). A retired cafeteria worker continues to spend her time in schools: "I'm retired and I'm working *back* in the school district, and I'm seeing the same plan there as when my kids were there" (p. 15). A vice-principal who has been working in education for over forty years told Dumas that although she could retire, she continues to fight to make education right. She surmises, "We never really desegregated … We remain a sophisticated, segregated system. How did we do that? We came up with something called the honors program" (p. 17).

Dumas empathizes with the participants in his study because he, like many of their children and grandchildren, is a product of their fight. He shares his own story that provides further evidence that the educational experience for African Americans, as a collective, is injurious. On the first day of sixth grade, Dumas vividly remembers that he was told he could write about *anything*. But his teacher then told him he was not allowed to write in his grandmother's voice. The teacher abruptly shut him down and Dumas, in turn, shut down to learning in school. "I would skip the classes of teachers who, even once, gave me that look that refused to see me" (p. 25). Participants in this critical study, including Dumas himself, repeatedly shared testimonies of the ways the school system—from inequitable funding streams to inexperienced teachers and/or racist incidents—attempts to shame, attack, and convince African Americans they are less than their peers and incapable of accomplishment.

Dumas' scholarship on the cultural politics of school desegregation is noteworthy; educational leaders rarely take into account how a policy is embodied and remembered. By peeling through layers of wounds he establishes the basis for *racial melancholia* that results from a collective experience of social suffering that impacts flesh, bone, and soul. Given the lingering institutional and cultural impact of slavery and the persistent racial politics around schooling, it is not shocking that patterns of marginalization continue. We still live in a society where demographics—measured by zip code and racial categorization—disproportionately define a person's destiny.

State of Emergency

In California, one in five Black students drops out and/or is pushed out of school. That's the highest dropout rate of any race or ethnicity in the state. And for those that make it to college, they are the least likely to graduate. Oakland reflects these national and state-wide trends.

The Alameda County Public Health Department (2008) released the report, *The Life and Death from Unnatural Causes: Health and Social Inequity in Alameda County*, that delineates:

Compared with a White child in the Oakland Hills, an African American born in West Oakland is 1.5 times more likely to be born premature or low birth weight, 7 times more likely to be born into poverty, 2 times as likely to live in a home that is rented, and 4 times more likely to have parents with only a high school education or less.

As a toddler, this child is 2.5 times more likely to be behind in vaccinations. By fourth grade, this child is 4 times less likely to read at grade level and is likely to live in a neighborhood with 2 times the concentration of liquor stores and more fast food outlets. Ultimately, this adolescent is 5.6 times more likely to drop out of school and less likely to attend a 4-year college than a White adolescent.

As an adult, he will be 5 times more likely to be hospitalized for diabetes, 2 times as likely to be hospitalized for and to die of heart disease, 3 times more likely to die of stroke, and twice as likely to die of cancer. Born in West Oakland, this person can expect to die almost 15 years earlier than a White person born in the Oakland Hills.

It is uncontested that we are in a state of emergency. Nationwide, African American students are underrepresented among high-achieving students[10] and overrepresented in incidents of school discipline (Gordon, Della Piana, & Keleher, 2000; Gregory, Skiba, & Noguera, 2010; Monroe, 2005; Noguera, 2003; Skiba & Peterson, 2003). Even though there is no evidence that Black males actually misbehave more than other students (Gregory et. al., 2010), they are twenty times more likely to be punished. Both Ferguson (2000) and Noguera (1995) turn to Foucault's (1979) concept of the "juridico-political" function of discipline to understand these unjust dynamics. Noguera asserts that in the context of the school, Black male bodies represent the ultimate threat to authority and that the disciplining of Black boys can be understood as the definitive reinforcement of security and order. Some scholars have argued that conversations about race are increasingly taboo in what has been called the "color-blind era" (Bonilla-Silva, 2009; Pollock, 2004). Discipline, in an era of purported color blindness, is a new mode of domination that purports individual characteristics for Black boys, as "bad" or "troubled" as code words that reproduce racist stereotypes. These newer, subtler forms are a masquerade for white supremacist policies and practices (Dance, 2002; Ferguson, 2001).

The battle cry to improve educational outcomes for Black children must be understood within this milieu of injustice. However, it is dangerous when scholars *only* examine the problems; constant pessimism and critique can be its own form of intellectual entrapment. Focusing exclusively on the disparities and despair rarely seeds solutions.

Given the current situation of most school districts in this country, Theresa Perry (2003, p. 19) in *Young, Gifted, and Black*, understands—like Dumas and others—that the children are suffering. She probes into some essential questions that penetrate to the heart of the struggle:

- Why should African American youth take school seriously if they cannot predict when and under what circumstances their intellect or intellectual work is likely to be taken seriously?
- Why should African American youth commit themselves to doing outstanding intellectual work if—because of the marker of skin color—this work is likely to be undervalued, evaluated differently from that of whites, or ignored?
- Why work hard at school—or at anything else, for that matter—if these activities are not inextricably linked to and concerned with addressing one's status as a member of a historically oppressed people?

Perry asks the above questions because she fundamentally believes that African American students are not the problem. This point has important ramifications when considering urban education reform. She provides a practical example of the ways good intentions can get misaligned in the pursuit of equity.

An administrator wants to close the achievement gap and starts to focus, exclusively, on the disproportionate data on African American students. The disparaging statistics become *the* conversation and in actuality, reinforce the ideology of Black inferiority. In other words, the focus on failure further victimizes the students under scrutiny. "The conversation about African-American achievement is problematic," she argues, "because it fails to begin with a careful examination of all aspects of the school, with an eye toward understanding how the school's day-to-day practices participate in the creation of underachievement" (p. 9). Perry wants the inquiry to move from *What is wrong with the children?* to *What is wrong with their schooling?* From this vantage point, the entire ecosystem of the school district comes into question as everyone interrogates the policies and pedagogical inequalities that result in drastic academic differences between Black students and their peers.

Perry encourages educators to adopt a pedagogy for engaging Black children and youth that does not focus on failures, but rather raises the bar of possibility. This measure of excellence relates to a counter-narrative that presumes African Americans are intellectuals who have, for centuries, demonstrated the brilliance and tenacity to transform oppressive systems, including schools. Perry offers compelling evidence of an intergenerational, shared African American philosophy toward education. She surmises (p. 11):

- "You pursued learning because this is how you asserted yourself as a free person, how you claimed your humanity."
- "You pursued learning so you could work for the racial uplift, for the liberation of your people."
- "You pursued education so you could prepare yourself to lead your people."

The principles above emphasize the importance of personal agency and resiliency to overcome adversities, inhumanities, and break the chains (Hilliard, 1998; Madhubuti, 1990; Evans-Winders & Love, 2015; Fanon, 1963; Woodson, 1933). This type of pedagogical framework is not just culturally responsive, but historically reminiscent. It reinforces that students—like all of us—are part of larger movements and collective memories.

Building on this point and returning us to the beginning of the discussion, various Afrocentric scholars (e.g., Asante, 2000; Hilliard, 1998; Nobles, 2006) assert that students need to fully understand their legacy and the immense power of their ancestors; this will provide both the pride and perseverance to dismantle the disparities. While this might be part of the puzzle, Shawn Ginwright (2004) challenges this panacea in a detailed case study that took place in Oakland. Specifically, he examined the history of Afrocentrism as an intellectual ideology and explored its implementation at McClymonds High School. He posits that the curriculum, though racially conscious, did not meet the immediate needs of the students. Whether or not their teacher was wearing a dashiki and relating course materials to Africa, students still dropped out. Ginwright argues that learning must relate to immediate, material circumstances (Ginwright, 2004, 2010; Ginwright, Noguera, & Cammarota, 2006). Present-day conditions need to be understood in a historical context; however, just looking backwards will not move us forward.

Pedro Noguera, one of the premiere scholars on urban education, has written extensively on ways to support students of color, giving particular attention to African American males (2003, 2008, 2012). In *Schooling for Resilience: Improving the Life Trajectory of Black and Latino Boys*, Fergus, Noguera, and Martin (2014) conducted a three-year mixed-method (qualitative and quantitative) study of seven single-sex schools for boys of color throughout the country. During interviews with school leaders and college counselors, Fergus and his colleagues consistently heard that "the greatest challenge our boys face is institutionalized racism" (p. 43). As creative, tenacious, and extraordinary as the students are, they are striving to survive in a society that has, for generations, been unjust. It is impossible to examine student achievement without considering the structures of discrimination. A powerful example sheds light on this reality.

The head of a foundation asked a principal in Fergus, Noguera, and Martin's study point-blank: "Well, what we don't really understand is why it's so important for these guys to go to college. I mean, maybe you should do some type of technical/vocational focus because it's important that we have people who deliver the mail and drive the buses" (p. 64). The frankness of this philanthropist reveals a fundamental zero-sum function of schooling that reproduces inequality. Understanding this quandary, the principal asked the donor if he had made the same comment to the private school his foundation just gave $1 million dollars to. He had not, and stated the private school is "different" (ibid.). Different was used as a polite code word to mask ingrained racist tendencies that impact funding decisions, access, and outcomes (Pollock, 2004).

As a summation, the legal construction of race (Lopez, 1997), the ramifications of desegregation (Dumas, 2014), the system of tracking integrated schools (Oakes, 1985), the cultural and social reproduction process (Dance, 2002; MacLeod, 1995; Willis, 1977), the ways schools are structured and funded (Bowles and Gintis, 1976; Coleman, 1966), and the information that is taught and how it is taught (Apple, 1995, 2004; Freire, 1970, 1998; Gay & Howard, 2000; Nieto, 1992) are all interdependent interlocking components inside an ideology of oppression (Leonardo, 2009; Patel, 2016). In other words, the dangerous hierarchies of patriarchy and white pathology establish intersectional traumas that are enacted throughout society—especially in our schools.

As a possible solution, Oakland Unified created initiatives throughout the district to disrupt underachievement by elevating a counter-narrative of Black educational excellence. Cognizant that the legacies of learning as the practice of freedom are wedded to existential conditions of oppression (Gordon, 1990; Perry, 2003), let us now consider the ways that the African American community in Oakland is making education their own.

Notes

1 Sankofa is a metaphorical symbol used by the Akan people of Ghana, generally depicted as a bird with its head turned backward taking an egg from its back. It expresses the importance of reaching back to knowledge gained in the past and bringing it into the present in order to make positive progress. The literal translation: "You must reach back to reclaim that which is lost in order to move forward."
2 http://www.pbs.org/wonders/Episodes/Epi5/5_wondr6.htm.
3 http://africanholocaust.net/africanholocaust/.
4 The Kongo comprises the modern-day nations of the Democratic Republic of the Congo, The Republic of the Congo, and Angola.
5 Peter Schjeldahl in *The New Yorker* (October 12, 2015).
6 http://www.pbs.org/wnet/slavery/experience/education/docs1.html.
7 To put the 100-pound penalty into context, teachers at that time had an annual salary of 60 pounds (http://www.history.org/foundation/journal/Summer02/money2.cfm).
8 For further reading, see also Scott, J. C. (1990). *Domination and the arts of resistance: Hidden transcripts.* Yale University Press.
9 http://usatoday30.usatoday.com/news/nation/2004-04-28-brown-side2_x.htm.
10 High-achieving as indicated by grades, attendance, and enrollment in gifted and talented or advanced placement classes.

5

INSTITUTIONALIZED RACISM
IN OAKLAND UNIFIED
SCHOOL DISTRICT

Throughout the school system, African American males are overrepresented in special education, lower-track courses, and on-campus suspension and under-represented in honors classes and gifted programs (Fergus, Noguera, & Martin, 2014; Gregory, Skiba, & Noguera, 2010; Howard, 2016). Consistent with national trends, Oakland Unified School District (OUSD) also had significant statistical inequities.

In 2010, Superintendent Tony Smith—together with the Office of Civil Rights, Oakland's Board of Education, the Urban Strategies Council, and the East Bay Community Foundation—examined longitudinal data and came to a jarring conclusion: past initiatives had done little to transform the experiences, access, or educational attainment of African American male students. Regardless of the reform or learning theory or even school site, en masse, the educational needs of Black children were not being met.

In response to disproportionality and racial bias, OUSD joined forces with com-munity organizers, religious leaders, neighborhood elders, teachers, parents, and students to launch the Office of African American Male Achievement (AAMA). Four years before President Obama's directive around *My Brother's Keeper*, OUSD made the formal statement that "African American male students are extraordi-nary and deserve a school system that meets their unique and dynamic needs." Although there was an impetus to reframe the system toward racial equity, my research interrogates the process of institutional transformation.

Over the past seven years, AAMA has made significant inroads. As discussed in Chapter 2, across the district, suspensions are down and graduation rates are stead-ily increasing for African American males. According to the students and com-munity members, these academic outcomes are the by-product of an intervention model based upon learning as a means of liberation. Prior to AAMA, schooling was detrimental to their sense of self as well as their ambitions. A student shared that before the Manhood Development program, "school had me believing I was a *bad kid* who needed to be fixed." Instead of education fostering a sense of empowerment for these Black children, it was still acting as a socializing instrument of disengagement and underachievement.

The School District's DNA

As reformers across the country consider the transformation of urban school districts, like the one in this study, let us pause and ponder what it is we are actually trying to accomplish. Studying the evidence around student outcomes provides critical information for educators trying to ameliorate the achievement gap. However, this focus can become too narrow and shortsighted. The work of transforming schools is powerful, political, and also historical.

Even in a city as liberal as Oakland, the remnants of racism have shaped the landscape and continue to paralyze the system. OUSD has a tumultuous history. It was founded in the mid-1800s and a century later, in 1970, Marcus Foster became the district's first African American superintendent. Three years later, he was assassinated.

During the early twentieth century, Oakland was the first school district in the nation to use IQ testing to track students. These particular tests were developed by Lewis Terman, a cognitive psychologist at Stanford University, and tested throughout Oakland Unified. Terman's research was grounded in an elitist ideology based upon the eugenics movement that championed the intelligence of whites as having higher levels of "complex cognitive functioning."[1] Terman is the author of *The Measurement of Intelligence* (1916) and *Genetic Studies of Genius* (1925, 1947, 1959), among other works.

Terman's scholarship has particular repercussions for Oakland schools because it was used to create course sequences that divided and categorized the student body from low achieving to high achieving. Students were not given access to the same classes based upon pre-determined, racialized measures of capabilities. Furthermore, Terman's graduate student, Dr. Virgil Dickson, became the head research director for Oakland Unified and carried out additional studies on how to use schools as sorting mechanisms for society (Dickson, 1920; Terman, Dickson, Sutherland, Franzen, Tupper, & Fernald, 1922).[2]

Again, historical context can provide poignant insight into a diverse urban school system that has been grappling with inequalities since its inception. The U.S. Department of Civil Rights conducted an investigation into the treatment of African American students in Oakland. When examining longitudinal data (1998–2012), a pattern of discrimination was discovered:

- In 1998–1999, African American students composed 53 percent of the total student enrollment and 75 percent of all students who received an Out-Of-School Suspension (OSS) [Risk Ratio: 1.42];

- In 2009–2010, African American students composed 33.2 percent of the total student enrollment and 63.5 percent of all students who received OSS [Risk Ratio: 1.91]; and 51 percent of the students who were expelled. White students composed 7.9 percent of the total student enrollment and 2.3 percent of the students who received OSS, and 2.8 percent of the students who were expelled.
- In 2011–2012, African American students composed 31.8 percent of the total student enrollment and 63 percent of all students who received OSS [Risk Ratio; 1.98], and 61percent of the students who were expelled, more than double the percentage of their enrollment in the District. White students composed 10.4 percent of the total student enrollment and 2 percent of the students who received OSS; no white students were expelled.[3]

The evidence demonstrated a glaring "risk ratio" for African American male students. The statistics paralleled the experiences, on the ground, of families who were struggling to hold the district accountable for the education of their children.

Generation after generation, Black families were sending their children to school, but the ideals of an oasis of learning were met with the realities of institutionalized racism, low expectations, and marginalization. A mom shares: "I'm convinced that schools expect Black children to underachieve. They don't push them as hard as they do the other kids. The way I look at it is, I sent three very brilliant young kids to school, and somewhere along the way, they got messed up. They got discouraged."

With pressure from all sides and evidence against the district mounting, Oakland entered into a Voluntary Resolution Agreement with federal civil rights officials to "reduce the number of suspensions of African-American students and eradicate bias in discipline." The decision was bold and unrivaled. Although it might sound like a victory, it was an arduous process that involved litigation and painstaking negotiations—many of which occurred internally.

Voluntary Resolution Agreement

The history of the Voluntary Resolution Agreement (VRA) is important. According to Chatmon, from the initial group of VRA stakeholders, he is the only one still working in Oakland Unified. Chatmon holds important institutional memory regarding the district's stance to no longer leave Black children behind.

In an exclusive closed-door session between Superintendent Tony Smith, Christopher Chatmon, and the School Board, a highly contentious meeting took place that shaped the school district's strategic plan. The exchanges between the adults were very harsh, remembers Chatmon. "It was a nothing nice kind of conversation," that consisted of cursing, erratic outbursts, screaming, chair throwing, leaving the room, coming out, and then eventually going back in. Superintendent Smith and Chatmon stood their ground because "we realized that this was a tipping-point moment. Given where the federal government was and what we were doing," he says, something had to change. "The reality was we were out of compliance." Oakland needed to leverage this opportunity to "go farther faster and get resources." "And this," describes Chatmon, "is where Smith was a visionary," because he was thinking down the line years ahead into the future. "Folks in the room didn't really get it," but in actuality, he was right "on multiple levels."

After years of political upheaval and debates, on September 28, 2012, the U.S. Department of Education announced a Voluntary Resolution Agreement between Oakland Unified School District and the Department's Office for Civil Rights. Dr. Jean Wing, executive director for Research, Assessment, and Data at OUSD recalls:

> The Office of AAMA was established as part of OUSD but funded externally (no public funds) *prior to* the Agreement to Resolve. ... Once the Agreement to Resolve Disproportionate School Discipline for African American Students was in place, OUSD moved the Office officially to district staff status, using federal order to trump state law that prohibits a race-specific focus.

As a result of this decree, AAMA became firmly established within the school district. "When they did the compliance review," shares Chatmon, "it provided a trigger" to move AAMA from outside the system into the district to officially address the patterns of underachievement for African American males.

The declaration to address and eliminate institutional racism was monumental and garnered national attention. "I commend Oakland for being the first district to directly confront this challenge" explained U.S. Education Secretary Arne Duncan because it offers a "model for school districts everywhere who are struggling with similar issues."

Up until this point, AAMA existed, but it was through piecemeal programs. During its first two years of operation (2010–2012), Brother Chatmon had a cabinet-level position with Superintendent Tony Smith, yet it was only because he was considered an "executive on loan" from *Urban Strategies Council* and later, *Partners in School Innovation.* These external organizations served as a safeguard and protective shield against the sickness of the system. In recollection, this proved quite important.

Dr. Derek Mitchell, CEO of *Partners in School Innovation*, elucidates: "It is hard for systems that are designed and defined to stratify ... to all of a sudden organize and unify." Looking back, he explains, it was strategic to "incubate the work outside the system" because it allowed AAMA to establish its own theory of change, accountability measures, and institutional prowess.

AAMA Is Alone

In 2010, the Office of African American Male Achievement was established and they hired one employee: Christopher P. Chatmon. When Chatmon first got the position, many stakeholders believed, in the words of a close colleague, "it was a set-up. I am a systems person and I was highly skeptical." The "word around town" was that AAMA would fail. Another close colleague told Chatmon: "Don't quit your day job. I give you less than three months." Without any employment security or retirement, without any staff or even an operating budget, Brother Chatmon took the helm.

Chatmon left his position as school principal in San Francisco to lead an issue as vast as educational inequity through the waters of Oakland Unified School District without a ship or crew. While many people saw the Titanic, Chatmon had, as he likes to say, "audacious hope."

Professor Macheo Payne, who participated in some of the first meetings, remembers, "Chris had access to a groundswell of support to make this movement happen," including the "Brotherhood of Elders Network (a network of elders in Oakland who work on strategies for addressing the health of Black male youth in Oakland) and the 100 Black Men of the Bay Area." However, "the scope of the problem was overwhelming: 32 schools with acute suspension issues [with] Black boys. The office had the expertise needed to begin the work but the capacity was limited. Trainings were not going to suffice."

Given the internal and external institutional barriers and inherent limitations, Chatmon used his first year in office to establish a strong foundation of sup-porters—philanthropic and otherwise—to build an organization that supported schools and the larger district, but was not dependent upon it for their survival. Chatmon's colleagues are insistent that his strategies shifted the tide:

1. Brother Chatmon has been able to raise a lot of money. If he had not secured external funding sources, OUSD would have shut it down.
2. His vision for gaining exposure and partnerships at the highest levels made the work bigger than him. At times when folks were extremely critical and skeptical, the naysayers could not stop the movement.
3. He has demonstrated that it is possible to impact students, families, teachers, and other leaders. It is possible to be in an institution and make a difference.

In all transparency, the Office of African American Male Achievement grew exponentially without actual funding from the district. This fact is rarely men-tioned, at least not publicly. Three years after AAMA had launched, in 2013, the interim Superintendent, Gary Yee, told the school board: "There is no line item budget investment in this work: in effect, making it an unfunded mandate." The board finally approved spending $700,000 to establish an infrastructure to do what OUSD promised it would do years ago.

Even with some financial commitment from the district, allies remained skeptical. "I want to remind you what is at stake here," urged Fania Davis, executive director of Restorative Justice for Oakland Youth. "Not only is compliance at stake, but the moral obligation that we in this district are very clear about eradicating discrimination." She proclaimed that "the whole nation is watching" what Oakland is going to do to address and eliminate institutionalized racism. Altogether, the community created the impetus and the rallying cry for change. The federal government got involved. And unsung heroes and sheroes from within the district emerged and took a stand. Because of the collective will of various stakeholders, a new kind of solution for Black children in Oakland was given a chance to develop and grow.

At the helm of the ship is Christopher P. Chatmon, the executive director of the Office of African American Male Achievement. He is the focus of the first portrait. To navigate the uneasy waters of school reform, his compass is the children, and his north star is racial equity.

Notes

1 https://alumni.stanford.edu/get/page/magazine/article/?article_id=40678 and https://en.wikipedia.org/wiki/Lewis_Terman.
2 For a thorough history of the sociopolitical context of Oakland Unified, see *A Different View of Urban Schools* by Kitty K. Epstein, 2008.
3 http://www2.ed.gov/about/offices/list/ocr/docs/investigations/09125001-b.pdf.

6
CHRISTOPHER CHATMON
In Service of Our Sons

In East Africa, a traditional greeting passed among the Masai warriors is *Casserian engeri*, which means "How are the children?" These infamous fighters of Kenya—whether or not they have children of their own—give the same calming answer: "All the children are well." This simple statement provides insight into a cultural tradition that prioritizes the needs of the young. This practice resembles core characteristics of Christopher P. Chatmon, the executive director of the Office of African American Male Achievement (AAMA). Throughout the arc of Chatmon's career—classroom teacher, youth development director, manager, school principal, administrator, executive director—a consistent thread continues to emerge that weaves his story together: he leads with his heart and listens to the children.

Brother Chatmon is the visionary behind the movement to uplift the educational experiences of African American males in Oakland. He is a force of nature; his inclination is to love, communicate, celebrate, and support. Even in a hailstorm of bureaucratic messes, Chatmon will find the slightest bit of hope, grasp onto it tightly as if it is a rope, and use it to climb higher, further elevating the work. His colleagues describe his optimism and his tenacity as unparalleled. They explain to me that each time they face a district-sanctioned reorganization that would normally feel like a defeat, Chatmon leverages it into an opportunity.

When Chatmon became the leader of this new initiative in Oakland in 2010, he was cognizant of the critics and disenchanted by the politics. He did not have any formal plan, so he relied upon his background in education and youth development to establish a listening campaign. Essentially, he put his ear to the youth. Student insights and experiences became the catalyst for an action-oriented campaign to move the mountain of school reform.

Along this journey, Chatmon has strategically fostered local partnerships on the ground in Oakland while simultaneously maintaining national notoriety. His network is a bit intimidating: text messaging with David Johns who leads the White House Initiative on Educational Excellence for African Americans; strategy conversations with Shawn Dove of the Open Society Foundations; launching economic development plans with Angela Glover–Blackwell, CEO of PolicyLink; and heartfelt walks around Lake Merritt with parents, program officers, and community organizers. His list of supporters seems unending. And yet he is quite transparent about his mistakes and misgivings. There are people he just does not get along with, but even then, he strives to find a point of connection. If you meet him, his warmth is so unassuming that the gravitas with which he walks can be easily underestimated.

★★★

"Brother Chris," as I have come to call him, contacted me after he read my book, *Learning to Liberate: Community-Based Solutions to the Crisis in Urban Education.* Although we had crossed paths over the years and have a lot of shared community, I actually knew very little about him or his work. I agreed to the meeting, but did not know what to expect.

It is the fall of 2012. At our first official conversation, I arrive at the AAMA office located at the corner of Grand and Lake Park. Behind the old district building, in the parking lot, sit rows of portables. There is no signage for AAMA; all I know is to find *portable number five.* Even though the space is a bit rundown, the location is great—just one block from Lake Merritt and diagonal to the legendary Grand Lake Theatre.

Upon entering the classroom-size space, I try to take it all in. Literally every inch of wall celebrates Blackness: posters of monumental historical figures, large photos of students, and even murals, hang everywhere. There are boxes along the floor filled to the brim with books, among them *Malcolm X, Nile Valley Civilizations,* and *The Pact.* The white boards are also busy: full of notes on teaching, agendas from staff meetings, and the like.

In the back left hand corner of the portable is a small, enclosed office that belongs to Chatmon. Like the rest of AAMA, it is packed to the edges with artifacts and accolades. As I peruse the walls, I discover that he was recently on the cover of the *Urban Advocate* and the *San Francisco Chronicle.*

As soon as I sit down, Chatmon offers me a bottle of water and then he begins to talk, in rapid succession, about the office and his need for a report that critically documents the work. I am still getting my notepad from my bag when he has already sped through the first year of AAMA. He is moving quickly and revving to go.

He acknowledges that "if you think of a seed … that's cultivated in the soil," then AAMA would not have existed without the wisdom and work planted years ago by "Demarcus Foster, Greg Hodge, Macheo Payne, Wade Nobles, Oscar Wright, Deshawn Wright, Alice Spearman, Brother Derrick (who started Triumph at Oakland Tech)" and, he leans in and states matter-of-factly: "I ain't create nothing new. Really, everything that we've cultivated was created through brothers and sisters in Oakland from the 2000s to the 1990s, the 1980s, 1970s, and 1960s." Altogether, he surmises, it was the actions of many people that cultivated the space "to question, to challenge, to agitate and to advocate." In other words, Oakland was fertile ground.

Engage, Encourage, Empower

"In my first year," explains Chatmon, "OUSD launched fourteen Task Forces to help initiate the Strategic Planning process for the district. All of the task force committees were led by adults and exclusively engaged adults." From his previous experience working with youth, he knew he had to "lift up the voices of our young kings."

One of Chatmon's first major initiatives was to design and implement a listening campaign for African American elementary-, middle-, and high school students. Brother Chatmon organized his colleagues and community members to "go around on school grounds with flip cameras and just interview students." He needed to "get a sense of how they were experiencing school and how they perceived their teachers and adults felt about them." Brother Chatmon shakes his head and looks down: "What came out of our listening campaign was humbling."

Chatmon learned firsthand that students felt that they were being treated like villains and suspects—even when they had done nothing wrong. School was not an oasis of learning and safety for these kids, but a space that reflected and reproduced society's racist ailments. "We learned," recalls Brother Chatmon, "that few adults even asked the kids 'How are you?' or 'What do you want to be?'" There was a general consensus that "our young brothers were not having a good experience." Moreover, these Black youth had little to no "access to positive African American men on school campuses."

As the leader of AAMA on the one hand and as a father of three sons in OUSD on the other, Brother Chatmon listened intently to students' jarring experiences. Their voices became the beacon of his platform: engage, encourage, and empower. Chatmon smiles and sits up in his office chair. With conviction he says, "In light of how our sons were experiencing school, we came up with the three Es." He delineates his response to the crisis of underachievement. "Engage Black boys as opposed to ignore them. Encourage Black boys as opposed to discourage them—*don't hate, appreciate*," and finally: "Empower Black boys as a way to equip them with the skills they need to master their content and community."

While Brother Chatmon recognizes that "It wasn't solely the work of one person," he felt it was his responsibility to lean on the system and hold the system accountable to African American male students and their families. In essence, his role was to leverage OUSD on behalf of the most marginalized.

Throughout his journey to uplift the students, there was skepticism from his colleagues. Maria Santos is currently the director for school and district services at West Ed. However, years ago, she was the deputy superintendent for instruction, leadership and equity-in-action for the Oakland Unified School District. She recalls:

> Chris took the office from the very student-centered standpoint. He immediately started working with kids and families. And that was the impetus for his work. And he created a community of support around him for the office and for the work of that office … Whereas another individual might try to work from teacher-driven or administration-driven or let's look at the data-driven kind of thing … but he started this office like let's reach out to the kids, let's get kids' voices in here, let's build up the kids. The design all centered on the direct kid experience, not necessarily looking at the institutional barriers. And to really address the issues, one needs to look at both.

In her own words, Santos was a bit doubtful. She suspected that Chatmon's impact would be minimal because he was not addressing larger problems of the ecosystem, like severe budget cuts to teachers or the lack of college counselors on campuses. She emphasizes the economic barriers to equity as well as the need to codify strategies for replication. In the beginning years, according to Santos, Chatmon was trying a lot of different strategies for students without a definitive strategic plan. She supported the vision of AAMA, but did not fully understand its application. Her perception and hesitancy were not that far off. During the first couple of years, Chatmon struggled to keep AAMA afloat.

Read to Lead

An overarching goal of the AAMA was to improve literacy rates. In the first year, Chatmon ambitiously tried to design culturally relevant reading programs throughout the district that would later be called Read to Lead. He describes a scaffolding strategy where a child learns the phonetics of words, then starts to read for content understanding, and eventually moves from "read to learn" to the inevitable objective of "read to lead." To initiate the literacy process, Chatmon organized African American men from the community to go to school sites and read to the children.

In West Oakland, Chatmon joined forces with the principal at McClymonds, Kevin Taylor, to create a full-day experience around culturally responsive literacy practices for the students. "Black men showed up. We all—I was part of it as well—had small groups of four to eight brothers and [we] read a book that was kind of a parable." During this gathering, a senior at McClymonds high school, "one of the basketball stars," pulled "Baba C" to the side to talk to him. This teenager confessed that he had never had his father read to him, or grandfather, or even an uncle. It was a completely foreign experience to interact with a Black elder around literacy and just have the opportunity to listen to a story. Chatmon was heartbroken by this testimony, and school principals started hearing similar accounts from the students. They decided they had to do something to fill this void in the lives of African American male youth. Chatmon pursued funding ("got a grant from Clorox") to expand the Read to Lead exposure strategy.

Building on this momentum, "brothers were assigned to a school and would come in, once a week, and read to classes." One of the books was based upon Jay-Z's, *Decoded*. They chose to focus on a particular passage about Jay-Z's process as a writer. As a youth, when Jay-Z started reading more, that is when his writing went from good to great. "We had a whole lesson around it … So we did all that," Chatmon says with speed and excitement, "and it was working!"

"It was our second year, first semester. We called all the brothers and said we were going to hit all the middle schools. So we had Black men hit eight different middle schools in Oakland" armed with relevant books and a need to read to younger generations. After the reading sessions, these African American elders and activists, like the spoken word artist, Ise Lyfe, started donating books to the schools' libraries. Altogether, Read to Lead was supported by members of the community who were willing to volunteer their time and a small grant that helped with the purchase of books and supplies. However, without a stable funding source, it was hard to keep the program going and eventually it disintegrated. Chatmon shares that "you either win or you learn."

In this moment of reflection, Chatmon looks a bit defeated and weary. He shakes his head. Chatmon was forced to acknowledge that this was an instance of misalignment between the district's focus on measuring ELA[1] scores and AAMA's insistence for cultural awakening. But, he insists and still seems to be pleading: "Just stop for a minute," Chatmon urges, "I just want you to ponder—whatever ethnicity you are—and think that no man within your cultural context ever read to you." A small solution is that the "first introduction to that is in a school. We have a man of your ethnic orientation and culture read to you." He shrugs his shoulders and folds his hands before telling me: "The fact is the system didn't value that enough." Even with a collective will to act, without a funding structure to support it, Read to Lead did not last.

Counter-Narratives of Black Brilliance

For every loss, there was traction being cultivated in another direction. Among the other activities were the Black Teacher Celebrations. Chatmon and his small team at the time (namely, Gerald Williams, Matin Abdel-Qawi, Brenden Anderson, and Anika Hardy) created a series of events to acknowledge and build with OUSD African American administrators, educators, and staff. At these gatherings, participants were encouraged to "bring a friend that is interested in becoming a teacher, which was one of our recruitment strategies." Chatmon is decisive: "People say there are no Black teachers. That's not true. Just get out of the box of what it means to be a teacher. Every Black man is a potential teacher; so how do you engage them?"

As Chatmon asks this rhetorical question, he takes a moment to reflect and then shares, "It was really through the journey of teaching and later, leading non-profits and working in youth development, that I saw I had a gift to organize people around a common cause: the service of children."

In another example, the African American family summits demonstrate Chatmon's skills as a community organizer. Between 150 and 300 parents would attend these Saturday sessions that took place at schools throughout Oakland. To involve the families, Chatmon would honor their children with awards for attendance, most improved grades, and various other forms of academic achievement. "Typically," he recalls, "we would have food and then we would start with a community circle to give thanks. We would have a testimony from some students and then student awards." The accolades were only part of the day, however.

Families would participate in "data walks." In close partnership with the Department of Research, Assessment and Data, Chatmon and his team would disaggregate school data and feature certain statistics, for instance around chronic absence, referral rates, literacy rates, grade point averages, and test scores. The entire community of people would go through the data walk with a sheet of paper so that they could write down their answers to the following questions.

1. What are the things you are seeing?
2. What are some of the themes?
3. What students are thriving in the school community?
4. What students are not thriving in the school community?

Although these questions are relatively simple, Chatmon underscores that it was important for the families to come to their own conclusions "as opposed to us stating it."

While some town hall gatherings might commence with a discussion of the problems, this is not the mode of AAMA. Subsequent conversations focused on "What does a school in service of Black children look like? What does it sound like? What does it smell like? Describe the aesthetic, describe the classes, and describe the experience. So we took the community through that process and began to reimagine what that would look like and began to prioritize those things."

These recurring community meetings came to be known as the Voluntary School Study Teams. These dedicated individuals were charged with helping design initiatives that would respond to Oakland's Voluntary Resolution Agreement. Ironically, but not surprisingly, the arduous task of addressing and eliminating institutionalized racism fell onto the shoulders of those stakeholders least served by the system.

Taking heed of the community feedback and the small size of the AAMA team, Chatmon made the decision to adopt a particular school that was disproportionately failing Black children and go deep to demonstrate what could be done at school sites throughout the district.

Chatmon explained to the school principal that it was going to be a process to activate the parents. He warned:

> Don't personalize their anger. Don't take it personally. That's part of the healing process. And if we can't provide an authentic place or space where they can just get it out, you're never going to get to any of this other stuff.

As a result of the community building strategies, "we were able to get close to 88 percent of the African American community at that school [to] participate in four African American family summits," recalls Chatmon. Over the course of two years, Brother Chatmon was determined to help turn the school around. "In addition to his administrative duties at the district office, Chatmon was "literally at Edna Brewer probably four days a week … and Saturdays."

The AAMA model was demonstrating important results. The school received an award for the most significant reduction in suspensions for any middle school. Plans were in place to offer, in the words of Chatmon:

> conscious and subconscious bias training, culturally responsive pedagogy trainings. I mean a whole new appreciation on how do adults need to show up differently in service of Black children and Black families. Working in partnership to engage and enlist and enroll Black families to provide you with many of the answers and solutions.

Then he shakes his head. "It got real. And the realer it got, the more resistant and just harsh that principal became." Unfortunately, activated Black parents turned into a threat. In other words, their actual empowerment was not valued or appreciated, but seen as an agitation. The animosity from the principal continued to get worse. "So much so," shares Chatmon, that "after that second year, all of AAMA was gone." The principal told Chatmon directly: *I'm going to divorce myself from AAMA. You all are too Black.* Chatmon leans forward and folds his hands together, his facial expression stern: "It took everything in me not to lose my professional character." But, he reconciles, there were important lessons that were learned:

> I still feel that that model and framework, although intensive, is one of the best strategies, but, as I learned the hard way, you have to have principal buy-in. With any strategy, if the principal is not bought in, they will undermine everything.

During the first two years of development, the Office of African American Male Achievement fought to survive. Even in these early stages, however, Chatmon was steadfast. The narrative around Black children had to change. The headlines of local newspapers were disparaging, reporting that "Black boys see bleak future at school" (*SF Gate*) and "Detailed reports highlight challenges facing black boys in Oakland schools" (*East Bay Times*) (see Table 6.1). Harkening back to what Perry (2003) warned about in the last chapter, these articles were reinforcing an ideology of Black inferiority.

To combat the dominant narrative of despair and delinquency, Chatmon continued to shine a light on the solution: the children. He held a "Perfect Score Celebration" to "lift up" the 21 African American students who achieved 100 percent on the California Standards Test (CST). As Dr. Wing notes, this was another point of collaboration between the Department of Research, Assessment, and Data and AAMA—"perfect scores" were elevated as part of the counter-narrative. And the media took note.

The *Oakland Post* (November 6, 2013) did a feature story on the "Perfect Score Celebration." In a news interview, Chatmon reiterated that he was trying to make success the norm in classrooms.

> We feel it's important for us to shine a light and celebrate the academic accomplishments of our children. I think within our city and within our public school system we've gotten too comfortable with normalizing and accepting mediocrity and failure. So we're trying to change that narrative, to remind people of the beauty and brilliance of all of our children, to raise the expectations, and to engage families.

It seemed momentum was building and people were taking notice. The Perfect Score Celebration was then picked up by *Jet Magazine* and even Professor Cornel West "shouted me out" by telling people to "go see what Oakland is doing!"

A media frenzy began, and it has not stopped. AAMA has been featured in over 100 news articles in the last seven years including stories in *The New York Times*, *Newsweek*, *Voices in Urban Education*, *Issues in Higher Education*, and

TABLE 6.1 Newspaper headings, 2012 versus 2015

2012	*2015*
SF Gate Headline:	*SF Gate* Headline:
Black boys see bleak future at school[1]	Oakland aims to lift students who are young, male and black[2]
East Bay Times Headline:	*East Bay Times* Headline:
Detailed reports highlights challenges facing black boys in Oakland schools[3]	Every black male student in Oakland can be a king[4]

[1] http://www.sfgate.com/education/article/Black-boys-see-bleak-future-at-school-4088520.php
[2] http://www.sfgate.com/bayarea/article/Oakland-aims-to-lift-students-who-are-young-male-6671320.php
[3] http://www.eastbaytimes.com/2012/05/22/report-reveals-challenges-facing-african-american-boys-in-oakland-schools/
[4] http://www.eastbaytimes.com/2015/12/19/every-black-male-student-in-oakland-can-be-a-king/

Ed Weekly. At the local level, a counter-narrative took hold that shifted the conversation. Between 2012 and 2015 an evident change occurred with respect to Black male achievement (Table 6.1).

The local victories alongside the national accolades and attention humble Chatmon because "I didn't grow up with a silver spoon in my mouth" and "I didn't have access to this kind of network." For the first time in our conversation, Chatmon leans back in his chair, takes a breath and looks up. He shares with me the motto inside his head that helps him stay the course and remain focused amidst a hectic schedule and juggling multiple initiatives: "My circumstances do not define me. Keep my head up. One foot in front of the other and move forward. Just keep building with good people."

As I leave his office, I feel a bit overwhelmed and dizzy from all the disparate activities AAMA is doing. Then, just a couple hours later, Brother Chatmon begins sending me a succession of emails with dozens of attachments (e.g., previous reports, curriculum samples, meeting notes). It was these materials that fully satiated my curiosity. "Oakland was alone in 2010 when it created a race-based program in its schools focusing solely on African American males. It was a controversial idea—an abandonment of a color-blind classroom to improve the lives of black boys," wrote a reporter. I became intrigued that a school district was naming and claiming to address institutionalized racism in both policy and practice.

Within a few months, I was given tremendous access to the AAMA. It seemed that each week I was getting sent a new file to review (dating back to 2010 when the office first launched), and so I began devouring the information slowly, making notes in the margins of emerging patterns, pressing themes, probing questions, and incongruous outliers. The documents became my guide as I searched for seeds to the AAMA story.

A Labor of Black Love

Nearly six months have passed and it has been hard to catch up with Chatmon. He is in high-demand, but we finally sync our schedules. As I enter into his office, he is sitting at his desk, surrounded by piles upon piles of papers and folders. On the right of his desk, sits his desktop computer that chimes with incoming messages every couple of seconds and directly in front of him is his laptop. Both his office landline and cell phone continue to ring and buzz sporadically as we talk, but he usually ignores them. The only time I really see him stop—even in mid-sentence—is when someone from his immediate family is calling or stops by the office. It's an admirable trait and much of his leadership style relates to fatherhood.

AAMA operates as an extended family—a village of care—that transcends the traditional school day and invites the entire community into the learning process. To name just some of the activities: Man Up Conferences, community Honor Roll Celebrations, robust summer internship programs, Seniors 2 Success College Fair, GradNation summit, community cook-outs at Lake Merritt, bowling nights, and basketball games. Some of the strategic input points that set AAMA apart from other interventions include this comprehensive approach.

Consider for a moment that within seven years, AAMA grew from a staff of one to thirty. And the highly acclaimed Manhood Development Program (MDP) is now in 23 schools. Programs have expanded, and now AAMA operates a Student Leadership Council and offers extensive case management services.

In 2013–2014, AAMA only had one accredited course, Mastering Cultural Identity (through MDP). Just a couple of years later, students can now take up to seven accredited classes that include, African American Power in the United States, World's Great Men and Women of Color, and Revolutionary Literature. These courses all are A-G accredited and meet California State University and University of California entrance requirements.

Between 2011 and 2015, African American male students (grades 2–12) had an 8.2 percent increase on the SRI. [2] The number of Black students who have made the honor roll has steadily increased each year:[3]

- 2013–2014: 20.4 percent (434)
- 2014–2015: 23.7 percent (474)
- 2015–2016: 31.7 percent (454)

Engaging students in meaningful instruction decreases disciplinary problems. From 2011–2012 to 2015–2016, the suspension rate for African American males decreased from 17.7 percent to 10.8 percent, and the raw numbers fell by 48.8 percent, from 1,200 to 614. Thus, the suspension rate for African American male students involved in AAMA was cut in half.[4] Moreover, from 2010–2011 to 2015–2016, the cohort graduation rate increased from 41.3 percent to 59.8 percent. While the district cannot attribute these changes exclusively to the efforts of AAMA, they do suggest significant improvements.

These powerful quantitative outcomes are the result of an African American community ethos and philosophy of education that is saturating Oakland Unified School District. A measurable impact has been made in this city as a result of the unwavering commitment Chatmon and his crew made to "save our sons."

Love echoes throughout the data like its own heartbeat.

A vice principal, Earl Crawford, offers a sentimental testimony regarding the need for the Manhood Development Program at his school.

> Our young soldiers, scholars, kings have gone from turning up to reaching up … This is indicative of the precepts of our forefathers; galvanizing, fortifying and expanding from within to overcome being without. I am grateful to have Brother Foster as a catalyst for this work on our campus and appreciate how he facilitates and models Black love for our young brothers to emulate.

For this administrator, it is not just love, but the *Black love* that is impacting kids.

This is about life over death, hope over nihilism. According to these equity warriors, the work, essentially, is about love. I remember when love as a pedagogical strategy was impressed upon me. I was collecting data at a Freedom School in West Oakland back in 2004. I was there to evaluate the significant increases in reading scores and I was speaking to the director about my findings. A decade has passed since that conversation, but I still distinctly recall the lesson. I was focusing on the culturally responsive curriculum and she said, "Yes, that's part of it. But the children love reading," and then she paused and leaned toward me, "because we love them." A love for learning begins with a love for the child (Watson, 2012). This thought is brought to the forefront of my mind as Brother Chatmon takes me inside his teaching philosophy and brings me to a soul-stirring moment that could have cost him his life.

Nearly two decades ago a high, riled-up young man ran into the Boys and Girls Club in East Oakland. He was waving a gun around, demanding money. An instantaneous, eerie silence filled the space. Everything just stopped, as if time itself was holding its breath, yet to exhale.

Chatmon vividly remembers this moment. "I didn't approach with ego. I wasn't trying to gain control of the situation," he recalls. "I met the young man's anger with love, that real love that can calm people down." He pauses and moves in closer as if sharing a secret: "It worked, Vajra. It really worked." The volatile situation was handled peacefully. Chatmon shakes his head as he recollects that "the police were not called."

I look anew at Chatmon, who is sitting across from me at his desk. His eyes are piercing and hold a certain sparkle; he exudes a contagious vitality for life. Chatmon's style of leadership is emotional, intuitive, and nurtures those affective qualities in himself and those around him. He literally and figuratively "feels things out." Even when he talks about AAMA's theory of change, where others might see a linear model, Chatmon explains the energy flow of institutions. Systems-change, for Chatmon, rests on relationships and the ways an organization, like a school district, enables and/or disables genuine human connection and growth. If the institution is an ecosystem, the question then becomes, is it healthy or dysfunctional; and, Chatmon wonders, is it loving?

I have witnessed love inside the classroom, but what about in a closed cabinet session? Or at a contentious school board meeting? How about during a professional development training? It is in these spaces that Chatmon has demonstrated a universal love for all people and an unapologetic love for Black children, especially African American males. He stands in this truth irrespective of whom he is with or where he resides. Like the brothers say, "It's just in him. It's who he is."

As we resume the conversation, Chatmon shares with me:

> Even at some point when I age out of all of this, I am still going to be volunteering at somebody's school, teaching a group of kids. That's what I enjoy doing. When you learn to love other people's children and, like, you love them and then you have children of your own too, that's a *pinch me* moment.

Chatmon opens up about his sons, and I inquire about how his own children are experiencing OUSD and AAMA. "Hold on, sis." Brother Chatmon says the word "wholeheartedly" and then stops abruptly. He takes a deep breath and leans forward. Chatmon's expression becomes tender, not anxious, vulnerable, not excited as he talks about the struggles of his oldest son, Amari. "If I let you know, as a father, what my son has gone through at Tech. He entered that school with a 3.2 and is leaving with a 1.6. He had full access to everything. He had one MDP class but the culture of just everything at that school—the level of mediocrity, the peer pressure," and Chatmon looks down. Amari is "relational," much like his father, "and if you don't show up with passion, he will not give it back." Amari will "disengage." "There are kids that I know in that cadre who are seniors," he admits, and one MDP class a day in high school was not enough to "inoculate and protect Black boys." There is nothing as painful as watching children "check out" of their future. This signal, in his own family, reminds Chatmon that students need more wraparound supports that serve as protective factors against the nihilism of oppression. The AAMA services continue to expand in new directions, which will be examined in forthcoming chapters, but what holds them all together is love. Education, in this millieu, is an act of love.

Parenting and teaching have many similarities, and the laborious planting of seeds into the mind and heart is certainly one of them. Even though we cannot control the wind, rain, or concrete, we do know that seeds, when cared for, watered, nurtured, and nourished in healthy settings can sprout into a forest of possibility and imagination. Chatmon wants to plant gardens of social justice where Black children bloom.[5]

Christopher Chatmon's convictions resonate with critical theorists and revolutionaries alike. James Baldwin taught us that, "If I love you, I have to make you conscious of the things that you do not see." Or as Che Guevara espoused, "the true revolutionary is guided by a great feeling of love." Along this same continuum, in *Teachers as Cultural Workers*, Freire (1998) discusses the importance of love in education, noting: "I do not believe educators can survive the negativities of their trade without some sort of *armed love*" (p. 40, italics added). bell hooks (2003) describes love as an important guide into the heart of community. She writes: "When I come here, or to any place and feel myself to be somehow not fully present or seen, what allows me to enter this space of otherness is love. It is the love that I can generate within myself, as a light and send out, beam out, that can touch people. Love can bridge the sense of otherness. It takes practice to be vigilant, to beam that love out. It takes work." (p. 162). Although love is personal, it is not a singular adventure. It is generated in relation with others.

Theory of Change

For many district-level administrators across the nation, their days are filled with strategic conversations and bureaucratic logistics as they go from one meeting to

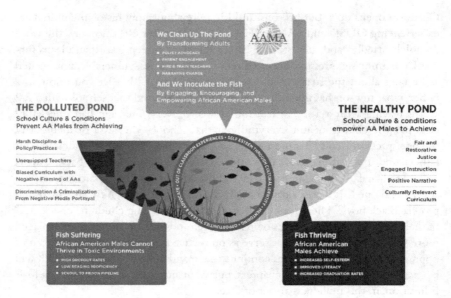

FIGURE 6.1 The AAMA theory of change

the next. Although this is definitely part of the job, Chatmon does not meet-to-meet, he meets-to-move. This slight difference has a cascade effect in the nature of his conversations, his impatience to get things done, and his relentless pursuit of actions that align systems toward social justice.

AAMA has been able to thrive because it is mission-driven with a specific focus, yet continues to be, as Chatmon likes to say, extremely alive and very dynamic. Chatmon describes "the curse and the challenge" of AAMA being moved time-and-again within the district structure. He has had six different supervisors in less than five years. He has had to be "in cold water" and then "in hot water, swim upstream, downstream, and then jump on a lily pad and then climb a tree." However, it was because of the inconsistency that he actually gained insight into the culture of the institution. "The blessing of that has been really learning the system." And, he adds, learning and having faith in the larger movement for equity. These experiences directly shaped his theory of change. In presentations across the country, he is sharing Oakland's vision of a solution (Figure 6.1).

To elucidate his theory of change, Chatmon uses the metaphor of the fish and the pond to draw attention to the toxicity of an educational system that under-values and undermines African American achievement. To alleviate the problem, AAMA strives to "clean up the pond" by changing the culture and conditions within the schools themselves through four target areas:

1. **Policy Advocacy:** Change school policy and practices to address the sus-pensions and expulsions of African American male students, and ensure that schools are intentional about the outcomes of these students.

2. **Hire and Train Teachers:** Enable teachers to have a better cultural under-
    standing of African American male students and therefore effectively engage
    them.
3. **Parent Engagement:** Ensure that parents are active in students' education,
    and are empowered to advocate for and support their children.
4. **Narrative Change:** Shift the conversation to report positive stories about
    African American male students, and to evolve school curriculum from a
    white narrative to one that reflects the contributions of African Americans.

While issues at the school site are addressed through the above measures, AAMA
simultaneously "inoculates the fish" by encircling the children with a conspiracy
of care and a consciousness-raising curriculum. This is accomplished through the
following wraparound mentoring model (Figure 6.2).

1. **Building Self Esteem Through Cultural Identity**: The MDP classes
    are the foundation of AAMA's work with students. The classes are taught
    by African American male teachers who form deep relationships with the
    students and help them navigate through school and life. Students develop an
    understanding of who they are as African American males, develop a broth-
    erhood among classmates, and boost their academic achievement through
    vocabulary and rigorously relevant texts (the sample reading list is available
    in the Appendix).
2. **Mentoring:** AAMA empowers older students to meet and mentor
    younger students one-on-one, as well as group mentoring through story

Policy Advocacy Æ Ban Zero Tolerance, Adopt Restorative Justice, AA-Focused Priorities

Cleaning Up The Pond

Changing School Culture
• Hire and train teachers
• Increased Parent engagement

Changing the Narrative
• Kingmakers of Oakland
• Strategic Communications

Moving Curriculum
• Khepera Curriculum
• 3rd-12th Grade

Inoculating The Fish

Self Esteem & Mentoring
• Manhood Development program
• Man Up Conferences

Out Of Classroom
• Field Trips/College Tours
• Conferences

Leadership Council
• Mentor younger students
• Advocate for better school conditions

FIGURE 6.2 Macro-institutional shifts toward a holistic social justice educational model

nights—benefiting both the younger mentee while building the leadership, confidence, and sense of purpose of the mentor. They also facilitate intergenerational mentoring and community building through bi-annual ManUp! Conferences.[6]

3. **Out of Classroom Experiences:** AAMA's field trips expand students' perspectives, networks, and horizons—allowing them to envision future possibilities and goals.

4. **Opportunities to Lead and Advocate:** AAMA's Youth Leadership Council provides opportunities for students to serve as advocates and ambassadors for issues related to educating African American male students.

Altogether, Chatmon has demonstrated that shifting an educational ecosystem is possible, but it is a slow, multi-dimensional process that works when teams of people align their priorities, politics, policies, and practices. This is not an easy task. Most school leaders are dealing with competing interests, exhausting schedules, and disparate stakeholders. This is also true for Chris Chatmon. What is unique to his approach is a constant refrain to be student-focused in directive and deed.

While the youth sustain his passion, he also strives to embody equity in his interactions with comrades and critics alike. When faced with push-back he will tell me, "I am willing to learn. We can all get better." This humility is disarming and I have watched him turn naysayers into allies. Another significant component of his character is that he tries, though its not always easy or spot-on, to not replicate patterns of oppression in his daily interaction with others. It is not about being liked—that is more about ego—but it is about authenticity and human kindness.

Irrespective of where Chatmon is within the institution he prides himself on building connections, a practice linked to a philosophy of inclusivity. At staff meetings and events, for instance, he has check-ins as part of the process. He prioritizes "having a sacred space that we can enter and leave in. Something to just appreciate and acknowledge who is in the room. These sorts of things I deliberately try to model" across the system, from board meetings to community gatherings. Chatmon will ask people directly:

- What is your passion?
- What is your purpose?
- And how do your passion and purpose relate to your profession?

Introspective questions can inspire social change. One of Chatmon's rare gifts is the ways he uses stories to bring people into the circle; absolutely no one is an outsider.

Even as Chatmon recognizes individuality, he is also cognizant that institutions, like schools, are by-products of the larger ecosystem of oppression. "You cannot deal with student achievement and not talk about race." He is weary that a lot of interventions—even those led by well-intentioned people of color—often "perpetuate the same system and get the same outcomes." A lot of reform efforts are still vested in linear modalities and a "European value system" that undermines the people, particularly "people of struggle."

It's all about people power.

Instead of partnering with the community in real, genuine, and authentic ways, district administrators often sit behind a desk "mapping out" solutions and think-ing, in relative isolation, "How do we get people to believe in what we're doing." Simply put, when the conversation gets isolated to an office or a boardroom, so does the solution, and nothing really changes. "Creating all of these things *around* families instead of *with* them" makes no sense. African Americans have been in Oakland for centuries. The system is silencing them—"not giving voice" to their expertise and experiences. He shakes his head in disappointment and shrugs his shoulders, "not even acknowledging them." Brother Chatmon is candid: "This is how systems underdevelop urban schools."

Chatmon is in rare form. He is tired of the political acumen and polite meet-ings that dissolve into more meetings that eventually dissolve into nothingness. This is about our humanity. This is about our children. The urgency with which he speaks is painstakingly honest.

Top-down modalities cause friction. Hierarchies tend to be inhumane. The system is broken. The principal and the janitor are equal; the child that lives in the hills and the child that lives in the flatlands both deserve to climb the mountain of their own dreams. AAMA is slowly demonstrating that any system constructed by the hands of human beings can be deconstructed, reimagined, and revivified. The power is in our hands—literally.

The Gold C

When I arrive on this late afternoon, Chatmon is sitting in his office sipping on some take-out soup. For the first time in a long time, his vibe is a bit slower. Maybe it is because it is winter and it is cold outside; he looks bundled up behind his desk, wearing a seemingly comfortable warm winter sweater. His presence is subdued and even his entire outfit, from his hat to his shoes, is varying hues of brown. I appreciate the calmness and casualness of the space today. We are able to reach a level of openness and candor, introspection and reflection. This stillness occurs as he simultaneously slurps his soup from a plastic container. And every so often, as he talks, he uses a pair of wooden chopsticks to pull out the noodles. Ironically, his office desk feels more like a kitchen table as we sit and talk, back and forth, about where AAMA has been and where it is going.

As the founder and executive director of the AAMA, Brother Chatmon acknowledges that, "it's my baby." The way Chatmon serves as the father of this initiative at work is inextricably linked to who he is as a human being outside of work. According to him, leadership is a living entity that exists in the dynamics ("that energy") of fostering community, building connections, and mobilizing care for those least served by the system.

Looking back on his life, Chatmon talks candidly about his own schooling experiences. "Going to public school in San Francisco," he shares, "teachers didn't understand me." In third grade, he was traumatized by his teacher who would lock him in the classroom closet, in the pitch dark, as a disciplinary action. Chatmon was energetic and considered unruly. And this particular educator tried to break his spirit with rituals of punishment and control. This experience almost cost Chatmon his education, because after that school year, his curiosity and eagerness to learn were squelched. He never quite trusted teachers the same after third grade. In middle school, he got banned from riding the school bus and was put into remedial classes.

As we are digging into his past, the phone rings. Brother Chatmon tells me to hold on. From the exchange, it sounds like Khalil on the other line, Chatmon's middle child who is in high school. "Hey son, you good. You walked Max? Are you done with laundry ... I'm cool with you hanging but then I'll take you to your basketball game so what time are you going to be home? Oh, okay. See you at 4:30. Be safe son. I love you." During all our interviews, he has only paused abruptly for his wife and children. I think about this as we go deeper into his story.

Although Chatmon struggled inside of school, there were other forces in his community that nurtured his lifelong development. In particular, he found refuge in the Boys Club (now the Boys and Girls Club). At this community center, he interacted with mentors and took life-changing trips that gave him self-confidence and self-determination and broadened his horizons. In particular, he reflects fondly on summer camp in Mendocino. He explains:

> The place where I was really a king was Camp Mendocino, that took me out of the hood and put me in the middle of the redwood forest. I felt like that was my home away from home. From the neighborhood to the redwoods and that transformed me.

Chatmon remembers, "swimming in the Noyo River at five in the morning ... I would get out of the water and literally, my body would be blue," in part because he was a scrawny kid and the water was freezing. These experiences taught Chatmon "how to push myself." He surmises that he has been "underestimated most of my life" and, as a result, he has had to learn to persevere with his own sense of direction and purpose.

By the time Chatmon was fourteen, it was his last year at Camp Mendocino and he was determined to get "The Gold C," an award given for a triathlon of accomplishments. One of the activities was to show survival skills by building a shelter and starting a fire without any help. Chatmon vividly recalls this night: being alone in the pitch dark in the middle of the forest, fighting through his fears, facing some of his most painful memories—from being abandoned by his birth parents to getting chastised into a closet at school—and persevering. He underwent a breakthrough that night that brought him into the light of his own abilities, resiliencies, and consciousness. The sunlight of that new day paved a bright path toward Chatmon's future; from that day forward, he believed, unequivocally, that anything is possible. "That moment, I knew that whatever I wanted to do in life, I could do." Chatmon was one of two youths to receive "The Gold C" that year and he "knew, even then," that was really the "rites of passage." With a positive sense of self, Chatmon's life started to turn around.

"My junior year in high school I made the basketball team and began to understand how to navigate the public school system. I made a commitment to graduate and come back and be an extraordinary teacher and transform the lives of all children that came into my classroom." Years later, Chatmon fulfilled his dream. He taught at Thurgood Marshall in San Francisco and he is still in touch with almost all of his students from twenty-plus years ago. "My modern world his-story and her-story class and the stuff we did there, like that was a Gold C moment." Brother Chatmon loved teaching—he still does—but he wanted more students to experience an amazing education, which inevitably brought him outside the traditional classroom context.

Brother Chatmon describes yet another, more recent Gold C moment: when he received a personal email from President Barack Obama, inviting him to the first anniversary celebration of *My Brother's Keeper* at The White House. "I called my dad and I cried. All I could do was say thank you." In this moment of recognition, Brother Chatmon felt humbled to his core. "It's a blessing to stay true to something and feel like you don't have to sell out to money or to positions." Chatmon is a career educator and youth practitioner whose goal in life was to be an extraordinary teacher. He grew professionally and built an astounding department in Oakland that has given him a national spotlight. He continues to leverage the system in service of children, Black boys in particular. So now, to be recognized as an expert in the field—"the president wants you and your guest"—is an unexpected victory that superseded even Chatmon's high expectations for himself.

Movement Building

For Chatmon, a moment turned into a movement. The work of AAMA is spreading. Mississippi, Seattle, New Orleans, Michigan, Missouri, San Bernadino, Antioch, and the list goes on. Inquiries are coming in from neighboring cities as well as from across the country. As leaders consider the comprehensive AAMA approach, it is important to contextualize and operationalize, modify and codify identity-based programs. The key is not African American males per se, but the way a district responds, through targeted universalism (Powell, 2008), to the group in need of specialized support systems.

Chatmon is busy sharing his insights with a group of seven district administrators from Milwaukee who want to create a similar office. We are all cramped inside the AAMA portable. I am diligently taking notes, enraptured by the discussion.

"I get people," admits Chatmon, "who are overly focused on policy, but if you do not have something that is genuinely engaging, encouraging, and empowering the people then all you really have is a policy." He explains to the visitors that after learning about what AAMA really does, on the ground, a lot of people are just overwhelmed because of the "layers and layers and levels and levels."

Dr. Derrick Mitchell, CEO of Partners in School Innovation, is at the table as well. Brother Mitchell reflects upon his own skepticism and then explains why he is a self-described "convert." He says, "the stars aligned in three pivotal ways," which is what made AAMA successful. First, Superintendent Tony Smith found the right person. This was so important, he insists, because "otherwise you will just get a darker version of a colonialist." Chatmon is about the children in word and in work, and he unapologetically focuses on the needs of African American students. Second, it was strategic to "incubate the work outside the system" before including it as a department within the district. Take something as simple as hiring people that the system might not deem qualified because they lack a formal credential, but they are the mentors the students desperately need in their lives. Maneuvering through the bureaucracy takes a certain skill set and tremendous flexibility, even just to get a payment processed. So the day-to-day operations of pushing against the system will often "grind the innovation out of you," says Mitchell. He speaks frankly and stresses to the administrators from Milwaukee that a lot of times, the "revolutionary spirit gets crushed inside of you." And then third, and finally, says Mitchell, the AAMA prioritized the data. Since "the people down in the trenches can't do the global analysis for community leaders, policy makers and funders," having the research component allowed the AAMA to "incorporate" those findings and narratives "into the work on the ground." This type of reflective praxis allowed the work to grow strategically—connecting the roots to the treetops. Mitchell underscores that although he always knew the work was necessary, it was Chatmon's "authentic relationship with the community" that drastically impacted the system.

As soon as Mitchell is done speaking, the team from Minnesota has a lot of questions. They are voraciously taking notes and asking clarifying questions. Brother Chatmon wants us to understand, "AAMA has never been just the Manhood Development program." In its totality, the AAMA is a "much more comprehensive strategy to treat the entire system. Manhood Development was one of those strategic activities that gripped and is getting a lot of support." Yet it is important to remember, he urges, that no one intervention "exists in isolation." Chatmon lifts his hands and mimics what it would look like to throw a rock in water—that's MDP—it hits the water which creates ripples of concentric circles that continue to radiate outward.

"Whatever we do nationally," Chatmon is clear, "Oakland is our lab." The commitment is to "stay deep locally." Even though Chatmon is being pulled in a lot of directions, "if you pull the roots out of here, it will not work." He laughs, "In our community, a suit-and-tie will actually get you put out." For the most part, "folks celebrate race and culture here. So to make moves here you got to have transparency and spirit in a way that people respond to as genuine." That is not the case everywhere. He admits, "There is a uniquity about Oakland." Acknowledging the local history and particular milieu—the fertile ground—that grew AAMA is intricately connected to the overall model and theory of change.

Chatmon does want to grow the work nationally, and he imagines an extended network and infrastructure that carries AAMA into new settings. He discusses the importance of being able "to pivot with a team" that can meet the urgent demand for services. "So all that to say," and he pauses before sharing, "there are places, like Mississippi" where it is "still very difficult" and people do not "have that kind of freedom" to "explicitly talk about the needs of Black boys." Chatmon recognizes that there is a "level of understanding and rhythm that has to be contextualized in every city." The contextualizing process is complex and crucial, because the work must reflect the particular realities and histories of its environment.

Chatmon continues to galvanize the group from Milwaukee and the rest of the stakeholders sitting around the table. He looks at each of us while talking decisively and fast: "There's not just one thing or one silver bullet. It's not just hire more Black teachers. It's not just change Black boys. It's not just curriculum." Then he claps his hands. "It's not just policy." He claps again. "It's not just restorative justice." Brother Chatmon claps one final time. He then uses his arms and stretches them out wide: "It's literally addressing the entire system … It's movement building" alongside "the collective will of the people" to fight for what is right, unapologetically. "We have to have the audacity to know what we are doing is necessary, but far from sufficient! So we have to stay in it and stay in it! We are nowhere near where we need to be!"

My field-notes from this moment: *The journey is the outcome. Without the embodiment of daily actions of radical love, people will just go through the motions, implement initiatives, and not ever dare greatly and courageously to transform systems.*

As I leave the meeting with the administration team from Milwaukee, I am concerned that they seemed overwhelmed by the task. I am equally concerned about Chatmon's level of exhaustion. He exudes so much energy to lift others up; I worry about burnout. As we walk out of the portable, I ask him sincerely, "When you get tired and dismayed, where do you find your energy and hope?" "The children," he says simply. Brother Chatmon's clarity on the importance of the young surfaces repeatedly. "The greatest thing I did for me, selfishly, is the Student Leadership Council," he tells me. "That brought me back to my roots. I'm a teacher." This is Chatmon's unwavering motivation and inspiration: "The way you change the system is through the children. It's the young people!

We Are Kings

A couple of his colleagues were a bit taken aback that during AAMA's moment of national momentum, Chatmon decided to reconstruct and lead the Student Leadership Council (SLC). When I ask him about this choice, he tells me that he did not want to lose sight of his purpose and as much as the students are gaining experiences, they are like his compass. He benefits tremendously from the opportunity to build alongside them twice a month; the exchange is mutually beneficial and reciprocal.

"I did not want to defer this anymore. I needed that reality check. I need to be evaluated and hear, intimately, what's happening." Chatmon laughs and shrugs his shoulders, "Ain't nothin' more humbling than being in a room of young brothers. Cause if they hungry, they don't care who you are." The group currently consists of twenty middle- and high school kings from twelve different schools. "That's my board. That's who's holding me accountable." The students ground him like nothing else.

With the satisfaction of a proud parent, Chatmon goes into great detail telling me about their trip to the University of Memphis for the Coalition of Schools Educating Boys of Color (COSEBOC) conference. "When we presented," he says, and then he takes a moment to clarify: "I can't even say 'we;' all I did was push the slides!" The young kings presented the curriculum, the theory of change, really everything. They were professional and the information shared was relevant and robust. "Just to see their level of agency shattered the bias" of what students are capable of doing—not just for themselves but for school reform! Afterwards, the students received a standing ovation and fielded questions long into the next session. It was a breakthrough moment that rejuvenated Chatmon.

Building on this conversation, Chatmon invites me to sit with him at the upcoming Youth Leadership Council meeting. He promises that this is where hope lives: in the raw, unabashed, bold, diverse, and colorful personalities of the young.

When I arrive at the SLC meeting, the rectangular tables in the center of the portable are full with students. I find a seat and squeeze in at the corner. Seeing the food on the table seems as important as seeing and hearing from one another. The students are devouring the afternoon snacks.

A middle school student arrives late to the meeting. Instead of him receiving negative attention, Chatmon gives him a special shout-out: "Welcome back to Brother Thyree. We don't break down; we build up. Give this brother some love." And after that directive, Brother Chatmon facilitates a quick check-in. He asks the students to share "one thing you think about this school year in its totality? What will you always remember when you're my age? … Lift up something that you will take with you." The students go around and provide windows into some of their greatest memories and lessons from the past school year. Once the opening commences, Chatmon says, "When I say *Man*, you say *Up*."

Brother Chatmon: *Man!*
Student Leadership Council: *Up!*

The side-talk stops abruptly and the group focuses on Chatmon's announcement about the upcoming field trip to the Lawrence Livermore National Laboratory, the upcoming family cook-out at Lake Merritt, summer internships and summer school. He then asks, "Are some of you interested in working at Freedom Schools?" And he proceeds to pass around a sign-up up sheet.

After the logistics, the dialogue centers around lessons learned in their Manhood Development courses. Students debate and discuss people they look up to, critical facts they've learned, and issues of identity. It's a space to challenge and to question with a group of peers from various areas of Oakland, but who are all committed to serving their communities.

The young men admire people like James Baldwin, Malcolm X, and Martin Luther King. A student critiques his peers, "Did y'all just forget about the women? What about the powerful females?"

"I don't look up to nobody," one of the students interjects.

> I don't put nobody on a pedestal. I motivate myself. When I grew up, I had to raise myself. Ya feel me? It was Top Ramen every night. Ya feel me? I was motivating myself to go to school. And then I motivated myself to sit down and watch Youtube so I could learn how to cut hair.

Another king sitting nearby puts his hand on the brother's shoulder: "Man, I know it's rough. That's real."

The conversation meanders, rather organically. "We can't really get mad at white people," a young king claims because "history is written by the victors." "How do you know white people won?" I prod. "They won because our story is not being told." Well, then, I ask: "What is the story that you guys are trying to tell?" They look at each other and start calling out answers:

> *We are not drop-outs!*
> *We are not thugs!*
> *We are kings!*

"We don't know enough about ourselves to be free" a middle school student interjects. Another young kid adds on sporadically: "You can only be so free with the knowledge that they gave us. The history that they teach us is a misconception." "They don't teach us anything about the greatness that Africans had before the slave trade," someone else adds. "Yeah," a younger-looking student pipes in, "nothing just started from slavery. There were thousands and thousands of years of greatness that happened in Africa. And they don't teach us any of it. Who is going to teach us our history, but us?" His question lingers for a minute. And then an older youth speaks candidly about how the literature in AAMA is "vital to our survival" because "it's the dynamic of realizing your power."

Watching the Student Leadership Council confer and build with one another reminds me of a recent conversation with Chatmon. Far too many adults chastise the young, so children get the message that something is wrong with them. He lowers his voice, and mimics: "You ain't gonna be nobody; pull your pants up." Chatmon pushes against this philosophy and says simply: "Elevate their minds, and we know our kings will elevate their pants."[7] I watch his words come to life throughout the SLC gathering.

A student shares lessons that he learned with his peers when he went to Africa: "I traveled to Africa. Seeing those things firsthand in Ghana was breathtaking." He wants the other kings to realize that:

> we come from empires like the Ashanti ... Even if we knew 5 percent of our history! Even if we just knew the history of one place: Nigeria. That country alone would be enough to empower us so much to do so many great things!

Another student adds to the analysis, and acknowledges that, "in all reality, the Ashanti Empire sold us." Even if the Ashanti did not know the extent of slavery, the Maafa would not have occurred without cooperation and compliance from Black people. The conversation continues to get deeper.

Building on the energy in the room, a student who plans on being an Astrophysicist discloses: "Freedom is knowing all of the possible choices and being able to make them. You cannot know your true potential if things are being held back from you."

In a final moment of reflection and to close out the meeting, Chatmon shares that he was adopted and throughout his entire life he has been led by "extraordinary people ... and typically, it was brothers ... For whatever the reason, outside of my dad, I just always had awesome brothers that were like *Nah, cuz, lift your head up.* They gave me the right dose of whatever to get me through that hurdle," he says, and "ultimately ground me" with "values" that were not necessarily monetary—"though some cats had the fly car." It was the integrity of particular individuals that inspired Chatmon to reach toward greatness and pursue his dream of becoming an educator. He wants nothing less for his own sons, those by bloodline and those, like him, who are adopted in one way or another, into this AAMA village of care.

Notes

1 A student's English, Reading and Writing scores are scaled to create combined English Language Arts (ELA) score.

2 Scholastic Reading Inventory (SRI) Interactive is a computer-adaptive assessment designed to measure how well students read literature and expository texts of varying difficulties.

3 Enrollment is based on all 8–12 students in OUSD district-run secondary schools, excluding charters.

4 This is based upon a cohort graduation rate; graduating in four years from the time a student enters ninth grade.

5 Chatmon's oldest son, Amari, is now a successful student at Cal State Dominguez Hills.

6 As a piece of history, explains a community member, "The West Oakland Community School, a middle school in 1996, was one of the first charter schools in Oakland and incorporated elements of Kwanzaa into the design of the rituals and themes at the school. Shortly after that school began, another school, an African-centered high school with a focus on science and African history and culture, opened in West Oakland. The founder of this school started a conference and called it the Man Up! Conference. This same conference was the template for the current Man Up! Conferences hosted bi-annually by AAMA."

7 http://vue.annenberginstitute.org/issues/42/lifting-our-kings-developing-black-males-positive-and-safe-space.

7

UNAPOLOGETICALLY BLACK

There is a parable in Africa that teaches: *If the young are not initiated into the village, they will burn it down just to feel its warmth.* There are many ways to interpret the burning of a community, but youth-on-youth violence is certainly one of them. According to the Center for Disease Control (2014), homicide has been the leading cause of death for ten- to twenty-four-year-old African American males and females for decades. On many social indicators, Black children are not surviving.

In response to this epidemic, the Office of African American Male Achievement (AAMA) strives to create various Rites of Passages—pathways of initiation—that nurture boys into healthier young men. The Manhood Development Program (MDP) inside schools, bi-annual Man Up! conferences, the Student Leadership Council, and the Summer Internship Program are just some of the examples that I alluded to in earlier chapters. Taken together, these services create a continuum of care and protective force that surrounds the children. Inside this village, students are taught to love their melanin, study their history, and elevate their cultures. This chapter focuses, specifically, on the insights from within community, those people who consider themselves part of the immediate and extended family of AAMA.

The findings I will now discuss are based upon data collected in the form of student surveys and writing workshops with various stakeholders. The results demonstrate key, recurring themes around Black identity development that the AAMA offers to students, their families, colleagues in the district, and even their own direct staff. A common ethos reverberates from their testimonies: a positive cultural community is linked to health, happiness, and hope. These ingredients foster a sense of personal agency and collective accountability that break cycles of underachievement.

Student Surveys

Five hundred and three students completed my survey over the course of two years (2013–2014; 2014–2015). Respondents ranged from nine to nineteen years old and attended the Manhood Development Program at twelve different schools.[1] All surveys were disseminated and collected by the MDP instructors at the school sites. Surveys were sealed in an envelope and all responses were kept anonymous. Sixty percent of the students surveyed have been in the program for almost a full year. Only 10 percent of them have been in MDP for more than two years.

Based upon the survey data, 37 percent of students live with their father in the house. Although the majority of students do not live with their dad, 88 percent of students said that they have a male adult who they can go to for guidance and support. Fifty-nine percent of students have been suspended from school at some point and 8 percent of students have been incarcerated. Thirty-seven percent of students have personally witnessed someone get shot. Five percent of students do not believe they will live to see their twenty-fifth birthday. In addition to this statistical data, I asked students to list three words to describe being a young Black male in America. They came up with a litany of words, which paints a dire picture of being menaced by society: underestimated, underappreciated, alone, statistic, ignorant, horrible, bad, sad, lonely, broke, and oppression. From the responses, the two most popular words were dangerous and hard. Juxtaposing these negative experiences, participant's self-identity very differently. When asked what they see when they look in the mirror, they wrote, for instance: "I am a scholar" or "I am a great thinker. I am an eighth grader with high potential."

Throughout the surveys, students seemed to vacillate between feeling *mistreated* on the one hand and *unstoppable* on the other. Through intensive coursework and a pedagogy of brotherhood, these young African males and their older African American male instructors work together to navigate through the root causes of racism and determine how to navigate oppressive systems, such as schools. This extends beyond the "codes of power" of Delpit's (1988, 2006) earlier analysis and goes into the fallacies of white supremacy. Focusing explicitly on a positive racial identity allows students to understand themselves in light of a society that often tries to dim and demean their shine.

It is not surprising that on multiple indicators, the vast majority of students perceive that AAMA adds significant value to their lives. Students were asked for three words to describe their Manhood Development class. All words associated with the program were positive, and the most popular were: brotherhood, educational/learning, caring, powerful, respect, interesting, fun, Black, awesome, and hard working.

Although the students used words of admiration to describe MDP, this was not the case when asked about their overall school. For 29 percent of students, they still consider their school "boring, ratchet/ghetto, horrible/terrible, ignorant/dumb, racist, and unsafe/dangerous, and dirty." These statistics almost parallel the neighborhood descriptors. While 68 percent of students describe where they live as "peaceful, quiet, safe, and nice," the other 32 percent, used words like "ghetto, dirty, dangerous, and violent" to delineate their neighborhoods.

Students were asked to mark boxes on an opinion scale (ranging from 1–NO! to a 5–YES!). The most popular, affirmative questions relate to expectations. Ninety-four percent of students report that their MDP teachers want them to succeed. Eighty-six percent of students state that their MDP teacher encourages them to get good grades and 86 percent also trust their MDP teachers. Students did not answer positively for all questions. The highest disagreements related to identity and relevance. One-third (31 percent) of students stated that their instructor does not look like them and 25 percent stated that they do not relate to their MDP teachers. Similarly, one-third (30 percent) of the youth report that MDP does not relate to their lives outside of school. Similar to other trends in the literature (e.g., Fergus, Noguera, & Martin, 2014; Ginwright, 2004), for a subset of students, the teacher's race and gender was not synonymous with relevance and relatability.

Students were asked to think back to before they started the Manhood Development Program. They were then asked a series of questions about the ways they perceive that their behavior and/or perspective has changed. Sixty-nine percent of students stated they have had a dramatic *decrease* in disciplinary problems at school and 66 percent report that they get into physical fights "way less." Eighty-four percent of respondents are now doing "way better" in school and 87 percent of them want to go to college "way more." Given that over 500 students took the survey, these trends are extremely high and paint a picture of AAMA's impact on academic ambitions.

At the end of the survey, students were asked if there was anything else that they would like to share. Many of the children and youth spent time writing additional feedback. Most of them were extremely appreciative of the program. For instance, one wrote:

> As a young man I have been through many struggles but still found a way to keep my work up. Many of my family members died and I was able to still feel empowered. The MDP program was the perfect fit for me and has benefited my life for the best. Without this class I would not have been able to discover my true identity.

Various students described their academic improvements: "I used to have a 2.5 but now I have a 3.6. I used to get in trouble A LOT!! But now I don't get into trouble at all." Another respondent said: "I went from a 2.3 to a 3.0. I did my work in class. I had some challenges and overcame them." Students repeatedly mentioned that the MDP class provided a unique support system that impacted their experiences in school: "This class is really helpful. It makes high school a lot more easier. Without this class I don't think I could get through as smoothly as I am now."

It is valuable to mention that one student described feelings of alienation within MDP. He shared anonymously: "I am a queer mixed male who lives in an unstable home. It would make me feel better if this class had more curriculum that is queer friendly." This student's transparency is vital. There are various inputs—in the form of intervention treatments—that influence and impact student behaviors, and what works for one child will not necessary befit another. Creating space that nurtures the diversity of Black brotherhood should be reflected in the literature and authentic practices that celebrate differences.

While children are the stars in the AAMA family, they are not the entire constellation. To accurately codify the "secret sauce" of this work involves a wide range of actors. On many levels, the organization operates as its own microcosm of racial empowerment, or as Chatmon would say "a healthy pond."

Community-Based Writing Workshops

A total of fifty stakeholders participated in an intentional writing workshop I designed for AAMA. Each session was two hours long, and we hosted three of them. The sessions were facilitated by Patrice Hill, my colleague at Sacramento Area Youth Speaks (SAYS).[2] At the end of each gathering, participants were given the option to identify themselves at the top of the page. About half of the people (twenty-two) chose to remain anonymous. Altogether, the respondents represented an array of AAMA participants, all of whom are strategic partners in the work. Contributors included the AAMA student leadership team, district administrators, parents, AAMA teachers, and the wide range of individuals that support the daily operations—from the twenty-seven-year-old white guy who oversees marketing and communications to the seasoned African American woman who handles a plethora of administrative duties.

Each writing workshop began with a call-and-response activity in which participants were asked to create a palette of words to describe the organization. This activity is simple, yet it has multiple purposes. First, the word palette represents the collective because everyone shares at least one word. This further substantiates that it is a community space and every voice matters. Second, the words that are placed on the board provide insight into the ways participants experience and define AAMA. Third, participants pick three words from the board and write them down on their paper as a starting point. In this way, nobody starts the individual writing process with a blank page.

The questions that I asked during the writing sprints were meant to illicit answers that were analytical and emotional; scientific and spiritual; theoretical and practical. Along this continuum, I was able to triangulate responses for patterns, accuracy, and answers to my research questions.[3] As is customary with qualitative studies, I coded and analyzed data sources for key perceptions and their impacts, using etic codes, like "identity development" and "institutionalized racism" derived from the literature, and emic codes that emerged from the data, such as "life-changing" and "brotherhood." Following Miles, Huberman, and Saldana (2014), I then constructed themes for my codes that addressed my larger research questions—specifically, scrutinizing social justice as a daily practice inside class-rooms (micro-level) as well as at the institutional level (macro-structural) to ana-lyze the impact of the AAMA in Oakland Unified School District.

Dream Work

At the first writing session at the district office on an early Saturday morning, the majority of participants were from AAMA's Student Leadership Council, or as the young kings like to shout: "SLC!" When asked to describe AAMA during the initial activity, a student hollers definitively: "dream work!" Heads nod; the facilitator writes the word on the board. This particular phrase, out the mouth of a babe, cuts deep through the data and into the spirit of a movement that this organization personifies.

When paired together, the words "dream" and "work" encapsulate something new and spectacular, existing at the intersection of who we are and where we want to be. Dream work lives on the horizon between imagination and reality. In daily practice, it looks like an email from Chris Chatmon that says, "Team work makes the dream work! Appreciate all of you for your responsiveness and grace. Onward and upward!" (Personal Communication, August 9, 2016).

Dream work is an overarching concept in AAMA and is a natural segue into the findings of this portion of the study. AAMA is not a panacea or a magic bullet; it is a work-in-progress based upon an unapologetic and undeniable commitment to fight for education to be/come a liberatory force. The empowerment, however, is complicated and sometimes compromised as individual actors work within and beyond the borders of the school district.

As mentioned in the introduction, many members of the AAMA village were doing this work long before Oakland Unified School District gave it a name. Through the writing workshop, Jerome Gourdine opens up that he has been "involved in the movement for Black male achievement" his entire life. He attrib-utes his passion to the "powerful African American male influences I had in my life starting with my father and both grandfathers." When Brother Jerome started teaching in Oakland, he worked at a continuation school where "most of my students were Black males." Later, he began working at Frick Middle School in East Oakland. One student, in particular, "became a son to me (God rest his soul)." Brother Jerome shares, "I watched him grow from a graduate of my mid-dle school, to a graduate of high school and college … After his passing, his best friend told me, *he loved you and you made a tremendous impact on his life.*" Beyond the job title, for Jerome and others, this is the their revolution—reaching, teaching and uplifting Black youth.

"As I continued through my educational professional journey as a teacher, assistant principal, and principal," Brother Jerome continues, "I have often tried to figure out multiple ways to positively impact the trajectory of our kings." The term king is important, and is something that Jerome started when he was a principal; it was later adopted by AAMA. "I coined the term kings" giving "particular attention to my Black male students to give them a sense of empowerment."

Even prior to joining AAMA, Jerome was the first school principal in Oakland to open up his school site to host the annual Man Up! Conference. On a Saturday in 2009, more than 300 kings and 100 mentors showed up. He remembers, "It was an amazing event with workshops, seminars, and activities. The interaction between the mentors and the kings was an incredible experience for all who participated." Brother Jerome's point that these events are transformative for everyone, not just the students, is important.

AAMA has created new safe spaces for staff inside the district. Although onlookers often focus on the children, the teachers discuss that the program has become their lifeline as well. As an example, Abdul-Haqq Khalifah, a technology teacher who is now affiliated with the Manhood Development Program at Garfield, explains that he has been teaching for a decade without any type of brotherhood or support system. He appreciates AAMA for the "true and sincere community and brotherhood that I have witnessed behind closed doors." He wonders, "How'd I make it this far without it?" "I think AAMA has done more for the people who work here" albeit as staff, than "all of their OUSD experience and interactions combined." "Why?" he asks rhetorically, answering:

> Because it is the voice for the voiceless who have been muted on purpose and there is no other vehicle that can do this heavy lifting in the district. Some growth outcomes are apparent, some are implicit, some will not reap for years to come, some don't reflect in the *what* but in the *why* and *how*. But they are all present and fully featured if one takes the time to dig deep, explore, talk to, question.

Brother Abdul-Haqq's appreciation for AAMA is based upon the professional support and growth he has received. As he shares about the impact it has on his own life, he imagines the layers of transformation he continues to see in the students. Building on this idea, Brother Jerome wants observers to enter these classrooms "cognizant of how the students are greeted and how involved they are in the process of learning. Please pay attention to the words the teacher uses to address them and direct them to complete their different tasks and projects. Also, notice the level of academic discourse that is taking place in the class."

Fighting Miseducation

The AAMA operates within a large urban school district that continues to wrestle with inadequacies. Nevertheless, being housed within the system has brought the program—and its teachers—tremendous credibility. John Smith, an AAMA facilitator explains:

> The greatest success of AAMA by far is that we are acknowledged as teachers in the classroom with all rights and accessibility to our student kings. We are not just a program like afterschool trying to grab any kid that wants to stick around. We are acknowledged by the district; we have the ability to track records and contact homes when problems arise; we need to know school issues, home situations, and the social-emotional status of the youth.

"If we want to service the child holistically," he asserts, then "we need access to the whole child."

Quinton Richardson is a teacher in the Manhood Development Program. He believes that AAMA is a large organization and it continues to grow, but "the teachers are the most important because they are the frontline soldiers in this battle to save lives." Toward that end, "we empower each student by allowing them to be heard each day. Every student is special and is seen through the eyes of love rather than discontent." Brother Quinton is proud of his accomplishments with the young kings. He proclaims that "each kid is different, but I am fortunate enough to work with a student that comes from a dysfunctional family background but has managed to maintain a B average or above over the last three years of being in AAMA. This student enjoys coming to class and participating. He enjoys being heard, and feels he has a place in society. Before he came to AAMA he was a failing student who didn't take himself seriously. Nowadays he's attentive and alert, and prides himself on being a leader in class and among his peers."

Another MDP facilitator, John Smith, states, "Our young kings have been historically and systematically ill-equipped to face the challenges of school, society, and life." To combat the mis-education, "We engage encourage and empower youth to understand their past, view their present, and strive for a future via transformational lessons and life experiences." "The frontlines of this war," he concludes, "is at the school ground. He who controls the minds, controls the heart, the sprit, and the soul of young kings."

Earnest Jenkins is the Director of the Khepera Academy and also still serves as an MDP instructor. He says:

> Being in AAMA allows me to fight against a system that I fell victim to as a student. I am here to vicariously reap the benefits that I feel I should have received as a youth. I fight because others have fought for me. I fight for my unborn children and family members who are next in line to encounter the bag of tricks that will be thrown their way by this district and country.

Earnest Jenkins is thirty-four years old and he shares that this is the exact kind of program "I needed at the age of high school." Even though he is grown, he admits:

> Youth allow me to feel, to let new thoughts and ideas enter my mind and with those I am forced to re-evaluate my life actions in conjunction with my life's purpose. I'm also healing myself and learning more ways to master myself with every lesson I teach.

As long as "this country continues to negatively brand our Black youth with imagery and systems to keep them within a mindset of inferiority," there will be people, like Brother Ernest, providing African American children with an alternative.

Bobby Pope is currently an AAMA case manager for middle school students. "My story with AAMA begins with my son," he discloses. Brother Bobby's son was in the first cohort of MDP students at Edna Brewer Middle School: "I knew at that time I wanted to get involved on a deeper level, but wasn't sure if my life journey would take me in that direction." Years later, a position opened up and Brother Chatmon told him to apply. "Once on the team, I quickly realized how powerful our work really is and the impact we have on the system." He continues:

> As the case manager, my role is to trouble shoot any challenges our kings and their families are dealing with inside or outside the classroom. I fight to make sure our kings have all they need to be successful. I'm fighting against an inherently racist system that treats folks of color unfairly.

Zarina Ahmad, principal of Piedmont Elementary School shares:

> In order to make this a reality I must fight against mis-education such [as] books and teachers that show African American history beginning with enslavement. I must fight against stereotypes and racism that limit their self-love and block them from access [to] education. I must fight against the negative images that makes them see themselves as men who glorify drug dealing, alcohol, drugs, or only see themselves as becoming professional athletes or players and pimps. I am in this fight because my goal in life is to help restore our people to our traditional greatness. I want for my kings the same that I want for my biological sons. I see them all as mine and truly when one is happy and successful then we all are.

AAMA has been able to combat underachievement with rigorous instruction, a culturally responsive curriculum, an army of African American male educators, and supporters of various races/ethnicities.

Josh Egel was skeptical that AAMA would have an impact, but what he has seen with his own eyes shifted his paradigm. A self-proclaimed liberal, Josh Egel "believed that human beings needed to obey rules that enforced respect. White people couldn't say the N-word. Politicians needed to listen to the masses and do what they say." His values were a bit one-dimensional and over the course of the last three years, Josh's self-perception has been challenged and stretched in unexpected ways. Brother Egel is the only white person fully employed by the AAMA. Although Josh is not in the classroom, he photographs and observes almost every class and event. "There's this idea that kids are good if they behave, stay quiet and do their work," explains Egel. He has come to believe that "these are insanely low expectations."

A case in point: "Remi's class," according to Egel, "operates out of love and functions as a highly rigorous academic class. In the heart of East Oakland, he's managed to counter the trauma with highly rigorous instruction and amazing engagement skills." Although the MDP instructors share a common curriculum created by Baayan Baakari, they each bring their own personalities into their pedagogy. Brother Egel recognizes that and shares:

> Sikkim is a different story. He embodies the idea of the classroom reflecting the real world. He operates out of core and skill. The man loves working on cars and audio equipment. His do-it-yourself start-from-nothing philosophy comes out in his lessons. Yesterday I documented his class. They learn[ed] about physics and engineering after completing a series of argumentative essays throughout the week. The kids constructed sailboats out of office materials and raced them on water. In one week they learned academic rigor, social engagement skills and practical engineering skills.

Even as an observer, Egel explains, "That class transformed me."

Living Transformations

Eddie is thirteen years old and attends James Rutter middle school. When asked to describe the first moment he learned about AAMA, he states: "That's exactly the point that my life transformed." Eddie shares that before the program he had no concept of "the future." Jakarri has a similar story. He divulges that in seventh grade "my grades were low and we were struggling. I needed help with basically everything in life." Brian Reed from Oakland Tech echoes these sentiments as well, saying: "AAMA is a life-changing program." Jakarri was recommended to the Manhood Development class by his school principal. He remembers:

> After I applied, my life started to change. I was surrounded by exceptional brothers and being a part of this program motivated me to do better in school. I ended up pulling up my GPA from a 3.0 to a 3.6 and that made me very proud.

Rickey, a senior at Oakland Tech, discloses:

> I was a young Black male that was not going down the right path … I
> wasn't always a model student, didn't always do what I was told, nor was I a
> scholar. I was a fuck up in my eyes. Joining AAMA was basically my turning
> point.

For each of these African American students, the Manhood Development Program
provided a life-altering intervention because it gave them a sense of self, a foundation of brotherhood and support, and lifelong aspirations. The academic outcomes
are the consequence of the consistent love and years of care that the students
receive from the AAMA community—from the adults as well as each other.

Willie Scott is now eighteen years old and is a senior at Oakland High School.
He has been an active member of AAMA for the last five years. In fact, Willie
joined the Manhood Development Program when it was just taking root inside
schools. He remembers: "We called ourselves *New Generation*. The first week of
class the camaraderie that was made was unheard of … I knew at that moment
that I wanted to be involved with this program forever."

The Manhood Development Program made a commitment to Willie five
years ago, and they have stayed a consistent and forceful influence in his life. "This
program is 24/7," he shares, because "I know I can call any of my instructors if
I am in any trouble." The AAMA family has not let him down when he was in
need; Willie's success represents their intention and years of service to his development and achievement.

As Willie sits at the table, writing intently alongside his AAMA brothers, I
harken back to the words of his first MDP instructor: "I look at Willie Scott. I had
Willie first in seventh grade at Edna Brewer and he used to tell me to lighten up,
you're too tough on us." Willie "used to be crackin' jokes in the back of class and
taking extra snacks. Now I am looking at him leading right now."

"If you compare day one to today," Willie reveals, "it is unbelievable how
far we've come and how much we are still beaming." According to Willie, with
each cohort, the program becomes stronger. He is emphatic that "this program
is changing the narrative of Black lives in Oakland." Willie lives what he has
learned. As an AAMA youth leader, he epitomizes a high school scholar-activist
who is boldly, in his own words, "fighting for institutionalized racism to be over."
For Willie, MDP is more than a class; it is his calling. He is not alone; countless
students share similar testimonies.

Andre McDade, a tenth grader at Castlemont High School in East Oakland, is
involved in AAMA because "it's one of the few places I feel wanted and loved …
MDP is more than a class, it's a brotherhood," he explains:

> Each year I feel like I am learning more than I ever could have. I feel like
> I'm improving my character more than I ever could have … Being in the

program has helped me want to learn more about myself and my culture and background.

While Willie is explicitly fighting institutionalized racism, Andre says that he is "fighting against the lack of positive role models and having one has made me feel like I have great power."

These outcomes are occurring in real time with real people. Another case in point:

When his closest friend in the world was murdered in middle school, Romelo Rims began isolating himself from his peers and even his family. His grades dropped drastically ("I wasn't focused") and he was not passing any classes. Recognizing the recent turn of events, Remi Bereola, his MDP instructor, took notice and worked with the school counselor to enroll him in AAMA. "Brother Remi called me," his mom remembers, and from that moment onward "Romelo changed." She noticed a drastic difference in her son's ability to communicate and participate in the world, including at home and at school. She is clear that there is a direct correlation between AAMA and her son's healing. Romelo is now a freshman in high school and he talks about going to college; he has hope. Romelo admits that "my eyes were opened." Romelo's mom saw a change in his friends as well: "They attitudes have changed. They more happier." "It works for these kids" and "as long as they keep this open, they got a chance." She encourages everyone to visit a Manhood Development class. The door is wide open—like outstretched arms—for anyone interested in experiencing a praxis at the intersection of relevance and rigor, healing and achievement.

Healing Our Hope

Precious Stroud found her way into the AAMA family after working in the private and non-profit sectors and still experiencing the antecedent rituals of white supremacy.[4] She began with AAMA as a program consultant but became more involved because "I needed to know that my father's legacy was being fulfilled in my daily life." On a personal note she shares, "after my father's recent passing ... I needed to be around positive men who were, like my father, men who stood up for people and grounded their work in love." For Precious, like other members of the AAMA community, this is not simply about a job. "There were times," explains Precious, "when I went above and beyond; my first payment was a $50 gift card to Target." Obviously, it was not about the money. She explains, "It was an honor to be in service. The time that I spent with Brother Chris on a weekly basis nourished my soul ... I don't question one day, one email, one effort, nor one hour spent on this work. It is soul filling and awe inspiring." "In my heart," she continues, "the greatest success so far is that Black students are learning to see themselves for themselves." Although the children discussed AAMA in terms of "dream work," Stroud says that when she visits the MDP school sites, she witnesses, "dream makers."

According to Brother Jerome, AAMA creates spaces for African American males to "have a different definition of who they are, where they originated from, and what they can possibly become. Now we have students (kings) who understand [that] their dreams, aspirations, and goals are limitless."

AAMA is unapologetically Black in purpose, policies, and pedagogy. From the structure of the classes, to the ways the educators scaffold lessons based upon familial knowledge, and the diligent love that is present, the barriers of the schoolhouse transcend into doorways of new futures. This form of social justice instruction turns nouns, like hope, into verbs. Hope becomes a doorway into the imagination, to a place where dreams are no longer deferred.

Notes

1 MetWest, Oakland Tech, Oakland High, and Skyline High Schools, Frick Middle School, Montera Middle School, Dewey Academy, Alliance Academy, Ralph Bunche, Claremont Middle School, Parker Elementary, and Piedmont Avenue Elementary.
2 SAYS is a critical literacy movement grounded in spoken word performance poetry: says.ucdavis.edu.
3 Sample questions from the Writing Workshop are available in the Appendix.
4 For more information on this particular area of her work, check out the *Black Female Project* at www.blackfemaleproject.org.

8

PEDAGOGY OF PATIENCE

Perhaps the recent racial tensions and unrest in this nation—from Ferguson to Baltimore to the presidential election—could have been alleviated if more children had attended schools that were using a multicultural curriculum and culturally responsive pedagogies (Gay, 2014; Ladson-Billings, 1994, 1995; Andrade, & Morrell, 2008). While this research is critical, it is improbable given the demographics of the teaching force described in Chapter 1. Plenty of studies reveal the ways white women can be effective, extraordinary educators (e.g., Harding, 2005; Howard, 2016), but it is unrealistic to expect teachers, at large, to critique systems of oppression if they were never given the tools to dismantle it within themselves. *How can we teach that which we do not know?*

The Office of African American Male Achievement (AAMA) was explicit and intentional in the ways they recruited educators for the Manhood Development Program. Harkening back to Chatmon's proclamation mentioned earlier that "every Black man is a potential teacher," this chapter discusses the process of hiring a transformative teaching force. Through the next two portraits, Matin Abdel-Qawi and Jahi Torman come to life and demonstrate practical and pragmatic tools for school leaders as well as hands-on strategies that can revivify learning spaces for all students.[1] For those who are struggling to do education differently in high-poverty, inner-city schools, these brothers illuminate that educators have incredible agency to subvert socially constructed limits on human development by changing the very schools in which they work to better serve the lives and learning of students (Catone, 2017; Mahiri, 1998; Oakes, Lipton, Anderson, & Stillman, 2015).

Building Success

School systems cannot improve without teachers. Teachers are the cultural keepers and dream makers. As discussed earlier, the AAMA doubled the number of African American male instructors in OUSD. To understand this result, I interview Matin Abdel-Qawi, the current principal of Oakland High School.

From the district website I learn that Brother Abdel-Qawi began working at Oakland High School after serving as Program Director of MDP. Starting in OUSD as a math and science teacher at Claremont Middle School, in 2002 he earned his administrative credential and a master's in educational leadership at the Principals Leadership Institute at the University of California, Berkeley, and became an assistant principal, and then principal, of the East Oakland School for the Arts on the Castlemont campus. He is the father of three teenagers: two sons and a daughter.

I arrive at Oakland High School to interview Brother Abdel-Qawi on a warm sunny day. As I drive into the parking lot, an older African American male security guard smiles and welcomes me onto the campus. My first impression of the grounds is shaped by the sheer number of students scattered outside, working in groups on projects. As I head into the building, the hallways are extremely clean, even the floor seems to shine. These thoughts run through my mind as I climb a flight of stairs and make my way to the principal's office.

Before we can begin the interview, Brother Abdel-Qawi needs to check-in with a student. I overhear an older African American male (in his late twenties or so) tell a younger student, "Mr. Abdel [pronounced Abdul] is Pops. That's Pops and he'll look out for you."

After waiting for my turn in line, I make my way into Brother Abdel-Qawi's office. Like most principal's offices, it is filled with the life of his school. His desk contains various sticky-notes of tasks to be completed and there are piles of papers strewn throughout. Amidst the usual clutter of running a site, this space feels distinct. He has a large bookshelf that also contains his prayer rug. Two large framed posters hang above his desk. The first is the photo of Tommie Smith and John Carlos raising their fists during the medaling ceremony of the 1968 Summer Olympics. The second is a painting of Che Guevara with the caption, "Against brute force and injustice the people will have the last word, that of victory."

To begin our conversation, I inquire about the comment the young man just made that Brother Abdel-Qawi is "Pops." Brother Abdel-Qawi shrugs and says, "That's nothing." He keeps it simple: "I was his teacher," he reflects back, "That particular older young man was my student fifteen years ago in middle school (sixth grade) and I knew him through high school, college, and now he works in Oakland for the probation department as a case manager."

In this short exchange, I am given a glimpse into a community network of fatherhood, brotherhood, and mentoring that involves a principal, a local case-worker, and a struggling young African-American male student. The paths of these three individuals serendipitously connect on a Friday afternoon at Oakland High School. Yet, the path that led to this moment was forged between a teacher and his student over a decade ago. A profound interaction that has given Brother Abdel-Qawi the title of "Pops," signifying a deeper role than that of a typical class-room teacher or principal, one that reaches beyond the walls of the schoolhouse into the heart, mind, and lives of those he seeks to educate. This relates directly to his role as an architect of the Manhood Development Program.

Groundbreaking

Brother Abdel-Qawi went to school in New Jersey in the 1980s. His graduat-ing class was over 500 students and over 90 percent Black. His father owned a local barbershop in town and the clientele was 100 percent African-American. Altogether, he grew up in a Black community where his neighbors and the "folks down the street" were all African American. While the nexus of his neighborhood was Black, this was in contrast to the teachers at his school who were almost exclusively white women. During his public school experience, he remembers having three African-American male teachers: "I had science, history, and PE teachers [who] were African American males." He does not speak about his white female teachers as ineffective or damaging, per se, but focuses on the interven-tions that exposed him to a world outside of Jersey. In his junior/senior year, "two brothers" ran a program that "took us to tour Morehouse and Spelman during Spring Break." During this experience, he was able to see an education system run by Black people for Black people. Historically Black Colleges and Universities (HBCUs)[2] represent a long-standing educational tradition—a legacy rooted in the struggle to use learning as a tool for personal and collective empowerment. Although all-Black schools are not a new idea, creating an identity and gender-specific program within a diverse large urban school district is groundbreaking.

When AAMA was still in its infancy, Superintendent Tony Smith approached Brother Abdel-Qawi about Oakland's new initiative. Brother Abdel-Qawi was excited about the vision. Superintendent Smith was "very specific and for good cause. If you look at all of the data, no one is performing worse than African American males. Every data point justifies the need to focus on African American males." He continues, for a "white male leader to have an agenda that focused on Black children, specifically, was interesting, to say the least" and was really quite "brave and brilliant."

In July of 2011, Brother Abdel-Qawi was placed on special assignment (vis-à-vis the district office) to help build a robust program in OUSD for African American male students. Under the direction and leadership of Christopher Chatmon, Abdel-Qawi's first directive was to oversee and manage the Manhood Development Program (MDP), which at the time, was still an idea. The lofty goal was to have it fully operational at all high school sites. This, Brother Abdel-Qawi chuckles, was nearly impossible given that school would be starting in just one month. Instead of feeling overwhelmed by the task, however, Brother Abdel-Qawi found places like Oakland and McClymonds high schools that "had the right people in place and were primed and ready to go." There were also critical partners like Destination College and the East Bay College Fund that had staff and expertise that they wanted to lend to the cause.

Based upon Chatmon's vision, Abdel-Qawi's contacts inside the schools, and a vast array of community partners, MDP began to take root. Since Brother Abdel-Qawi had served as a teacher and principal in the district for over two decades, he had well-established partnerships with teachers, school personnel, and principals. "I did not come in with a really fancy book or a lot of curriculum in place," he recalls, but people knew me and there was "a lot of trust" and "we did it on the strength of relationships." I wonder about pushback; did any of the site administrators feel like a program such as this might alienate other students? Brother Abdel-Qawi is adamant that "there was no resistance from anyone." While there were "a lot of questions" because we were still building it, everyone was eager for a solution. "No one was happy with the data on African American male students. It was an easy sell."

Throughout the fall of 2010, Brother Abdel-Qawi was focused on, "developing relationships with administration to get the school sites ready, made sure we were on the master schedule, and found students." Overall, the schools were ready to embrace a class on manhood development for African American teens; equally critical was finding the right facilitators.

I ask Brother Abdel-Qawi what kind of attributes he looked for in the MDP instructors. He leans back in his chair, smiles, and responds with a calm serenity: "Patience." I am surprised that he mentions this first and he must sense my reaction because he shares, "It might sound silly, but we needed to find brothers that had a tremendous amount of patience, an unbelievable wealth of patience," and that is not something that can just "come across in an interview. So we sat at cafes for long periods of time," he explains, "and had long conversations about why do you want to teach, how would you approach this type of situation. In addition to patience," Brother Abdel-Qawi continues, "we looked for brothers" who majored in African American Studies in college, worked with African American male organizations before, demonstrated some kind of connectedness to the community (through art, hip-hop/spoken word, faith-based work, etcetera), and who were, "personally and professionally connected to African American people in general and African American boys specifically." Essentially, they sought facilitators who would not see their position as merely a job, but a calling. Using their networks throughout the Bay Area, AAMA began to develop a strong team of nontraditional teachers who had a genuine "love for the work."

As it turned out, "Some had college degrees. Some didn't. One facilitator was a college professor and found time in his schedule to do this four days a week." Although the skill sets were all different, admits Abdel-Qawi, "the foundational pieces were there in all of them." A set of common values, an unrelenting commitment to Black people, and personal qualities, like patience, far out-weighed any particular credential. The teachers were expected to be culturally competent, caring, and compassionate and to devise lessons that would complicate one-dimensional caricatures of Blackness and masculinity.

In its first year, MDP targeted low-achieving Black students with disciplinary problems. But the demographics of these classrooms looked more like On-Campus Suspension (OCS); this was an unintended problem that needed to be fixed. The AAMA team paused and reflected. Soon thereafter they built a model similar to AVID[3], but were deeply attuned to racial identity development and empowerment.

To date, each manhood development course is comprised of a diverse group of teenagers: "one-third of the brothers struggled a lot academically, one-third on the bubble [i.e., were on the threshold between success and failure], and one-third who demonstrated academic success," remarks Brother Abdel-Qawi. The goal was that this cross-section of students "would support each other in different ways" that impacted the learning environment and eventually, "the classroom and school culture." The configuration of the class is significant:

> Students who are straight A students sitting next to a kid who comes to school two to three times a week and try to get them to have a serious conversation about what it means to be a brother in this society and valuing both of their perspectives can be very challenging.

Nevertheless, for one class period each day, approximately twenty-five African American male teenagers grappled with their own identity and belonging in school and in this world.

Brother Abdel-Qawi desperately wanted this experience to "lift them up. I wanted to help create an environment that they looked forward to coming to, that would build them back up." Too many of these students experience poor treatment in their communities and even in their schools. "They go from class to class and get beaten down and disrespected" and they start to believe that they are menaces to society and that they are destined for failure, even an early death. As I listen to Brother Abel-Qawi, I am reminded of the student surveys; hundreds of students wrote down the way the world negatively perceives them. Just for these same students, urges Abdel-Qawi, to "feel good about who they are and what their potential is" and that they are capable of advocating for themselves and using their voice to get what they need out of school is monumental. "I want them to know they are an asset to their families, community, and homeland" and gain a real understanding of the "African American experience" in terms of the "challenges and the blessings."

After all his years in education and the intense work associated with MDP, Brother Abdel-Qawi admits that when it comes to a child's destiny, there is no definitive "rhyme or reason" to who a person will become. As educators, then, it is our role to nurture their brilliance while they are in our care and further each student's ability to think critically, act wisely, and advocate for themselves and their communities.

I am interested in what these ideals look like, on the ground, inside a high-poverty school in Oakland. I backtrack a bit to ask, "Given that there is no rhyme or reason, what would you say are some best practices for reaching and teaching young African American males?" I continue to prod, "Does it even matter what we do?" Brother Abdel-Qawi appreciates the question ("that's a good question") and provides four key definitive points:

---

1. **Create a safe space for African American young men** *inside of school*
    "Our schools in general don't do that. I think that a lot of our brothers feel alienated, isolated, picked on, and just to have a class, at least one-hour a day, to just breathe, exhale, and be who they want to be without judgment."

2. **Recruit and retain** *African American* **male mentors and educators**
    "Having a brother in front of the classroom who is articulate, intelligent, and caring is a shift from what a lot of them see on a daily basis. This helps disrupt the stereotype. It also creates an intergenerational brother-hood and network of support to help these students succeed."

3. **Utilize a culturally responsive rigorous curriculum**
    "We must have an opportunity to learn about who we really are and the legacies that we come from. Schools have a responsibility to be inten-tional about fostering that. Black children in this country actually believe that who they are started with slavery and that history is not even taught in a functional way. It does not connect you to Africa or to ancient civi-lizations. So all you feel connected to is East Oakland, drug dealing, negative hip-hop, misogyny, and that's all you experience about your people. Someone has to take responsibility for showing us the beauty of who we are by demonstrating a counter-narrative to the stereotypical images that surround us."

4. **Provide opportunities to experience life** *outside of school*
    "Exposing them to life outside of their neighborhood and school with col-lege tours, going to the beach, and so on. With all these other aspects in place, the field trips and experiential learning opportunities make African American manhood development a really special adventure."

As previously discussed in the theory of change in Chapter 6, these four ingredi-ents continue to be ever-present in MDP at elementary, middle and high schools throughout OUSD. The class serves as an oasis for the students, but it also under-scores the deficiencies and, at times, discrimination, apparent in their other courses.

Case in point: Three MDP students came to their MDP facilitator to express concern with their poor grades in another class. The students were adamant that even though they were turning their work in, the teacher was marking it missing. They were no longer willing to accept a "D" or an "F" grade. The MDP facilitator mediated a conversation between the students and the teacher and subsequently created academic contracts that had to be signed daily to hold both parties equally accountable for the learning. According to the MDP facilitator log, this small-scale intervention proved quite successful and gave the students the leverage they needed to earn higher grades in that particular class.

In the best case scenario, confirms Brother Abdel-Qawi, MDP facilitators are on campus full-time and can serve as a powerful mentor within the MDP classes as well as act as an advocate, case manager, and change agent for the whole school. At one site, the facilitator noticed that On-Campus Suspensions was comprised, daily, of a classroom full of African American males. Prior to having the Manhood Development Program on campus, a student would be sent to OCS for an entire day, but with the AAMA advocate at the school site, he was able to point to the problem, name it, and then devise a solution. Now teachers can only send students to OCS for one class period and during that time a reflection needs to be completed that helps identify the root causes of the behavior. This shift changed the structure and culture of the entire school and, "drastically reduced the number of students in OCS," explains Abdel-Qawi.

Teachers are instrumental in cultivating a cultural shift at schools; they are the gatekeepers that can resuscitate learning. Again, how does it happen? Jahi Torman provides an answer.

★★★

When Brother Chatmon decided to go to a KRS-One concert in 2011, he was not expecting to meet someone that would become an MDP instructor, but then he saw Brother Jahi on stage and listened intently to his uplifting message. He was moved. After the show, he approached Brother Jahi and there was an immediate connection: the use of creative expression and critical thinking as a liberatory tool. Brother Jahi explains "timing." Chatmon and Jahi were "on the same page without realizing it." Today, Jahi is a program manager for AAMA, but when he first started, he was hired to run the Manhood Development Program at Edna Brewer Middle School.

Edna Brewer is located on 13th Avenue in Oakland. Brother Jahi "lived up the block" and "wanted to do something in my neighborhood." The Manhood Development Program served as his doorway into the school system and he was eager to lend his expertise to the cause: academic achievement for Black youth. Brother Jahi was excited to have a presence "on a daily basis." His ambitions were clear: "Be of service. Inspire kids. Make an impact."

Prior to engaging the students, Jahi was insistent that he needed to get to know their families. "Before I did anything," he says, "I had a family gathering with food and music and laughter." At this inaugural event, Brother Jahi literally served the parents. It shifted the power dynamics because Jahi told them, "Don't get up, I'm here to serve you," and proceeded to fix each person a plate. As a result, the parents opened up in profound ways. "My real leverage" is families. Jahi explains that the "Mama, Aunt, Grandmama all knew that I cared." A parent shares that Brother Jahi was effective because he constantly reminded her son "how great he is." A father echoes these sentiments; his "efforts with my son have been helpful not just in his classes, but in life."

Brother Jahi boasts that through the MDP community at Edna Brewer Middle School, he watched families become advocates for their children. According to him, there was a shift underway; they were moving from recipients and by-standers to active agents. He provides me with an example.

"I can remember Brian who *they* considered special needs, he was being treated unfairly and the parents had a meeting with the school." Although Brother Jahi had been asked to attend these types of meetings before, this one stands out in his mind. As he watched the parents, he realized that they were modeling his behavior. In previous meetings, they sat back as school personnel dictated to them about interventions for their son. Now, the parents had a notebook full of questions and they wrote down the entire conversation. At one point, they even asked the Individualized Education Program (IEP) team, "Weren't we supposed to receive a phone call prior to this decision?" He relates this experience to larger issues of family engagement and school improvement. When everyone is on the defensive, learning slows down. In parent-teacher conferences, for instance, families get "run through like they fast food" and a lot of teachers "already assessed [that] your kid is bad" so there is no real conversation. But through community and relationship, he stresses, "We can get a lot further" on behalf of kids.

Brother Jahi's reputation precedes him, and the MDP team holds him in high regard. Because, he acknowledges, "I tried to make an impact. I am serious about my work. I wasn't playing." Jahi's colleagues explain that he was at an extremely difficult school where site administrators were highly skeptical. Nevertheless, Jahi was relentless because, "We got to win." While parents were critically important to his overall feat, it was equally important to have teachers on his side.

From the onset, Brother Jahi explains, he would "take an assessment" and just ask the students directly: "What teachers are you cool with?" and "Who are the teachers that you are having problems with?" Once he had his list, Jahi would meet with his colleagues. For those teachers that students identified as particularly effective, Brother Jahi would approach them with the following script, "Johnny identified that you are a cool teacher; why would he say that?" As the teacher would open up, Jahi would, "make a friend and ally" because, "both of us want this child to succeed." Conversely, for those teachers the students designated as difficult, he would, "be very strategic in saying *how can I support you and help you with this child*?" From this conversation, Brother Jahi could gauge where the teacher was at, not just with a particular student, but also with their profession.

Brother Jahi is direct: "Any time a teacher would talk to me about a student, I would say, *tell me something good about that child. Tell me three things he did well.*" He boasts, "I was instrumental in creating a paradigm shift."

Brother Jahi understands that children develop in an ecosystem. Therefore, just having a great MDP class was not enough. He needed to foster connections to students' families and work with the staff to shift the dynamics of the entire school. Having his other colleagues at the site discuss positive attributes of his students was a small, but significant pivot in the right direction.

Collective Accountability

To create a classroom culture that empowers students, Brother Jahi allowed the middle schoolers to choose a class theme ("They decided that the theme was *greatness*") as well as set the rules. First and foremost, "The rules were set up by all of us. I am done trying to set up rules and giving them to kids." He shakes his head as he describes horrific approaches to classroom discipline. "When they have to be held accountable to it," he surmises, "It's not like *uh, somebody imposed that on me.*" Brother Jahi retorts, "Oh, I didn't say you couldn't be late three times. You know, that was *your* rule." In effect, his style fostered collective accountability—"the students disciplined one another because it was *their* rules, not mine."

Once classroom order is established, children just need a space to "grow and blossom." Similar to Abdel-Qawi, who also discussed the importance of safe spaces, Brother Jahi intentionally wanted his students "to be themselves, be a child in a safe environment" that nourishes them to "grow" with "somebody who truly cares about them." Furthering this metaphor of a garden, for Brother Jahi, he intentionally creates lessons that explicitly relate to the context, environment, and roots of students' identities; for African American youth, this has particular significance.

The curriculum in MDP classes is culturally relevant, and Brother Jahi has a gift for making content, no matter how rigorous, accessible to the students. When teaching Malcolm X, for instance, he started by having the students dissect his life from age zero to fifteen "so they could find out Malcolm was a foster child. That Malcolm's father was a Garveyite; he studied Marcus Garvey. That Malcolm wanted to be a lawyer and his teacher told him to be a carpenter." If he had just pulled out the *Autobiography of Malcolm X* and ordered his students to read, they probably would not have been as engaged with the text. His scaffolding approach to literature and other lessons demonstrated a keen awareness for developing their analytical skill set. Essentially, it simultaneously increased his students' depth of knowledge and knowledge of self. Brother Jahi chuckles a bit under his breath. His students thought they knew about Malcolm because of the popular phrase, "*By any means necessary,*" when in actuality, "I want you to know what Malcolm was like when he was twelve." As a middle school teacher, Brother Jahi met the youth where they were at and introduced them, anew, to leaders like Malcolm X using a relatable age-appropriate frame of reference.

Jahi and I have a common passion for teaching. The conversation flows naturally as we discuss best practices. I am a little taken aback, however, when he describes his pedagogy. It is a beautiful combination: simple and powerful.

Teaching, according to Brother Jahi, is straightforward. Building on decades of his work with young people "around the world," he has developed a three-step process that continues to prove effective. Brother Jahi's pedagogy: *I Do. We Do. You Do.* These three phrases are plain enough, but listening to his description of the process is powerful. I ask him to clarify what his tactics look like inside the classroom ("Break that down brother, please"). He elucidates:

I Do: "In the first five to ten minutes, it's what you as an instructor have to do to take control of your classroom; you have to know exactly what you are teaching for the day. You set the tone and the energy: if you come in slouching, then don't be mad when your kids are slouching. Inversely, if you come in organized, prepared, and energized, then it will be infectious."

Once "I Do" is established, then "We Do is what we will do together."

We Do: For instance, "Today we will learn about Malcolm X. We will watch the video together and we will critique what we watched and we will have a conversation about what we saw. That's the '*We*' part." He advises, "As you facilitate the conversation, you are giving away your leadership, every time you can. Somebody raises their hand, '*Ah, you lead.*' Someone is an outlier and is not paying attention and not focused, '*Ay, can you tell your brother to pay attention.*'"

Learning is a collective process, but students also need to take personal responsibility for what they comprehend. This leads to "You Do."

You Do: In this stage, students have to "Demonstrate critical reflection and competency with the task at hand." In a lesson about Malcolm X, each person needs to explain, "How does Malcolm's experience relate to you?" At this point, "I back completely up."

The arc of the lesson comes to a close ("There's the exit") when the students are told to jot down a fact and figure on a note card. It could be something as simple as what are two things that you learned today like, "Malcolm X was born on May 19th and he joined the Nation of Islam." These note cards provide the instructor a quick glimpse into each student's grasp of the content and serve as an important bridge to tomorrow's lesson.

Jahi is methodical in his approach to teaching. And his students excelled in the environment he created for and with them.

Clearly, Brother Jahi had some outstanding success at his site, but given my experience working in urban schools, I feel compelled to ask: "Do you think there was any perception, especially among the white teaching force, that you are only successful because you are a Black man working with Black boys? Do you think there was any scapegoating there?" Before I can even finish the question, Brother

Jahi responds with conviction: "There's always that." Some people rationalize Jahi's success as a race issue. He laughs and responds, "You are a teacher. You decided to be a teacher." He goes on to explain that when a person becomes an educator, they should not be so narrow-minded as to think they will only be effective with kids that look like them, talk like them, or are from the same economic or ethnic background. That is not realistic and it is not the core of good teaching. "I am not going to let you off the hook because what I am doing, you could actually do. Now, there might be some unique skill set, like I'm an artist, but," he reiterates, "You decided to be a teacher. Here are some universal principles that you can use so that I can stop being your scapegoat." Brother Jahi takes a breath and I jump right in: "So give me your universal principles for teaching. What are they?" He responds immediately, in rapid succession.

"Number one: All children are inherently great. Number two: They are always one opportunity away from succeeding even more. And three: There is no such thing as failure. Failure is an illusion; there are only various degrees of success." Brother Jahi speaks with clarity and precision. He seems personally invested in these principles and as the interview continues, I realize that this is not just about how he teaches, but reflects how he lives. "I hold myself to an incredibly high standard," he shares. Even so-called failures "are part of my success plan" because "it is only when you reflect and have introspection that you become better." He urges anyone who dares to improve schools and society to courageously and carefully look into the mirror: a precipice of self-actualization.

Unlock It

While the focus of MDP is the students, in the conversation with Jahi, I learn that the program also provided a new type of brotherhood, camaraderie, and network for the educators. As much as Chatmon, Abdel-Qawi, and others sought to create services that would impact African American students, they, too, became integral agents in this collaborative process. Manhood development is not just for the youth. Being a part of a community that cares, shares, and whose members hold one another accountable is powerful for the adults as well. This is a recurring theme.

"The Manhood Development Program," explains Brother Jahi, "Does not just enhance the leadership abilities of students, but also provided leadership opportunities for African American men." Brother Jahi was able to grow as a teacher and facilitator. He also gained important skills in leading professional development, designing curricula, and directing and overseeing activities. He discusses the vital mentoring he received from Brother Chatmon ("Just being around him, period— was great") and the guidance from Brother Abdel-Qawi was inspirational.

Jahi leans back in his chair and looks up. There is a pause between us. He does not appear to be bothered or even notice the loud game of air hockey right next to us; students are screaming and the puck seems exceptionally loud moving from one side of the table to the other. Still, this backdrop fades away as Jahi leans in, with a sense of excitement and a twinkle in his eye, and shares with me a typical morning. Brother Abdel-Qawi "would call me," grins Jahi, and he would only say, "I love you, brother. Have a good day," and then hang up. In turn, Brother Jahi felt compelled to, "Tell my students, *I love you, brother.*" This ritualistic, unapologetic Black love had a cascading, expansive affect that created a harmonious dynamic in/ out the classroom. Even in staff development trainings, it was evident. Jahi and the other facilitators would be advised: "You know what, we got to love these brothers. We got to love these brothers!"

In keeping with Jahi's comment, love is the heartbeat of the story. A student at Dewey Academy writes, "This class has influenced me to love and cherish the people around me while staying true to who I am." Loving students might sound simple enough, but it's the way the MDP instructors love that is key. For instance, a particular student with "emotional explosions" who had recently "witnessed a murder" and had "some PTSD," had a break-down in class and "broke our foul language rule." "His classmates," shared the facilitator, "were holding him to the class expectations," but the student continued on a volatile tirade. "I let him know that if he could not follow along with our agreed upon rules, he'd be taking some unwanted steps toward being pulled out of our program." The student expressed discontent and said blatantly that, "He didn't care" and that, "He wanted to be out of the class." "The next day when he came to my class," explains the facilitator, "I gave him his new class schedule." About a week later the teacher got a visit from the student's mom and IEP teacher.

> After hearing their arguments, I let them know that he could return, but it was going to be under two conditions: One, he must do the push-ups that he owes the class for his foul language violation. Two, he must formally apologize to the class for not holding his end of the agreement.

The student eagerly rejoined the class. Upon further debrief, when the MDP facilitator sat down with the student to better understand why he wanted to be back in the class so badly, he admitted that he "missed the brotherhood and men- torship." "Today," explains his MDP teacher with pride, "this young man is one of the model students of the class." When examining student-created poster boards I discover the one that belongs to this particular young man. He writes enthusiasti- cally: "What I like about the class is it's 100!"[4]

I think about this student—who went from having emotional explosions to being a leader amongst his peers—and wonder, what accounts for the transforma- tion? Brother Jahi provides insight. He is critical of shortsighted conceptions of learning. He explains that some educators are so preoccupied with making sure students get their homework done, that they completely ignore a child's develop- ment. I concur: "We are not teaching math or science or English, those are just the subjects. We are first and foremost teaching human beings." Jahi nods and states poignantly that in his first year as an MDP facilitator, "I learned to keep my humanity in the room. Like be a human. Sometimes you want to safeguard that and create this image. Nah. My students saw me some days tired. Some days, super energized. Some days challenged." In order for his students to keep it real with him, he had to be honest and authentic as well.

With his own vulnerability Jahi was able to show—not just tell—the kids to open up. To foster trust and community, he would sometimes put a "do not disturb" sign on the door. The students would love it because, "It's going to be just us." Those conversations and lessons, recalls Brother Jahi, "That's when it got really real." Jahi discloses:

> I would say to them, you know you been waiting for somebody to tell you
> to be smarter. You know you smarter than this. And you've been waiting
> for somebody to tell you it's okay for you to just unlock it—now's the time!

When the door was closed, hearts and minds became even more open; the students and Brother Jahi became closer as a family, as brothers. A student shares, this class is different than other classes, "Because it is a type of brotherhood." The bond of brotherhood is a ritual of AAMA resistance—I hear it in conversations with parents, at staff meetings, in the MDP classroom. Creating a protective force around the students gave them the space to thrive. Even the guidelines emphasize ways to build one another up.

CLASS GUIDELINES

Our Standards for *The Brotherhood*:

Respect for Ourselves and Each Other
Keep it 100 (Tell the Truth)
Lift Ups, No Put Downs
Look Out For Each Other
Play Hard, but Also Work Hard
Represent Your Best Self at All Times
Be On Time
Be Responsible for Your Actions
Build the Brotherhood
Trust Yourself and Others in the Brotherhood

"School is about education," Brother Jahi continues, so, beyond the rhetoric, "let's educate the whole child. It is not just about reading and writing, there has to be a class on who you are." Self-discovery is as "vital" as any subject. He continues, "you are a being in this world and you need to understand yourself." The Manhood Development classes are a special, sacred space because "you can kind of put yourself on the experiment table [and] get a chance to learn from yourself. ... and then out of that, you're able to function and understand more about yourself, your sensibilities." This is not just about an existential knowledge of self; a youngster might be wondering, "Why am I growing, why are my feet getting bigger, why is my voice cracking? Like those are things that you can talk about" in this class. Brother Jahi gets excited, "That's why I love middle school!"

I wonder how Brother Jahi defines manhood. He quips, "If you ask a hundred different men, you might get a hundred different answers." He adamantly wants his students to "define manhood for themselves." He is cognizant of his positionality and does not try to impress his ideas about manhood—or anything else for that matter—on the students. "The one thing they learned about me," he states, "is that I never try to pull *here's your motto of manhood. It's me. Do what I do. Act how I act.*" No. Brother Jahi wants each kid to be able to "grow up and find your own uniqueness."

I continue to prod, "If manhood is deeply personal, then how do you define a successful African American male youth?" "Hmmm," he nods, "that's a good question. Umm ..." he repeats, "that a good question." For the second time in the interview, a moment of silence enters the conversation. I lean in a bit closer, waiting for Brother Jahi to speak. When he begins to talk, his voice is stern and calm:

> Success has a lot to do with them determining where they want to go. Success is when they can identify where they want to go and then take the steps they need to take and are proactive on a daily basis, in their own unique way, despite their challenges or family issues, they are making some step toward their goal—that's a pathway and success happening at the same time.

He says practically, "If you had five missing assignments and now you are just missing three, you are on a success track. I think it's the lens," because, "we're lifelong learners."

The idea of setting personal goals is pivotal to manhood and achievement. As an illustration of this concept, one of his student's responds to the daily quote: *You must eat an elephant one bite at a time.* Jodiah writes in his journal:

> I like this quote because it expresses the fact that even if you have a huge dream to become a college professor, you must first do your work, get good grades, graduate, go to college and then get your degrees—slowly but surely you'll get to your goal. One example for me is when I was in the sixth grade I wanted to get a 3.0 so I did my work studied and when I got my grades I had a 3.7. I take from this that you can't just jump to your destination you must get there step by step.

According to this student, the class quote helped him understand that small accomplishments lead to big dreams. In many such examples, it is evident that students in the Manhood Development classes revel in the camaraderie and life skills; for many of them, like Jodiah, it spurred their drive to do better in school.

Jahi was also acutely aware that not all of his students' teachers were going to care about their holistic development. He acknowledges that personal ambition, alone, is not enough to overcome adversities. To prepare them for success in school, Brother Jahi would tell his "young kings" to "be first to raise their hand" in all of their classes. Unfortunately, it was not always well received. His students would complain: "My math teacher still didn't call on me today." Brother Jahi did not want his students to feel defeated. He told them:

> Well, you can raise your hand here and we can talk about it. Tomorrow I want you to raise your hand, but the only difference is that I will be in your math class with you tomorrow so that I can see first-hand what is going on.

This is significant because it demonstrates that MDP was not just a class, but also an opportunity for campus-wide advocacy. Brother Jahi continues:

> That's the leverage I have as an instructor because I can really be with the kids who need me the most during the day. I'm already in the school. I don't need to stop at the principal's office or get a pass. I can go directly into the class.

When Brother Jahi showed up, the dynamics between students and teachers started to change: he became a pivotal partner in the learning process.

Time to Grow

When Jahi was growing up, he needed a Manhood Development Program. He reminisces, "I failed the eighth grade. Luckily they had summer school for free. I was the kid beating on the table, writing rhymes in Cleveland, Ohio." He shakes his head. Looking back, "I realize how much culture I was not exposed to or around" but, "Public Enemy and Poor Righteous Teachers was happening." Inadvertently, hip-hop "became my cultural education." In eleventh grade, Brother Jahi's mom "got a good job and moved to the suburbs where it was all white kids" and he was called the "n-word." Experiences such as this inspired Brother Jahi "to go above and beyond to culturally empower our brothers because you need that armor to be able to function."

I inquire, "What is that armor that you are trying to give them?"

> A sense of self. A sense of validation. You do not have to adjust, let the world adjust. Stand in your manhood. Stand in your Blackness. Shoulders back. Back straight. Some of them things my grandfather used to say. Be comfortable in who you are. Don't try to front like you better than anybody, but be authentically who you really are.

I take a closer look at Brother Jahi. I jot down in my notebook: *humble confidence*. He seems to exhude the very attributes he wants his students to emulate. I realize that even his name has significance. Jahi is a Kiswahili word that means "Dignity." In 1992, after studying with Rastafarians in the Clarendon Hills in Jamaica, he legally changed his name "to reflect the person I strive to be." He continues to describe his last name, Torman. "Tor" is a Yoruba word that means King, and he added "man" because, "although I am a king, I am also a man, meaning balance. I never use my last name in public. I use only my first name. Why, because it's my right and my own personal freedom to do so."

In closing, I ask Brother Jahi if he has any advice for executive director Chatmon. Echoing the MDP philosophy, Jahi wants Brother Chris to:

> Lean on your brothers and keep pushing forward. Be aware of your team. Your team represents you and if you have weak links on your team, call it out, because there is no time for weak links. Be courageously honest about that.

He urges Chatmon to identify the strongest aspects of AAMA (people, programs, and policies) and build upon the strengths in order to move the work into the future. "The reality of it is this is not just cultural work; this is not just manhood development facilitators and young brothers." It is bigger and bolder. He tells me, "We could make Oakland an example of changing the world." Suddenly I get a rush of goose bumps up my spine and down my arms. Jahi is adamant: "We can actually change the lens about how we look at Black men. There was a group of strong brothers who came together to save our sons." It is not a miracle that a movement was created inside a school district to drop suspension rates and increase engagement in school: "This should be the norm across the nation. Doesn't this country realize that there's a million Jahis?" What is stopping all of us from lending a hand to "actually make that happen" for more brothers, young and old? Brother Jahi leans to the side and speaks with his voice as well as his hands: "It's crucial right now. It is not a time to stop. It's a time to grow."

Notes

1   The portraits of Brothers Matin and Jahi come out of my earlier study of the Manhood Development Program as depicted in *The Black Sonrise* (Watson, 2014).
2   Historically Black Colleges and Universities (HBCUs) are institutions of higher education in the United States that were established before 1964 with the intention of serving the African American community.
3   AVID stands for Advancement Via Individual Determination and was founded by Mary Catherine Swanson in 1980.
4   "100" refers to being all the way real and truthful.

9
EDUCATIONAL EMPOWERMENT

In another serendipitous moment, executive director Chatmon needed help streamlining the curriculum, and Brother Baayan Bakari came onboard to carry the torch. Bakari was "intrigued that MDP was in the schools" and he was excited by the possibilities. It was a natural fit. In 1997, with a prestigious fellowship grant from the Echoing Green Foundation, Bakari had created his first African American male curriculum. Throughout his career, he revised it based upon experiences he had teaching inside the schools, working at The Mentoring Center,[1] and coordinating several community-based programs, including Oakland Freedom Schools. Over a decade later, he was compelled to join the Office of African American Male Achievement (AAMA).

After the murder of Trayvon Martin and the George Zimmerman verdict, Bakari felt called to lend his expertise to AAMA. "The value of our Black boys was evidently zero by greater society." He was moved to action and even changed professions:

> I stepped out of the tech space as my sole focus after Trayvon Martin because I was so angry that this society was just dismissing our Black boys. The Trayvon Martin verdict is to me, personally, the darkest stain on modern American society. If I think about it too long, I get angry all over again.

Brother Bakari made the following commitment:

> If I can get the curriculum that I have been working on into our boys, at least I can help raise up the value of how we see ourselves and how others see us so that Trayvon never happens again.

To counteract the narrative of underachievement, the AAMA curriculum links present-day injustices to a historical context. Bakari intentionally devised lessons to address and complicate the stereotypical notions of Black masculinity that have shaped the way young Black men self-identify (Nasir, 2012; Nasir et. al., 2013). Consequently, a paramount goal inside these classrooms is to "cultivate healthy identities amongst Black male students," he explains, "as a means of improving Black male achievement."

Although Bakari designed scripted curricular units, he understands that it is a living document based upon the ever-changing dynamics inside schools. While the content is not prescribed, per se, there are pedagogical components that shape the rituals, routines, and assignments that result in healthier class-rooms for African American males. Specifically, facilitators rely on a Freirean teaching style that emphasizes open-ended questions, group dialogue, critical thinking, and consciousness building. Lessons are multi-modal and often utilize various media forms, such as texts from popular culture, to intellectually excite the students.

For Bakari, it was these same texts about Black people that changed his life. Growing up in the toughness and roughness of Richmond, CA, Bakari thought there were two types of African American men: those who were strong and those who were intelligent. When he was in middle school, he picked up the *Autobiography of Malcolm X*. Malcolm's image widened Bakari's horizons:

> The image of the glasses, the suit and tie, standing very, very strong and yet, nobody was going to run up on him—to use the colloquialism to say—that he was fully capable of defending himself. Malcolm gave me a vision of manhood I could grasp onto. He dispelled the fear of being seen as a nerd.

Brother Bakari considers himself a philosopher and thinker. As a widespread reader and historian, he is quick to compare Malcolm to Paul Robeson and the Moors of Spain. He references these people and groups to emphasize that Blackness is multi-dimensional: "I can be a warrior and at the same time a poet. I can be and do a range of things." The curriculum naturally reflects Brother Bakari's paradigm and experiences; he intentionally tries to complicate what it means to be an African American male living in Oakland.

Homegrown Educators

When Kevin Jennings was growing up in the nineties in West Oakland, he felt part of a close-knit, safe, and loving community. He was not particularly athletic so did not find a brotherhood through sports nor was he lured by the streets or gang culture, another place many youth find camaraderie. He found solace in his church and school. Nevertheless, Brother Jennings always felt like something was missing. AAMA became that space he had been yearning for his entire life: a peer-group based upon Black identity, history, and leadership. Now in his mid-twenties, Jennings has full-time employment as a classroom teacher and a community that brings him home to himself.

Brother Jennings teaches the full-credit elective, *Mastering Our Cultural Identity: African American Male Image*, at Montera Middle School. As a teacher, he begins each class with a daily affirmation: "I am focused. I am ready to learn. Let's turn up!" Although he definitely brings an immense amount of energy and positivity to his students, when I stop by his class, I am most struck by the ways the children proactively run the class. Without any direction from Brother Jennings, an African American middle schooler moves to the front of the room: "fist up, mouths shut." Another student proceeds to start a "soul clap." Five minutes before the bell rings, I watch as the students clean up the space and prepare it for the next MPD class. Jennings explains that this is a simple "ritual of respect and brotherhood."

Jennings began working for AAMA a couple of years ago and soon realized his calling as an educator. He recently completed the credential program at UC Berkeley extension: "The program focuses on the mechanics of teaching, like how to create a rubric and measure student work." While these tools are important, it is the professional development that he continues to receive from his AAMA family that impacts his pedagogy: "We talk a lot about bringing passion to the work. If you're not fired up, they're not going to be fired up. If you're not prepared, they're going to see through it." In these sessions, the instructors share best practices and talk through their struggles. "Our professional development is about pedagogy, brotherhood, about what we all do ... Because we all do different things in our classes, we'll have different rituals, a different rhythm. Some of the other teachers like to meditate and they're great on meditating 'cause they do that in their life. I'm a problem solver, and so one thing I tell my students: you're in this class to learn how to become a problem solver."

When Jennings first started teaching, Brother Jerome Gourdine came to observe him and offered insightful feedback. "If I was a boxer, I would need a coach. It's the same thing in teaching" and "Brother Jerome really helped fine-tune my pedagogy." As an example, Gourdine told him to use the old *popsicle stick trick*[2] to make sure he was calling on students throughout the room (not just the ones who sit in the front or are quick to raise their hands). He also told him to "move around the room" which helped Jennings tremendously. When I observed Jennings teach, I was amazed with his use of the space. He seemed to teach from every angle of the room and had lessons on every wall. "Jerome helped me push the limit," he explains, because he "helped me have more courage in my classroom."

AAMA provides an archetype for a "new type of educator," vows Jennings. "You can't come in with 'I know all the answers, I have my college degree, I've got a teacher's credential.' That should not—and does not—qualify you to be a teacher, or to be a *good* teacher." When other teachers in the school approach Jennings and ask for help ("some teachers who have been teaching longer than twenty years") he advises them to:

> open their selves up more and allow a student to learn about them in the most authentic way and then also be able to learn about other students in an authentic way, not from a pity perspective or I'm going to save you perspective, but let me learn about you. Ask the students to come in and have lunch with you, I bought a burrito for you today—sit down.

Although it might feel anecdotal, it can become medicinal. This healing is not just about the students; it is about inoculating the entire ecosystem with a greater sense of humanity.

The goal is that the ethos of AAMA permeates the system, shifting the culture of schools to become more teacher-driven and student-centered. Chatmon provides an example. "We asked teachers to go out into the hallway and to greet every brother they saw, to call them by their name, and give them a compliment." At first, for some adults it felt uncanny to target African American males with a positive accolade, but then something unexpected happened. "We found this had implications not just on the African American student receiving the compliment," shares Chatmon "but even on that adult." Positivity is actually infectious. The administrators reported that their jobs improved just by "being much more aware of putting out into the universe a light of positivity and engagement." Consequently, explains Chatmon, tardies decreased and so did disciplinary infractions. But the educators started feeling happier about their day so they started "lifting up" all kids with constructive feedback. Targeted universalism worked: "Initially," recalls Chatmon, "it was just for Black boys. But that practice started permeating the culture of the entire school."

Dare to Dream

Healing is palpable—it lives within our will, our words, and the ways we reach out toward one another. Proponents of this kind educational transformation exist throughout the district. Dr. Devin Dillon, the chief academic officer for the district, wants other courses to embrace the AAMA pedagogy. "Young Black males who have been silenced by a system," she explains, are "now asked to read empowering literature and view popular cultural portrayals of race through a critical lens." She is equally impressed that this type of consciousness-raising curriculum is "naturally rigorous" as students deconstruct "racism in our world."

Since the curriculum is highly analytical and radical, the educators are constantly pushing against their own normative assumptions about what it means to be a teacher. Brother Jennings explains: "I'm constantly making sure that I get rid of that ideal of what school is, how a classroom should be." He acknowledges that, "you do need certain things in place in order for a class to flow," but that he can also be intentional, and radical, about ways to shape-shift the space. "We have to start engaging African American males and boys of color in a different way and have a different set up." I think back to how his students, without any direction, cleaned up the classroom and set it up for the next group of brothers that were coming in.

When I prod for his advice to other teachers, Jennings just wants his colleagues to "be on your A game." He repeats: "You have to be on your A game." As a teacher with " twenty-something boys in the room" and he shakes his heads "I have to see an argument before it happens. I have to see a joke before it happens. I'm zoning the room and making sure this class experience is the best experience it can be within fifty minutes." Jennings is methodical with his prep time: "Making sure the video cues up the right way and I have to ask the right question or ask it in the right way that gives me multiple answers, just all of that."

While many of his colleagues at the school site complain that they are over-worked and underpaid, Jennings does not agree. He describes himself as highly valued and appreciated. He shares with me that there was recently a teacher-led strike in the district. He did not participate because he did not want to lose valu-able learning time with his students. Brother Jennings is adamant: "I work for my students and their families. They don't work for me." The school system is preoc-cupied with standards, but, he chimes, "we need to stop trying to meet standards and start trying to meet people."

> As I leave Montera Middle School, I am inspired and intrigued. I write in the margins of my field-notes, "AAMA is the beginning of the answer, but it's going to take *all* teachers to move the mountain."

To codify the AAMA philosophy of teaching and learning so it can be applied more generally, I examined two years of classroom logs. Each month, the AAMA instructors submit a narrative that gauges some of their moments of successes and challenges. Similar to most classroom teachers, they struggle with disinterested students. They, too, feel overwhelmed when a child is homeless or being told to "sell this weed to pay the bills." There are times when students enter into their courses in middle and high school, but still do not know how to read. The dis-tinction, however, is in the way the AAMA teachers frame the problem. Students are not blamed for their weaknesses or deficiencies. This asset-based paradigm allows educators to hold students accountable for their work, without demeaning their struggles.

As a representative sample, the quotes below provide a window into teachers who perceive that all children can achieve.

- **Engaging students *is* classroom management:** An MDP teacher spent his weekend looking up the discipline and transcript data for each of his students. He was shocked to discover the "pervasive and excessive discipline" problems with 90 percent of his students. He shares, "When I saw their records I had a hard time believing these were the same guys in my class because we haven't had those same issues."

- **Learning who students are *outside* of school impacts learning *inside* of school:** An MDP teacher's presence in the neighborhood and at community events provided important insights into his students. An example, "I saw Asim turf dancing on a Friday night. At this event I was amazed at the precision of his moves and I now challenge him to set aside the same amount of time studying as he practices for his dance events."

- **Affirming excellence creates a *culture for success*:** An MDP teacher finds success in the little things that others might overlook. He compliments his students when he notices improvements, no matter how small. "Harry now carries a back pack," mentions the MDP teacher, "which is something not common to what he is known for." This educator describes his student Harry with pride: after participating in MDP, "He takes initiative in making sure his grades are improving, he's not as confrontational as he used to be, and he has truly shown his promise and proven his potential to be a positive contribution to his community and his own self-worth."

- **Building a *continuum of care* reinforces student achievement:** As if it's all in a day's work, an MDP facilitator explains in his weekly log that, "I have talked with at least seven teachers on campus to ensure time for late work to be turned in, for students to retake/make-up quizzes or tests. I have collected work from teachers to hand deliver to certain students for completion. I have even hand delivered work to students in their neighborhood."

- **Classrooms are *fertile ground* for transformation:** For African American children in Oakland, there is now a place on campus to discuss what is happening in their lives. An MDP educator reiterates this point: "During our routine check-in process, this young man wanted to share what he was going through… His grandmother is addicted to crack and his mother was getting very sick and needed to have surgery." The MDP facilitator continues, "Now you must understand, this is one of the so-called 'class clowns.' This brother is rarely serious about anything. For him to open up and feel comfortable sharing something like that made me realize we are slowly but surely helping these brothers feel safe."

The testimonies from these teachers demonstrate a pattern of behavior rooted in a love for students that drives the MDP instructors into the community to see their students in their own cultural terms and on their own neighborhood turfs. In this educational setting, neighborhood knowledge is a resource and an instructional tool, like the way the AAMA teacher learns about Asim's self-discipline when it comes to dancing and uses that to push him in school. As a result of authentically meeting students where they are at and from, these educators are able to necessitate difficult conversations inside the classroom. Consequently, for some of these teenagers, they go from trying to survive on the streets to thriving in school.

Rickey Jackson, now a senior, almost failed his freshman year. At the time, his mother was in and out of the hospital with cancer. "I gave up, so to speak," he said.

Rickey and his siblings lived on their own, and when their mother passed away, Rickey called his MDP teacher, Brother Hancock. Rickey recalls that it was a life-saving intervention. Hancock helped him re-enroll and re-engage in school. He now has a 3.6 GPA and recently went on an airplane for the first time to visit colleges. So far, he has gotten into six Historically Black Colleges and Universities.

Rickey is among a large group of AAMA students headed to college. More than half of the first cohort (52 students) received scholarships from the East Bay College Fund and are now headed off to college. "We got brothers that are entering two-year and four-year institutions across the nation," shares Chatmon. "Some of their universities include: UCLA, UC Berkeley, Hampton, Howard, Morehouse, Tuskegee, Cal State Dominguez Hills, Cal State East Bay, Arizona State, Arizona University, and Xavier," he says proudly. Since students want to stay engaged with one another as well as the AAMA, Chatmon and his colleagues are thinking about how to carry the network of brotherhood onto college campuses. These students, in particular, are pulling Chatmon to the side saying, "Baba C what can I do? I want to stay involved." Chatmon grins, "Aw man, come on! There's many things you can do!"

As mentioned by Chatmon in Chapter 6, teaching is about planting seeds. And the fruits of that labor are "in bloom." But Chatmon understands that the work is bigger then AAMA, it is about repurposing educational systems. The Manhood Development Program provides a beacon for what our schools could become. A counselor at Castlemont High School poignantly states,

> This class provides a very much-needed safe, comfortable, almost sacred space for young African American men... This class rebuilds self-esteem, relieves the feeling [of] personal responsibility for symptoms of an unjust and racist social system that most severely affects African American males. The class allows for close connections with positive role models who teach, lead by example, and encourage the members of the class to dare to dream about their futures.

An MDP facilitator underscores the significance of learning for liberation:

> If we can continue to deliver a positive uplifting message to the youth that they can understand and implement into their daily routine, we will be building a front line of young Black soldiers [who] will rebuild their communities with the betterment of their people and the generations to follow.

These young men "represent the future of us as a people, and once they realize their power it will drive them in mind, heart, and action." The legacy of resistance is real. We continue to make the road by walking, intentionally planting the seeds of social change along the way.

The pathways that AAMA has constructed over the last seven years represent a transformative lifeline to the traditional schooling model. The knowledge base and brotherhood grounds students to their own greatness. From this seed of consciousness, the roots grow deep and the tree stands tall. College does not become yet another stepping stone in the assimilative white washing process wherein students of color, and African American males in particular, are made to feel misplaced and displaced which does nothing to foster personal success and collective empowerment.

To harken back to the legacy of education as an emancipatory tool, I close this chapter with a reference to Dr. Carter G. Woodson. Because of financial hardship, he was not able to attend school regularly. But eventually, he graduated from high school and became a school principal. Later in life, he received his doctorate from Harvard University. The year was 1912. He is considered one of the first scholars of African American history and went on to found *The Journal of Negro History*.

In his seminal text, *The Mis-Education of the Negro* (1933), he presented a theoretical framework for understanding the functions of schooling within an oppressive ecosystem. In the early 1900s, he argued against compulsory education models stating that they would further disenfranchise African Americans from their communities and locus of power. He warned that just going to college, in and of itself, is a trick. He elucidates,

> It may be of no importance to the race to be able to boast today of many times as many 'educated' members as it had in 1865. If they are of the wrong kind the increase in numbers will be a disadvantage rather than an advantage. The only question which concerns us here is whether these 'educated' persons are actually equipped to face the ordeal before them or unconsciously contribute to their own undoing by perpetuating the regime of the oppressor...What Negroes are now being taught does not bring their minds into harmony with life as they must face it...The so-called education of Negro college graduates leads them to throw away opportunities which they have and to go in quest of those which they do not find.
>
> *(p. 3)*

As we consider the transformation of urban school districts, like the one in this study, let us pause and ponder what it is we are actually trying to accomplish. Is success simply measured by the number of African American males that get to/through higher education? I surmise that for Woodson, nearly 100 years later, he would still hold fast that education must become a forceful liberating tool that breaks oppression from its roots.

Social justice demands new ways of learning and living, being and becoming. A critical consciousness continues to permeate and saturate schools throughout the district. Along this journey to change the world, there are countless people— young and old and of every hue—who are trying to help a school district regain its humanity by addressing and eliminating institutionalized racism.

In this next portrait, an unlikely "brother in the struggle" is introduced. As a white man, he was not particularly aware of the severities of oppression. But in East Oakland, he experienced debilitating traumas and newfound aspirations. In this place, he also discovered his calling. Brother Charles provides a keen lens into AAMA as a system-wide solution.

Notes

1 The Mentoring Center trains and supervises mentoring programs in the Bay Area. They also provide direct services to incarcerated youth: http://www.mentor.org/.
2 This discussion technique ensures that all students have an equal opportunity to participate and share their responses in class. The randomness of drawing a student's name using the Popsicle Sticks method also helps with classroom management: http://www.theteachertoolkit.com/index.php/tool/popsicle.

10

CHARLES WILSON

Reflective Resistance

Charles Wilson is the deputy network superintendent for Middle Schools in Oakland Unified School District. He began working for the district in 1994 and in these two decades has served as a researcher, classroom teacher, principal, and district administrator. In each of these positions, Brother Wilson has exceeded expectations and willed a solution, even in the most dire of circumstances. He is well-known in a number of capacities, one of which is for co-founding Fred T. Korematsu Discovery Academy, a public elementary school located at 10315 East Street in Oakland.

Today I have the opportunity to interview him about the Office of African American Male Achievement and why he sees the work as a beacon for critical discourse that needs to be embedded into all levels of learning.

I make my way to the sixth floor of the district's office on Broadway in downtown Oakland. His office views are expansive and natural light pours in from the rows of windows. When I arrive, he is busy in another meeting down the hall. One of his colleagues invites me to have a seat and tells me "I'll text Charles to let him know you've arrived."

Soon thereafter, an older white man comes into the large open office space. He appears to be in his early fifties and is wearing sharp, modern-framed glasses and a blue button-down collar shirt. He smiles wide in my direction, shakes my hand, and introduces himself. Within what seems like just a few minutes, we are immersed in a heartfelt conversation about identity development, school politics, and the possibilities of an education system that successfully serves *all* students.

Reproducing Inequality

The first time Charles Wilson met Chris Chatmon was at a speaking engagement for the League of Women Voters. Both men were in the limelight of school reform. Wilson was getting accolades because of his leadership at Korematsu, including a nomination for the National Blue Ribbon award for being one of the most improved schools in the country.[1] AAMA was also being heralded, but for the ways they were reaching and teaching African American children and families. From this first encounter, Wilson was struck by how much Chatmon knew about him and the deep ties he had to the community.

At the voters' event, recalls Wilson, Chatmon "stood up and it was so funny because he was [saying] Brother Charles and I couldn't figure out who he was talking about." "Who is Brother Charles?" Then he realized, "I'm a *brother*. He's talking about me!" "Chatmon was so sincere," from that very first moment, and Wilson was genuinely taken aback by his "generosity of spirit."

Even though Wilson and Chatmon have different vantage points within the district, they both hold tightly to the belief that systems-change is relational work and that their job is to leverage the institution to better serve students. It is not surprising that these two educators would find a way to partner. Soon after their first encounter, Wilson and Chatmon worked together to bring the Manhood Development Program to Korematsu elementary school.

At that time, a number of Wilson's African American students were experiencing a "disconnect" at school and MDP offered a solution. "These students now have a support network" attests Wilson. "The manhood development courses are addressing a real need" and are "incredibly necessary." Wilson applauds the ways the instructors have provided students with the "space to be emotionally soft," showing "young men that they can be respected *and* emotionally available." "There was a student," he mentions, "whose mom passed away unexpectedly … and just to see him smiling and excited to come to school" demonstrates what an authentic network of care can really do. "The Manhood Development Program has been a life-saver," urges Wilson and he goes on to name specific students that the course drastically impacted. Evidence such as this reinforces the need for comprehensive services that are vested in the lifelong development of the whole child and whole family; but I push back on this idea and ask if this is the responsibility of schools? According to Wilson, it is the soul purpose. He points to AAMA.

Over the course of seven years, AAMA has created a particular model of engagement that has measureable results. So Wilson naturally—like many others in Oakland as well as nationally—want to "see the program grow and expand." Through this process of replication, however, Wilson urges Chatmon to codify particular elements of the work into instructional strategies that can be used "with everybody." Again, this is a recurring theme: integrate AAMA district-wide and provide tools to *all* teachers.

Although many stakeholders discuss the need to integrate AAMA, will the program's power get diluted through the process of assimilation? In other words, will the instructional strategies permeate throughout the system or will it eventually dissolve and disintegrate, losing the special fervor that drew students into the brotherhood in the first place? This tension is real and Wilson and I discuss the potential traps and areas for opportunity.

Part of the appeal of the Manhood Development Program is the special selection of instructors, many of whom are, in the words of Wilson, "mentors that come from the community." Wilson recognizes that "some of these guys are just really young. They're fiery" and they can have real, legitimate issues with "authority." AAMA needs to be "more conscious about how those mentors show up and see their work within the larger system," especially when considering how to expand the model. Wilson asks a very real, pertinent question: "What do you do when this person might be an oppressor and slow down the work and still maintain professionalism and work with them?" As an answer, Wilson lifts up the work of one MDP instructor who was a "great mentor because he was a fierce advocate of his young men and was pushing them to be better and better" and he was simultaneously "intentional and super reflective about his work" and was "constantly going to other leadership on the campus," strategically building partnerships with staff on behalf of the students. For Wilson, then, MDP instructors are most effective when they are not isolated to a classroom, but are active in shifting the school culture. This echoes the sentiment that Brother Abdel-Qawi, Principal of Oakland High, had as well. AAMA can inspire other educators to do education differently.

Across the twenty-three school sites that currently house the program,[2] I continue to hear that teachers and staff want to know what is going on, in the words of Wilson, when "that door is shut." It seems a large part of their genuine curiosity comes from the changes they are seeing in the students. Why is MDP so successful at building that connection and consciousness among children and youth, and how can other teachers partake in the process?

Wilson's answer is striking. When he thinks about the work of AAMA, he finds it transferrable because all educators, even the "trigonometry teacher," need to have the skillset to "create a space where students feel safe enough to bring their identities into the room. You don't just want to be *a student*. It is really important to be a *Black female* in the honor society or ... trigonometry. Our world gives us so many messages that that's not supposed to happen," so AAMA helps give students a sense of belonging that is critical to academic achievement and lifelong aspirations. AAMA signifies "a successful way to bring kids together," asserts Wilson, "and give them a *subaltern* identity."

Without going into too much detail, unpacking the concept of subaltern is valuable. Subaltern refers to populations that are socially, politically, and geographically marginalized. In describing "history told from below," the term subaltern is derived from Antonio Gramsci's work on cultural hegemony, which describes groups that are excluded and denied voice and power over their own lives (Gramsci, 1973; Guha, 1983; Kock, 1992; Scott, 1985; Spivak, 1988, 2005). Kristen Buras and Michael Apple (2006) in *The Subaltern Speak: Curriculum, Power, and Educational Struggles* discuss the contention over what counts as knowledge in a range of educational contexts. They write, "Whether in boardrooms or classrooms, home schools or school communities, universities or foundations, each arena is characterized by the dynamics of differential power and the complexities and contradictions of identity and agency" (p. 6).

Building on this work and the insights of Wilson, subaltern, as a framework, is quite apropos to an analysis of the ways schools can address and eliminate institutionalized racism. Wilson is forthright: "There is no predetermined destiny unless we give up the work." So as AAMA strives to elevate the voices, histories, and current needs of Black students, it is critical to recognize that their work does not exist in isolation. It is embedded within a larger ecosystem of power and privilege that reproduces inequality. Going against these hegemonic forces takes more than good-will and passion; Chatmon must simultaneously "build capacity, generate a lot of light for the program, which he is really good at, and he also just has to keep the ship running." In doing the day-to-day work that can be arduous and relentless, Chatmon and others are helping "de-stigmatize all of the kids in Oakland."

Underbelly of School Reform

Since the focus of this study is AAMA's role within the district, I still want to get a clearer understanding of how Wilson's leadership fits within this larger movement for racial equity. Essentially, I am trying to unearth the seeds of his convictions. I learn about a critical moment in his career when he became the principal at a high-poverty school in East Oakland.

Wilson's account unfolds, and it could echo the remnants of a *Dangerous Minds* or *Freedom Writers* movie: the stereotypical Hollywood storyline about a white savior who arrives at an impoverished school on a mission to save urban kids of color. As he describes it, Charles Wilson, a well-intentioned white man, put on his superman outfit and flew down into the hood to rescue students from themselves, their neighborhoods, and their families. For many of us in education, this narrative is not far-fetched. Wilson admits that this type of rendering is "deceptive" because it boasts the ego of the "savior" while further disempowering those being served. As a thoughtful practitioner and lifelong learner, Wilson starts to unpack this pivotal moment in his career—moving from a teacher in the hills to an administrator in the flatlands. We delve into the underbelly of the story. He promises to be "transparent."

Wilson began his career as an elementary school teacher at Sequoia and then moved on to teach middle school at Montera. Although he loved the classroom, he yearned for larger systems change. He remembers, "I was really dissatisfied with some of the leadership that I had been experiencing" and began thinking about next steps. Soon thereafter, Wilson was told by one of the district directors that if he got into an administrative credential program, she would immediately place him at a school site as the vice principal.

After just a week and before he had a chance to enroll in an admin program, she told him she had a new job for him: Wilson would become the principal—the "seventh leader in five years"—at Highland Elementary in East Oakland.

Up until this point in his teaching career in Oakland, Wilson had never been below the I-580 freeway line, which is "one of our dividers around race, class, and geography." "I had never even been to East Oakland," he gasps. He proceeds to grin and even chuckles a bit about his new job because "I hadn't even taken an administrative class!"

What made Wilson qualified to lead a school on 85th Avenue? The answer is disturbing, but essential to any adequate analysis of school inequities.

After some critical reflection, Wilson started to understand why he was chosen for Highland. He is clear that there were other schools at the time also seeking principals. For instance, "Why wasn't I being considered for Joaquin Miller?" Especially "because I know those families and I've been working there."

At the onset, Wilson looked the part: he is a "white, mono-lingual, male." This somehow superseded the fact that he had no administrative credential or experience. While Wilson clarifies that there was not any malicious person at the district conspiring against these students, it was a quick-fix to a problem that needed to just go away.

The reality is that Wilson "was the go-away" and "good enough" to oversee the education of poor children of color. The message seemed to be that the "babies on 85th didn't really count," he surmises. While the Joaquin Miller parents would not put up with "an inexperienced white guy," the children in East Oakland should be satisfied with anything. He repeats with particular disgust: "I was good enough. I was fodder," which refers to animal feed, and, he pauses, "Their kids are fodder." He speaks with his hands: "It was all throw away."

For the next decade of his life, Wilson grew to love his students and the community. As much as he strived to better their school, it was reciprocal; East Oakland bettered his humanity. Although he "never liked categories," his work on 85th Avenue pushed him to look at other people's lives—no matter how seemingly different—and find a place for connection. He shares one of his most powerful tools: simply "experiencing people as people." Building on this relational work, Wilson continues, "I do believe change can be made through the work of individuals, even if it's micro-change." He talks about seeing genuine partnerships between teachers, a parent, and a child, and witnessing the transformation of a student who at the "beginning of the year is clearly frustrated about being in school and totally off-track to by the end of the year seeing this same student excited to learn because we've found that hook."

Even though Wilson arrived at Highland as a Band-Aid on a festering wound of low expectations, disorganization, and underachievement, it was one of those rare moments where "the Band-Aid grew into a solution" because the healing was intentional, consistent, and personal. I prod Wilson on his effectiveness in a setting that others were ill-equipped to serve, referencing that fact that he was the seventh leader in five years. Wilson smiles, his grin contagious: "I've been waiting to tell this story for awhile."

Conspiracy of Care

> I am a gay man and I am a bit older. I came of age in the early 1980s. I came out to myself and my family in '83 when AIDS didn't have a name and it was still "GRIDS" which stands for "Gay Related Immune Deficiency Syndrome."

"I really developed my identity as a young man in my twenties" under the belief that there was a "systematic and systemic effort to exterminate us." His face is solemn as he shares, "When you start losing literally dozens of young friends within a couple of years" and then he stops abruptly, takes a breath, and discusses what it did to his psyche and outlook on the world. Wilson speaks with his hands as well as his heart. I can feel his conviction from across the table. "It is my obligation to take the privileges I have been given and use them to blow up the system. I do not believe in the ability of the status quo to take care of the oppressed!"

The gay rights movement shaped Wilson's activism, but he believes that it is "not the struggle that needs to be fought right now" especially compared to addressing structural racism. In the fight for equal rights, Wilson recognizes that within a couple generations, tremendous strides have been made in the LGBTQI[3] community. Today he is "a gay man with a good income." He and his husband live in "a beautiful home" and "I can buy my way out of uncomfortable situations at this point, *literally*." An unremitting injustice is that "kids of color, kids in poverty, can't do that." I prod him for some real-life illustrations.

Wilson provides glimpses into a reality riddled by oppression. One of his students was sleeping on the floor of his apartment building's laundry-room. He was displaced and had nowhere to go. This particular young man still managed to come to school every day, but when he started to smell "two-weeks' worth of dirty," the teachers and staff began to inquire about what was going on at home. That's just one example. Wilson continues, "Staying at school until two in the morning with two kids waiting for the police to come pick them up to take them to the Alameda County Processing Center because no one ever came to pick them up." Wilson pauses, leans in, and discloses that he does not want to blame the families; yet he is cognizant and compassionate that the child is in pain. "I get why things are so difficult for people, but it's just so hard to be watching it getting processed through the eyes of a nine-year-old."

Wilson knows what it feels like to experience the loss of an entire peer-group, and he deeply empathizes with the "incredible level of sustained trauma that our kids are facing and bringing to schools." He recognizes that it's too hard for a lot of people to bear: "It just emotionally burns you out and is crushing to your spirit."

After seven years at Korematsu, Wilson was not ready to leave, but he was determined to transform the "local feeder" pattern. He left Korematsu to ambitiously lead and impact the next school in the pathway of his students, Alliance Academy Middle School. "We were working really hard to get kids to a certain level at Korematsu and then it was just really disappointing to be knowing these kids and knowing their families and watching them get to these middle and high schools and for what?" He folds his arms and speaks matter-of-factly: "they were ending up in the newspaper as casualties and very rarely as successes."

"That was the year," he recalls, "that Lee Weathersby was murdered on New Year's Eve. He became the first murder of Oakland for 2014." When I look up this case, I discover that Lee Weathersby III was thirteen years old and was fatally shot while walking home. Two weeks later, his older brother, Lamar Broussard, was shot and killed while driving. "I have no more kids," their mother cried to reporters. The pain is beyond cognizance.

How does a school leader create an environment of high expectations amidst a neighborhood saturated with present (not post) traumatic stress? For Wilson, the answer comes in the form of code-switching on multiple levels: linguistically, mentally, and cognitively. While traditional code-switching often refers to language use, having an "ability to move language to fit different contexts and to really be bilingual," he expands this notion to include trauma. Code-switching also entails the ability to be in crisis in one area of your life and still high-functioning in other areas, like school. He talks briefly about "mindfulness work" and providing students with a "sense of belonging" which, when done successfully, can provide the nourishment that helps students to survive and thrive in multiple contexts.

The schoolhouse needs to become the "most important institution in the neighborhood. It is more important than the liquor stores or the gangs." Schools will take precedence over other community ailments if they embody excellence, equity, and healing. In other words, if the schoolhouse is just a pathway to the jailhouse, what is the point of engagement? For Wilson, educational spaces are meant to be alive with the hub of learning and neighborhood interaction, where families gather and needs are fulfilled. "I wanted parents when they walked into the school to feel like this is their second home. ... We would be the place that a family could come to fulfill almost *any* need." Wilson is proud that "we started to get to that place at Korematsu."

Reframe Resources

Wilson's charisma and love for students radiates throughout his narrative. His philosophy of schooling is informed by his own experience attending private schools. As our interview draws to a close, Wilson's vision of learning emerges.

"If you go to an elite private school," he explains as he adjusts his wireframe glasses, "you are going to see a different type of relationship between students and teachers based upon mentoring. Teachers create provocative situations that encourage students to think critically through a process of intellectual discovery."

Those moments of "push," rigor, and challenge are *the* education. Wilson asks rhetorically, "Why can't that happen on 85th Avenue inside a non-charter school?"

Instead, for far too long, the students in East Oakland were receiving subpar schooling and the pattern was to "just send the inexperienced guy" and it would be "good enough." Wilson's voice raises, "The good enough mentality has to go!" He names things like classes taught by long-term substitutes, classes taught solely with handouts. He sits up and proclaims: "Our metric should not be that no one dies!"

He pounds his hand on the table and speaks emphatically, "What we feel obligated to provide to a privileged community is what we should provide to everyone! That's the baseline!" Vast variations between what schools offer children is the "expression of the inequities that our system has been maintaining."

But how does Wilson's obvious passion for learning translate into institutional transformation? Now, as deputy superintendent, how does he enact equity? Again, the answer is found in relationships.

Wilson's mom used to tell him to speak "with honey rather than vinegar" and this advice has served him well. It's quite simple: Brother Wilson uses kindness to get things done. "I understand that we have to work inside big systems" so he personalizes the process, which echoes Chatmon's strategy as well. Essentially, both of them get to know people and genuinely try to understand their jobs in order to ask informed, productive questions that push the institution in the right direction—that is, to better serve students and their families.

For the upcoming school year, Wilson "wants to be able to create the conditions for principals to really listen to the needs of their community and start responding beyond the baseline." To help "shift the mindset," he is trying to raise the bar: "my goal is *every* kid in *every* school *every* year needs to have a life-changing positive relationship with an adult at that school." Wilson is dedicating time and funding for advisors whose sole purpose is to foster trust with children and serve as an advocate and ally. He is realistic that they are "flying the plane while we build it" but he also knows that "the reason some of my kids started going off-track when they got to secondary school is because they were so used to having trusting relationships."

His insights remind me of a conversation I recently had with a high school drop-out. He told me point blank: "I don't care about school. When did school ever care about me?" I commend Wilson's approach because it offers a solution. As a district leader, he is trying to implement and institutionalize an ethic of care with built-in time for mentors for every child.

Wilson knows that people and systems can improve. In the beginning, "I was the guy that I tell stories about that you should never be" because "I made really bad decisions and said some horrible things to students." But he stayed, reflected, and learned to be more effective. Now, "I have been in the district for twenty-one years working and there are a lot of us that have been here for a long time … We're dedicated and most of us stay because of the relationships that we have."

As we sit above the Oakland landscape on the sixth floor in downtown Oakland, Charles Wilson continues to find inspiration from his work in East Oakland. The only difference is that as deputy superintendent, he is charged with having a "larger impact on the same type of work."

Wilson concludes the conversation by bringing up, what he deems, is an American atrocity: the murder of Michael Brown. He tells me that directly after Michael Brown's murder, his mother told a local reporter, *Do you know how hard it is to get an African American male to graduate from high school? I am so proud of him!* In the wake of her son's death, the reporter was shocked by this pronouncement made by Brown's mom. This is what she wanted to talk about? His schooling? Then, upon further investigation, the reporter discovered that the Normandy school district, from which Brown graduated, is among the poorest, most dismal, and segregated in Missouri. It ranks last in overall academic performance, and by the time Brown graduated, it lost its accreditation.[4] Michael Brown persevered in a school system that was designed to fail him and he was headed to college. Yet at the hands of a racist police officer, he did not make it out of his neighborhood alive.

There are layers of injustice in just this one case—from the mis-education to the murder. Recognizing the deep-rooted oppression and institutional, personal, and communal traumas that continue to saturate the inner-city, Wilson says that it is "my job ... to make that difference" because that is the meaning and duty of an educator. It reminds me of something Chatmon said: "If you join my team, this is a lifestyle because of the sense of urgency; it's a 24/7, 365-day sense of being." As I sit across the table, the balance between critical thinking and thoughtful action beams from Wilson. He shrugs, "That's my own rallying call: angry gay man fighting for kids of color."

★★★

Another unsung trailblazer in OUSD is Dr. Jean Wing. "In building community," Chatmon remembers, "I needed some early wins and I also needed to know who is in the choir because you don't have enough time to convert." He nods his head and points his finger in the air: "Jean Wing, that's the choir!" He shares with me that "Jean's brilliant" and in the early stages, the way she framed both the problems and solutions, became "pivotal to pointing us forward."

In the beginning of this book, I referenced the work of Dr. Terman and Dr. Vigil, two scholars with far-reaching effects on Oakland Unified. Fifty years later, the position that was once held by an architect of eugenics and tracking, is now led by Dr. Jean Wing, the executive director of Research, Assessment, and Data for the district. For the past eleven years, Wing's mission has been "to support the whole district to create a culture of inquiry around equity using all of the different kinds of qualitative and quantitative data" to better understand the "actual experience of children as they make their way through our public school system." Jean is unwavering in her approach that research needs to serve students, not just study them. In many respects, people like Charles Wilson and Dr. Jean Wing paved the way for AAMA. But even they did not fully envision the breadth and depth, the strength and drive that Chatmon would bring to the job. Amidst a desert of despair and hopelessness, Brother Chatmon found fertile ground to grow one of the most comprehensive initiatives for African American male students in the twenty-first century. His bold approach within a large urban school district inspires his colleagues, even the newly appointed superintendent.

Notes

1 The National Blue Ribbon Schools Program recognizes public and private elementary, middle, and high schools based on their overall academic excellence or their progress in closing achievement gaps among student subgroups.
2 This figure encompasses twenty-three elementary, middle, and high schools throughout the district, out of a total of eighty-seven district-run schools.
3 LGBTQI stands for Lesbian, Gay, Bisexual, Transgender, Queer or Questioning, and Intersex.
4 http://www.propublica.org/article/ferguson-school-segregation.

11

SUPERINTENDENT ANTWAN WILSON

Lessons in Leadership

I am on my way from Sacramento to Oakland to sit down for a 7 a.m. interview with Superintendent Antwan Wilson. We have carved out time to discuss his first year serving as the superintendent for Oakland Unified School District. Just getting on his calendar felt like a small feat. It took patience and finesse, but underscored the web of communication systems that exist among those who yield a lot of power, albeit behind-the-scenes. In this case, it was Berlena Gullett, Office of African American Male Achievement (AAMA) office manager; Tanara Haynes, AAMA project manager; and Precious Stroud, communications consultant. These queens worked together on my behalf and linked up with Julia Gordon, the superintendent's senior executive assistant. As the result, I was given the necessary time to better understand Wilson's insights for Oakland in general and his vision for the AAMA, in particular.

On June 1, 2014, Wilson, an African American man in his early forties, was hired to take the realm of a district that has had inconsistent leadership; he is the eleventh superintendent in eighteen years, the third since AAMA opened in 2010. He inherited a system that pays teachers considerably less than other Bay Area schools, and by some measures, the salaries in Oakland are the lowest in the nation. This long-standing divestment in educators is coupled with severe debt, which is partly caused because of the loss of state funding tied to attendance.

Given this calamity, Oakland Unified desperately needs a particular kind of school leader, and naysayers are skeptical that Superintendent Wilson can do the job. Before coming to Oakland, Wilson was the assistant superintendent in Denver, Colorado. He also has experience as a principal and classroom teacher. Although his background in education definitely prepares him for the position, there are no promises. It can be incredibly grueling trying to advance racial equity.

Social systems, like schools, which are rooted in human interaction and development, are complex organisms that are slow to change and intense to improve. Leaders exist at the nexus of polarities, simultaneously pulled in opposite directions. With hundreds of employees and thousands of students, Superintendent Wilson is constantly wrestling with divergent needs. It would be impossible to make everyone happy, and that is not what drives him. Rather, he faces battles with political acumen, a diligent consistency, and a somewhat shrewd focus.

Dysfunctional Organization

I witnessed his stoic resolve and patience just a few nights ago, in the fall of 2015, when members of the group, By Any Means Necessary (BAMN), organized a rally against Superintendent Wilson and his cabinet. According to the Oakland Tribune and Contra Costa Times, since the beginning of the school year, protesters have fiercely railed against Wilson, carrying signs, chanting songs and lambasting him at school board meetings for being "the face of the new Jim Crow."

Tonight, a young Caucasian-looking woman in her early twenties speaks vehemently at the podium. "I am a former intervention specialist with OUSD and now I am a current substitute teacher." She points to Wilson and addresses him by name:

> Antwan Wilson, the first day that I was a sub at Grass Valley there were twenty-two kids in that second grade class. Three of them were special needs students: one with severe ADHD, the other with an ED [emotional disorder], and the other with some spectrum of autism. There were no aides in that class! I was the only one who could provide the necessary support with my background as an intervention specialist! This whole board was responsible for dismantling special education!

You are part of a policy," she bellows, "to re-segregate public education and take things back to the period of Jim Crow. There is a new Jim Crow! We are building a civil rights movement and you will *not* be successful and you will be *removed*!"

The anger in the space is venomous.

Superintendent Wilson sits on the other side of her rage, listening intently. He looks a bit emotionless and his voice is calm, even monotone as he retorts back to the young white woman: "I can sit here and listen to a lot of things, but I'm not going to sit here as an African American male and have someone that doesn't look like me talk about Jim Crow whatsoever." Another board member comments that whenever you start "labeling" people in a disparaging way with caricatures like "Uncle Tom," it is naturally divisive, "jarring," and diminishes opportunities for collaboration. The racist tones of tonight's board meeting are like a canary in the coalmine; I am reminded, once again, that we are so far away from racial harmony inside school systems, let alone society as a whole.

The rage bequeathed to the board stems from a number of issues, one of which is Superintendent Wilson's implementation of a full-inclusion model for special education students with moderate to mild disabilities. Wilson's decision is based on a national trend and various research studies that critique racial disparities in special education. In particular, this data pinpoints the subjective process of labeling students—overwhelmingly students of color—with disabilities such as speech/language impairments and emotional/behavioral disorders (e.g. Artiles, 2011). Nationally, for instance, Native Americans are 24 percent more likely than their peers to receive a learning disability label and African Americans are 59 percent more likely than their counterparts to be identified with emotional/behavioral disorders. Once placed into special education, these children have a higher rate of dropping out and a substantially higher probability of being incarcerated. So it is no wonder that Superintendent Wilson and other school leaders across the country are trying to address these patterns that disproportionately impact Black and Brown students. Yet shifting the tide of underachievement is political and controversial.

For many teachers inside schools, they are overwhelmed, lack support, and feel ill-equipped to meet all of the social-emotional and academic needs of their students. From this perspective, dismantling special education creates learning environments full of even more challenges and puts tremendous pressure on them as educators already juggling too many urgent and divergent needs. These sentiments are real, as well, and far too often teachers express that they are made helpless by top-down directives that impact their classrooms. The result: cycles of dysfunction and feelings of powerlessness.

Unfortunately, without adequate opportunities for dialogue, policies pull people even farther apart. A lot of education reform is driven by blame and cynicism coupled with hurtful and unproductive quick fixes that essentially disregard the needs of students. Tonight's board meeting in Oakland was just another example of this pattern. It was the racial epithets—and not the children—that took center-stage.

Research undergirds that institutional transformation will not occur until drastic shifts are made from finding fault to developing partnerships, from documenting problems to discovering solutions (Watson, 2012; Rodriguez, 2015). The intense politics of trying to raise the bar of achievement does not surprise Wilson, yet I wonder if it seems daunting and exhausting. When given this question, he is candid that one of the reasons he came to Oakland is because he admired the district's emphasis on community schools that provide support beyond just academics to include social and emotional services and health centers. And he was drawn to Oakland's boldness in calling attention to African American male student achievement through an office specifically devoted to that. Wilson is straightforward: "Oakland was the only place I went after, and I went all in."

No Excuses

At his previous job in Colorado, Wilson adopted the mantra of "Success for all. No excuses." He even made plastic bracelets with those words and handed them out to his staff and students. When he accepted the job in Oakland, his wife, a career educator in her own right, presented him with a black and silver version of it. He wears this bracelet every day: "Success For All. No Excuses."

This relatively simple slogan frames Wilson's outlook on education. "Being able to say that I was able to perform well in school, that's what changed things for me; well, that's what we want for all kids" he chimes, "high achievement." "If we are going to have to fix poverty or apathy *before* we educate kids," then that will be a long time coming, he explains. "Helping all students achieve is one of the solutions for addressing poverty."This is not rhetorical for the superintendent; it's personal.

Wilson's transparency and vulnerability comes to the fore when he goes out to school sites for his weekly visits. On this winter morning, he is speaking to an auditorium full of students at Madison Park Academy in East Oakland. "Poverty is not an excuse for low achievement," he discloses. He expresses frustration with the people who "want to give us reasons as to why every student can't be successful" because of "those neighborhoods that students live in, the zip codes, the family backgrounds," and he pauses, rests his hands on the edges of the podium, and scans the room. As he makes eye contact with students he proclaims, "I can assure you that you don't have to come from a middle class background or even a remotely wealthy background." In actuality, he advises, "You can come from a poor background, grow up on public assistance, move from house to house, have a single parent raising you, and you can go on to do whatever you want to do, because that's what happened with me." He urges the children to see their capabilities and realize their potential.

Although Wilson appears friendly and approachable with the students, he does not necessarily have this same reputation with adults. He is incredibly fast-paced, a bit impatient, and talks with decisive speed. In the face of political unrest, threats to his family, and the toxicity of prejudice, he remains stoic, even a bit cold.

Oakland has brought him on a long road: from inspirational speeches and working directly with young people in Colorado to heralding the mandate by the board that the district *will* address and eliminate institutionalized racism. The gravity of the task can become burdensome and overwhelming, rather quickly. I recall an exchange with Chatmon when he advises: "Don't get caught up. I can't fight that, that's a nickel fight, I got to stay in the dollar fight." Those smaller battles will "derail you" and "drain you."With Chatmon's advice swirling in my head, I look across the table at the current district leader. He is definitely striving, to the best of his ability, to move the mountain. But this is not about quick directives; it is a slow, long battle over the purpose of schools. Wilson acknowledges the pace, but his destination is non-negotiable: "Helping all students achieve is one of the solutions for addressing poverty" and, he claims, "that is what we will do here in Oakland."

Thurgood Marshall

"I did not intend to be in education," Antwan Wilson shares with me during our conversation in his expansive office on the sixth floor of the district building at

1000 Broadway in downtown Oakland, but he "always wanted to help people" and "impact injustice." He explains to me that when he was younger he wanted to "become Thurgood Marshall."

Growing up in Kansas, Wilson had several teachers of color at an early age: "My kindergarten teacher was Latina, my first grade teacher was African American, and my third grade teacher was African American—all women." "Then my mother moved us to Lincoln, Nebraska," he remembers, "and then all I saw were white teachers." Although he had some phenomenal educators throughout his schooling experience, he specifically remembers an "African American male teacher who ended up going on to be a principal and he was a mentor to me and hugely impactful. I gravitated to him just because he looked like me. And I know that's all it was." Then, when Wilson was in high school, he had a social studies teacher who broadened his horizons. Thomas Christie taught him about what it "means to be an African American male, what it means to be a leader, what it means to perform at a high level, and what it means to give back." "The idea of service and that you owe ..." Wilson pauses, looks down, folds his hands, and shakes his head humbly. He repeats, "That was Thomas Christie."

These life lessons that occurred during school shaped Wilson's pursuits. "I always had a feeling that the education system could be better but while I was in college, I had an opportunity to meet an outstanding teacher who helped me understand that education could help me address the social justice issues I cared about." He is referring to Linda Murray, an award-winning social studies teacher at Hyde Park Career Academy in Chicago. He actually went to observe her classroom and see for himself the ways she engaged students. In her classroom, he witnessed an educator who was "tremendous at her craft, loved her students, and got a great deal out of them." When he left that day, "I did not leave fully sure I would teach," but, he continues, "She inspired me to add education to my pre-law focus." Evidently, his dreams of being a lawyer started to diminish while his aspirations for teaching started to grow.

In Wilson's education courses, in particular, he learned lessons that inform his leadership style and vision for OUSD. One of his professors told Wilson that regardless of their home life or other circumstantial situation, "if the students didn't learn it, you didn't teach it." Decades later, he is still grappling with this idea. He speaks candidly: "We can't ask young people and families to adapt to the way we want to teach them; we need to teach them in such a way that is conducive to how they learn." This approach is rooted to student-centered learning practices and culturally responsive pedagogies, all of which the AAMA exemplifies.

In order to replicate programs like AAMA locally as well as nationally, it is critical to identify strategies other district leaders can use to launch similar initiatives. Superintendent Wilson poses three questions to his peers—other superintendents—and then delineates the answers:

1. **What does the data say?**
   "In your district, it might be Latina females or Asian males. And don't accept people saying you can't do this because you somehow are showing you don't care about all kids. No, we care about all children here. Each child matters! But recognizing that sometimes in systems you find that some students are disproportionately impacted by not getting the additional attention—they are hidden in the average. So we need to show up as a district and respond."

2. **Who are the people being least served and what do they have to say about it?**
   "Here in Oakland, the data spoke quite clearly about what was happening with African American males. The students and their parents were saying we're not being served well."

3. **What are the insights of the educators who care and are keenly and acutey aware and willing to do something about it?**
   "The teachers were clear that there are more pieces to this child than what they learn in their classes. We start with high academic achievement, but there are more pieces. This child is a physical being, a mental being, an emotional being," and all of this needs to play a part in the puzzle of their school success.

The three above points, when taken together and answered honestly, can move a district in the right direction, much like a compass. Throughout this trek to shape the system, it is the superintendent's role to "lead" and "determine what should be done." "Don't be afraid," quips Wilson. "The past superintendent, Tony Smith, made a decision and said I am going to jump in this pond and I'm gonna lead here and it doesn't make any difference if other people are not there. We are going to do it for no other reason than it needs to be done."

Antwan Wilson is carrying Tony Smith's vision forward. He is the first superintendent to participate in professional development meetings with the Manhood Development Program instructors. At one particular session at the beginning of the school year, Wilson shared with the brothers the importance of reading and writing as providing a gateway into achieving in all other content areas. By the time he was done, the two white boards inside the AAMA portable were covered with information and ideas for rigorous instruction. Wilson is an esteemed educator who became a district leader. But effective teaching is not synonymous with management, and time will tell if it is the right fit.

Breaking Barriers

Beyond the rhetoric, how does a school system actually eradicate racism? First, we have to face the facts. Institutional change is based upon the "people within the [institutions]. This is ultimately about people. We have to hire people that care about this issue and want to do something about it. This is a people business." Second, although it might be hard to reconcile, the fact is, "Good people perpetuate institutional racism." "Institutional racism persists," he claims, "because we are looking for a magic pill. It takes more than a magic pill. There are not any magic pills that can change people." Third, leaders need to ask the hard questions, "call out" the challenges, and then stay committed to advancing the work. Fourth, once institutionalized racism has been "called out" and, in Oakland's case, they put "eliminating inequity" into the mission, the next critical step is to fully understand "What is equity and how will we address it? What do we want it to impact?"

Building upon this fourth phase and answering the directive for impact, Superintendent Wilson outlines his vision, discussing the importance of "affirmations, access, acquisition, and achievement." In terms of affirmations, "The culture and identity that young people bring to us matter. It is important in-and-of-itself. We should care about that and how we educate them should take that into consideration." Yet just tending to who students are and where they come from is piecemeal if other institutional hurdles impede their academic success. This leads him to an unwavering commitment to eliminate the roadblocks so all students have access to success. For Wilson, the district office needs to be "very pro-active in trying to get rid of exclusionary practices" that inhibit learning and high achievement. We know full well that there are skills that students are going to need whether it's a social-emotional skill, whether it's an academic skill." And, quite frankly, "it's our job to provide it … I used to say to people all the time who would tell me this child can't do this or can't do that in terms of education. 'Well,'" he smirks, "'that's really good then for them and their parents because they came to school and that's what we do: We teach.'" Finally, it is achievement. Do not "accept achievement gaps as natural," Wilson states insistently. "For me, while we need to recognize that there are certain factors that contribute to achievement gaps, we can't accept them as reasons to accept the achievement gap. Poverty is something that *impacts* achievement. Since poverty is an issue, we may need to provide more mentors, more early childcare services, or more access to books," but what "we can't allow" is for extraneous factors to somehow dictate who a child is capable of becoming.

The AAMA is a special place because, "In order for students to do well in school"—he takes his hand and points to his heart—"they need to know themselves." Wilson leans toward me and speaks rapidly:

> They need to know who they are. They then need to believe in themselves. That's extremely important. Then they need to know that other people believe in them and have high expectations for them. Not as a matter of favor, but just as a matter of fact. We are not doing you a favor because you

are an African American male [rather] we expect a lot of you because you are you.

He repeats, "We have high expectations for you. *Period.*"

The AAMA, led by Chatmon, has been able to demonstrate—with real students in Oakland schools—that achievement is not just possible but probable, given the right mix of input points. "Our Executive Director Chris Chatmon comes in," explains Wilson, with a fearless ferocity to change learning outcomes for the most disenfranchised students. Oakland needs "people who unabashedly are going to say we are going to do what we need to help this population of kids and we are going to get it done." This no-nonsense, no-excuses approach to learning outcomes is results-oriented; yet impressive numbers should not be the only focal point. Significantly, improvements on achievement within AAMA are a by-product of a process that envelops students in a continuum of care and support, and provides them with teachers who elevate their students (young kings) as scholars every single day.

Become the Change

At an AAMA community gathering, Superintendent Wilson addresses the crowd of students, families, and community members. For most people in the crowd, this is their first encounter with him. He steps to the podium and then asks the participants to join him in a call-and-response affirmation:

> If you want love, be love.
> If you need hope, be hope.
> If you long for a hero, be heroic.

Superintendent Wilson enlivens the space with his energy. He then asks all the students of color to take a stand. As the children rise to their feet, he declares, "There is a community here that believes in you, that knows you are awesome. We expect you to be successful!" With this momentum, he applauds Chatmon and his team for raising the bar—not just for Oakland, but for the nation. Superintendent Wilson stands with these students, as a leader and role model, not because they are African American males, but because they embody a new kind of achievement that raises the bar, expands the heart, and elevates the mind.

12

OBASI DAVIS

New Generation of Education

The district office on Broadway in downtown Oakland is six stories high; it houses hundreds of offices and thousands of cubicles. On each floor, adults are busy at work, often sitting quietly at their computers, carrying out the day-to-day operations of running a school system that serves 46,000 K–12 students and employs more than 6,000 people. It is a large business—a business, however, with a lofty mission *to serve the whole child, eliminate inequity, and provide each child with excellent teachers every day.*

The only area of the building where the buzz of young people can be heard is the corner of the third floor where the new Office of African American Male Achievement (AAMA) now lives. It is summertime and because the youth are out-of-school, AAMA has established internships for students throughout the city. For a handful of them, they have the privilege of working in the district office, directly under Brothers Chatmon, Jerome, and Jahi. As part of their work, these students are designing programs for their peers, participating in a summer study session, attending weekly writing workshops, and making presentations at various conferences across the country.

Today I have the opportunity to interview the summer internship coordinator, Obasi Dumasani Davis. He is nineteen years old and a sophomore at the University of Madison-Wisconsin, majoring in fashion design. He grew up in East Oakland, graduated from Berkeley High School, and was Oakland's Youth Poet Laureate in 2013. Since he was going to be home for the summer, he wanted to lend his hand to the AAMA movement.

Unstoppable Greatness

Brother Obasi has been around AAMA since 2010, serving as a performer at community events. However, he has known "Baba Chris," as he calls him, since he was five years old and considers him "my uncle." Obasi and Chatmon's sons attended the same preschool, Nikesemu Emu, an Afrocentric school in West Oakland and have been "extended family" ever since. At an early age, Obasi had African history "instilled in me" which provided a foundation for "knowing my history and knowing who I am in the world." Growing up in Oakland, he saw first-hand that many of his peers did not have that type of opportunity. "In high school you start to see the change in people in how people limit themselves or are limited by certain structures and systems. AAMA is trying to break through those limits and get the kids to realize their power."

For the dozen AAMA interns that Obasi is working directly with in the office, he wants them to fully grasp that "they can do anything." To accomplish this goal, he focuses on critical literacy in the Freirean tradition: reading the word, the world, and oneself in a new way. He understands that this type of self-actualization is "a growing process" and that for AAMA youth it develops out of "fellowship" and "brotherhood." Obasi grins as he describes the ways his students are genuinely "soaking up" what "I am giving them as an older brother."

Obasi recognizes that he is a role model in some respects: he is a successful college student who was born and raised in their same neighborhood. He affirms that because of his background, the students can relate to him and he is able to shine some light on their path. According to Obasi, "I am just passing down everything that I have learned in all of my experiences and just hoping that they can grow up a little faster than I did." I prod for some examples. "We were just talking about this the other day," he chimes, and leans forward in his chair, adjusting his eyeglasses as he speaks.

These bright African American males are really struggling, Obasi insists, "with being in a system that is not conducive to them and not looking out for them. Oakland Unified does not have the best reputation for handling African American males."

Obasi understands that the AAMA youth interns are "so smart," yet this fact, unfortunately, does not necessarily equate to academic success. The students were sharing that by their senior year most of the "messages of victory" they received revolved around playing sports or making music. While these stereotypes do not come solely from the school sector, Obasi is discouraged that teachers rarely view it as their job to disrupt them. He elucidates: "To be at a school where that is what you are being taught and that is the realization that you have come to after all these years, to come out of school" and "your possibilities have been limited to music and sports just shows the failures of this system." I shake my head and respond, "It is disgraceful."

To combat these implicit and explicit breakdowns in achievement, Brother Obasi is using the summer as an opportunity to open up the minds of the "young kings" and expand their horizons. For instance, he chose *Can't Stop, Won't Stop* by Jeff Chang as the summer reading. According to him, the reading is significant for students on three levels because the book:

1. Provides a historical understanding of hip-hop culture.
2. Recognizes the ways Black culture and hip-hop are intertwined.
3. Demonstrates a real-life example of young people creating an international social movement.

These themes connect to writing workshops that Obasi facilitates with the youth; he uses spoken word prompts to better understand "what's going in their heads."

As Obasi uses critical literacy exercises as a doorway into his student's consciousness, he is acutely aware that often their traumas are perpetual and embodied. The interns, like most young people in their neighborhoods, have lost friends to street violence, and all of them know someone that is incarcerated. On a larger scale, with respect to African Americans, in the last couple of years, these students and the world witnessed the state-sanctioned murders of Oscar Grant (Oakland, CA in 2009), Tyrone Smith (Sacramento, CA in 2011), Trayvon Martin (Miami Gardens, FL in 2012), Tamir Rice (Cleveland, OH in 2014), Eric Garner (Staten Island, NY in 2014), Laquan McDonald (Chicago, IL in 2014), John Crawford III (Dayton, OH in 2014), Freddie Gray (Baltimore, MD in 2015), Sandra Bland (Waller County, TX in 2015), the massacre that took place inside the Emanuel African Methodist Episcopal Church where nine African Americans were murdered during a prayer meeting (Charleston, SC in 2015), the physical assault of an African American girl inside her math class by a school resource officer (Spring Valley High School, SC in 2015), the murder of Philando Castille (Falcon Heights, MN in 2016), and on and on and on. This death, at the hands of racism, is the current tableau of these students' lives. Obasi is all too aware that the crime is still Blackness.

This world that students inhabit—which is wrought with jarring inequalities and murderous injustices—should provide a moment for reflection, silence, and sorrow. According to Obasi, students experience white supremacy but often lack the language, communication skills, and analysis needed to articulate their pain and perceptions of a society and school system designed to fail them. There is an unspoken anger that African American children live with because of colonization and the residual and perpetual patterns of disenfranchisement.

As young Black males in the United States, Obasi says, "We can feel in our gut when something is wrong." He continues:

> It's like this rage—that is particular to Black children—because you see what your parents go through, you see what your cousins and everybody who is older than you goes through and you don't know why good people are treated like shit. You don't know why your school looks like this when the other school down the street looks like that. Or why you have to wear this same pair of clothes two times in the week while they get new. You see everything happening and you understand it as being wrong but you don't know why it's happening to you and only people who look like you.

So you're just angry and you want to lash out at something. So when your teacher is like 'read a book, sit down, shut up,' it makes you really combative like, 'No!' You don't listen to authority as well. Authority doesn't mean anything to you.

According to Obasi, teachers and school leaders need to know that "every Black person has this anger inside of him and when you're young, you don't know why. You talk back to your teachers. You do what you want. You cuss. And that's just how we get our anger out." Until schools learn to address the intergenerational and institutional trauma of oppression, asserts Obasi, African American students, at large, will not be successful academically. Healing has to happen! "We need to know why we are angry," he states with conviction.

I nod my head, immersed and a bit taken aback with Obasi's generalized views. Of course, not all Black children are angry, and there are certainly plenty of non-Black children enraged as well. I try to clarify. "So basically," I prod, "you're being asked to respect a system that does not respect you." "Exactly," he chimes and continues:

So you get angrier. The more you don't know, the more you are just fuming ... Now you want to do is release anger and that's violence—then immediately violence becomes release of anger—and then that maybe becomes drugs as an escape from anger.

It is a vicious cycle of self-destruction that stems from "the anger that you are born with."

Instead of trying to control the ailments of anger, Obasi says the educational system needs to address the root causes. This is very important, and something AAMA does extremely well: deal with racial identity development and white supremacy directly. When it comes to school, "Teach them why they're angry" because it will provide an opportunity for authentic recovery and resiliency. Obasi challenges programs that just get kids into college or pressure them to wear a suit and tie as if that, alone, signifies transformation. He is adamant: it does not! "If you just put a suit on them and don't deal with the anger," proclaims Obasi, "they're still going to snap."

The AAMA offers a solution to the pain. Students are provided with a myriad of cathartic outlets for their implicit and explicit, conscious and unconscious rage. As an example, he experienced something "very powerful" at a recent *Man Up!* conference.

Flesh and Bone

The auditorium of Oakland High School is filled on a Saturday morning as approximately 150 African American boys and young men trickle in from the dew and rain. First-timers take a minute to say goodbye to their families while the returning students leap into action, pounding fists and clapping hands with their peers. There is a distinct murmur through the space with greetings like "Hey, brother" and "What's good, young king?" The beating of drums pounds methodically underneath the low hums of chitchat and breakfast clatter. As everyone settles in, Jahi steps to the front of the room—mic in hand—and announces, "Welcome to the 10th biannual *Man Up!* Can we give it up for ten? This is number ten!" The students, some of them still wearing sleepy faces, begin to clap their hands. As the day progresses, elementary, middle, and high school students participate in goal-setting activities, experience a health session with Stic Man from the hip-hop duo Dead Prez, meet with various African American male professionals, and participate in cross-generational dialogue about what it means to be "brothers."

A particular highlight, however, came when spoken word artist Amir Sulaiman took the floor and left Obasi and the entire crowd in awe with an electrifying piece about the recent deaths of young African American males killed by police officers. "Maybe I am overreacting, maybe seeing Black dead babies shouldn't phase me. But it does, it does! Are we not flesh and bone? Are we not minds and souls?" asked Sulaiman.

Sulaiman's question lingered in the air and raptured the crowd—young and old alike. Reflecting on the *Man Up!* conference, Obasi is a bit speechless. He experienced Sulaiman's words as an endless echo, somehow etched through time by freedom fighters of yesterday, today, and tomorrow. These legacies simultaneously came together by way of a single pulse, a vowel spewed, a future coming to fruition. It was intimate and infinite. Obasi did not speak; he just watched and witnessed. One of his interns, however, Toussaint Stone, a junior at Met West, described experiencing something quite similar. "At today's conference," he admits, "I learned that mind, body, and spirit is very important when it comes to happiness. Eternal happiness at least."

Beyond the woes and wails of the world, amidst atrocities unfathomable, and persistent mis-education, police brutality, and inhumanity, spaces are being created—through brotherhood—that are "necessary" to survival, explains Obasi:

> Just growing up in this city and knowing what I was exposed to at those ages and in those schools, it just feels really powerful to have that coalition of young people led by that coalition of brothers who are really there to teach them something. It's essential to have that space that's all Black males because we don't get that—ever. There's never a time when I'm walking down the street and I'm just surrounded by Black people. Seeing people that are successful who look like you and seeing other people who look like you that are in your same boat. It's just important to know that people exist because a lot of times we are stranded in our own little circle of struggle. We have to realize that it's a lot bigger than that! There are people that actually got out of that and are trying to help us get out too!

The "out" Obasi describes is not necessarily a good job or a "better" neighborhood. It is getting out of the pain—the wretched pain—of living in a powerless state.

As young people actualize their potential and discover their agency, the diversity of the world opens up, literally and figuratively. Obasi has experienced this first hand, during his first year of college. Although Obasi faced instances of prejudice growing up in the Bay Area, nothing quite prepared him for higher education. "Going into Madison where it's pretty much all white people—the Black community is a speck on a blank canvas—it's interesting to see how people react to someone who is confident in themselves even though they are different." Obasi takes me on a journey into some of his college experiences, as he shares intimate moments of living beyond the borders of Oakland.

Microresistance

Most Black people in Madison, Wisconsin, Brother Obasi discloses, are very poor and severely dis-empowered. So to meet a powerfully articulate and intelligent African American young man from Oakland whose father is a famous activist-educator and whose mother is a corporate attorney as well as an esteemed African dancer just baffles them—both Black and white folks alike.

He repeats, "It's interesting." He shakes his head and says again: "It's interesting."

After a moment of silence, Obasi talks about the countless times when he is leaving a building on campus or turns a corner and white people literally "jump." Obasi was shocked by the fact that "people are just scared of you a lot. You can see the fear; it's evident. They want you to be violent and they want you to be everything that they assume that you are. But you are not." That fact, he concludes, "just scares them even more."

"When you are around people that don't know your culture," he explains, "then they view it as something alien" and it has the potential "to alienate you within yourself." For Obasi, his close friends are part of his fortress; he is not trying to lose his mind while pursuing his degree. He provides an example. Obasi and his roommate, Jahleigh, who is from Chicago, were playing basketball and were talking trash. People got scared and tried to intervene: "Are you guys about to fight?" He grins wide and chuckles as he remembers the obliviousness of his classmates: "No, this is basketball!"

Instead of allowing *microaggressions* to undermine his success (Solorzano, Ceja, & Yosso, 2000), Obasi shields himself with a strong peer-group. In this way, his resiliency tactics serve as a form of *microresistance* to systemic oppression and ignorance. This helps him survive and thrive in an academic environment that is overwhelmingly ignorant to racial diversity and difference.[1]

As a fashion design major, Obasi is often the "only dude" and "only Black person." The environment is definitely a "struggle" but it has forced him to "learn how to navigate" in these extremely white spaces. I am curious if navigation, for

Obasi, means code-switching. He is adamant that "code-switching is a form of cooption. I don't have to code-switch. I am the same person in every conversation. *Their* discomfort is not my problem." He recognizes that he could "be what we call a 'Chad' but I don't do that because that's not who I am."

"Then who are you?" I prod. Obasi leans up, puts his elbows on the table and looks me in the eye: "I'm Black. That's what I am." He elucidates, "For me, the term "African American" has a sense of complacency. I don't feel like I am an American. My ancestors did not come here because they wanted to. We were born here in an unjust system." Obasi explains that "Blackness" symbolizes both a loss and "finding of identity" because it signifies a "rejection of the identity you were given." Obasi decrees rather decisively: "If the system that is disenfranchising you gives you this label, I don't want that label. I need to make my own and I need to have my own way to address my own people" and "I can't say I'm African because I've never been to Africa." "I was born in America," he explains, "this life, this country—all the good things and bad things about it—is all that I know."

Building on this idea of identity development, I ask Obasi for his definition of Black manhood. Similar to Jahi, he posits that, "For me, I could not answer that question." He folds his hands, straightens his back, and takes an analytical dive to deliver his answer. There are a lot of stereotypical images of Black masculinity and Obasi is critical of both extremes: the head-high *I don't give a fuck* misogynistic gangster on the one hand and the head-down *I want to be accepted* subservient butler on the other. Obasi, like most African American males, does not fall into these falsehoods. Rather, he surmises, "There is no definition of Black manhood. It's really about being comfortable with yourself and having confidence to do anything no matter the barriers around you."

Teaching Matters

A lot of the participants in this study want to fully integrate AAMA, opening up certain classes and coursework to *all* students. "I would definitely support that," Obasi declares with quick decisiveness, "because it doesn't help Black boys if we're the only ones that know we are great! We can't be the only ones to know that we're smart!"

As much as Black children—and all children—have been mandated to succumb to and participate in Eurocentric education models, the same should hold true for schooling processes that facilitate consciousness-building, critical thinking, and social justice. When African American students are isolated and taught about their histories there is often a natural inclination to get indigent and resentful, explains Obasi. Upon learning the facts about Black history, a lot of students might even leave class with a certain level of disgust for their white peers. Consequently, the white students will have no idea what is going on because they have been mis-educated. Naturally, these students, in turn, get scared and react in other ways that reinforce their privileges. As a result of this cycle, both groups continue to suffer because a space has not been created for people to understand one another. "We need to teach the white kid in the class the same thing that we are teaching the Black kid in the class. If they don't get that same information then they are just going to be more at odds."

When thinking about his white peers he is empathetic: "Ignorance is not the fault of the ignorant. Ignorance is the fault of the people who didn't teach them. You can't necessarily be mad at them for just following along." There are lessons that white people need, in particular, if the cycle of racism can ever be fully addressed and destroyed.

According to Obasi, white educators need to sincerely "try to get to know" their students, have a "conversation" with them, "connect with them on a human level." Basically, he shrugs, "meet them where they are, not where you are." Conversely, he is extremely weary of teachers who enter urban areas with some kind of savior mentality. Obasi has direct advice for white folks who enter places like Oakland with a missionary complex. I am reminded of Charles Wilson's critique of himself when he headed into East Oakland. Similar to Wilson, Obasi surmises:

> Don't save Black children. Teach Black children. They think we need saving but we don't because if we don't save ourselves why would we want you to save us? Like literally, we love it! We love where we are! We love what we're doing! Because we don't know … there's no way to know … I went to a party recently in East Oakland: They love the music, they love the life, they love everything. They're jubilant! It's not like everyone's going through the world, shoulders down. You trying to bring them out of something that they love is not helpful.

He reiterates insistently that the job of an educator is not to save students, but to "teach them!"

Obasi comes from a long line of teachers. His parents, grandparents, and mentors are all "adamant and diligent" about "uplifting our people and educating us." In Obasi's eyes, these heroes and sheroes, like his grandmother Laroilyn Davis who is a career educator and school leader, demonstrate that "even if you do not want to be a teacher in the classroom, you still have an obligation to teach and to give back to people. Everything that you've learned is not for you, it's for the next person." His sentiment reminds me that "the more you know, the more you owe" (Watson, 2012, p. 148).

Obasi and I sit across from each other in this pristine conference room at the district office. As I listen to him I hear echoes of Baayan Bakari's testimony about the diversity of spirit—be a scholar *and* a dancer, a thug *and* an intellectual—but in all that you do: be you and do you. Along the way, be bold, brilliant, and unapologetically Black with it. Obasi is light-hearted, jovial, critical, angry, and intellectually astute. He is a fashion designer, a poet, an activist, and so much more. To onlookers, he is a lean and tall, dark-skinned 6'2" young man, with four-inch dreads and a beard, a nose-ring hoop that hangs from his right nostril, brown-frame eyeglasses, and a bright smile, that he wears often.

As our interview draws to a close and he reconnects with his students, I see the way his ethic of care permeates his classroom space. I watch him working with younger mentees. He chuckles a bit as he gives these brothers in the AAMA family their tasks for the day. Although he does not consider himself a teacher per se, he seems to naturally guide the next generation to recognize their greatness.

Note

1 A growing body of literature discusses "microaffirmations" that educators can utilize to foster a healthy learning environment. See https://www.gse.harvard.edu/news/uk/16/12/accentuate-positive for further information.

13

ENGAGE, ENCOURAGE, AND EMPOWER SCHOOL DISTRICTS TO TRANSFORM

Educational spaces are contentious terrains where ideological and political battles are fought and particular futures won. Consider the University of Virginia's recent resurgence of explicit white racial rage, hate, violence and death at an institution of higher education (August 2017). And then a month later, motions were set into play to repeal the Deferred Action for Childhood Arrivals (DACA) program—impacting the legal rights of children of immigrants to attend school. Each of these cases demonstrates that schooling (who is taught and what is taught) is an ever-present battlefield. The innovative work of the Office of African American Male Achievement (AAMA) is part of a larger legacy and struggle to reimagine schooling as powerfully inclusive and unapologetically democratic.

The AAMA has been in operation for eight years (2010–present). In the last year, however, a lot of has shifted that informs the ways we think about our liberation from miseducation and the role school districts can—and must—play in this fight.

In Chapter 1, I referenced issues of displacement with a focus on the histories of colonial settlement and its impact on Natives and African Americans. Forced migration and loss of homeland is not a concept of the past, but continues to shape the power dynamics between marginalization and privilege. Over the past twenty years, there has been a steady move of middle-class white Americans into cities. The phenomenon, often called gentrification,[1] is reshaping the urban landscape. Between 1970 and 2009, income-based neighborhood segregation increased (Schneider, Wilson, Corak, Grusky & Waldfogel, 2016); this problem has intensified because of a decline in subsidized housing for poor families. Altogether, people of color are disproportionately being pushed out of urban areas all across the country; this impacts school policies and practices (Lipman, 2011).

Urban education is part of a larger social system. Schools are both shaped by and deeply implicated in the dynamics of remaking cities because these new urban areas are producing and intensifying inequality. In other words, forces outside of education directly impact the dynamics inside the district. Specific to my research, the gentrification process in Oakland has devastated lower- and middle-class communities who are overwhelmingly Black, Brown, and Southeast Asian. Families have been forced to relocate.[2] The Alameda County Health Department reported that between 1990 and 2011, Oakland lost half of its Black population.[3] This displacement has impacted the school district as well. Since AAMA first began in 2010, OUSD has lost over 8,000 Black students.

Other changes are afoot as well.

As depicted in his portrait, Superintendent Antwan Wilson, has an unflinching commitment to social justice issues, but that, in and of itself, does not sustain institutional transformation. I learned a lesson when researching my first book on community-based educators:"It's not enough to be down for the cause," explained Jack Jacqua, co-founder of the Omega Boys Club in San Francisco, "you've got to be down for a particular community. If you're just committed to the cause or youth in general, you won't be able to make a steady impact over time." He warned that us equity warriors need to "get some roots somewhere so you can make a real impact" (Watson, 2012, p. 144). These words hold true in Oakland.

In November of 2016, Superintendent Wilson announced a mid-year departure from the district. He left Oakland to become the next chancellor for the District of Columbia Public Schools in Washington, D.C. Although many of us were surprised by the announcement, we should not have been. Around the country, the average urban superintendent stays two to three years. Oakland has been led by eight people in the last sixteen years. While I do not know the personal details of Wilson's departure, there is something inherent in the job that creates instability; how to effectively support and sustain urban school superintendents is still an understudied domain.[4]

In May of 2017, the decision was made to hire Kyla Johnson-Trammell as the next superintendent. Over the past eighteen years, she has worked for Oakland Unified as an elementary school teacher, middle school assistant principal, elementary school principal, and then worked her way up to the district's director of talent development, associate superintendent for leadership, curriculum and instruction and elementary network superintendent. "She is third generation Oakland. She is a native," said board President James Harris to a room of reporters. "I would argue that you have someone before you who embodies what it means to be of this town. She is someone who knows the difference between East and West." "I want to commend the board for actually making a decision that matched a lot of the checklist items the community demanded," said Oakland Education Association President Trish Gorham. "I believe that she will bring Oakland back to Oakland and serve the students of Oakland. And I am going to take that leap of optimism to say she is the candidate who can start the healing in this district."[5]

Amidst good intentions and a wealth of expertise, Johnson-Trammell is inheriting a system wrought with wounds, both systemic and spiritual. OUSD continues to have a $25 million shortfall that is expected through next school year, which has been worsened by the fact that top-level salaries at the district have skyrocketed by 566 percent since 2013. Pecolia Manigo, executive director of Bay Area Parent Leadership Action Network (PLAN) and an Oakland parent, explained in a recent interview, "It is not right to say you call for equity to improve outcomes and then cut, reduce and eliminate dollars from classrooms and schools."

Although Brother Chris is acutely aware of the shifting terrain, political upheaval, and financial shortages, it does not define his course. AAMA's flagship Manhood Development elective course is now being offered at twenty-three elementary, middle, and high schools throughout the district. As previously demonstrated, these academically rigorous classes are taught by African American male teachers who form deep relationships with the students and help them navigate through school and life. Students develop an understanding of who they are as African American males, develop a brotherhood among classmates, and boost their academic achievement by building their vocabulary and studying challenging, culturally responsive texts (Givens, Nasir, & de Royston, 2016; Nasir, Ross, Mckinney de Royston, Givens, & Bryant, 2013; Watson, 2014).

The AAMA has contributed to the system-wide transformation of OUSD. Because of AAMA's theory of change and strategies, significant shifts include: 75 percent of the AAMA instructors are now funded through the district, accounting for 1.2 million dollars in base budget funds. From 2010 to 2016, the suspension rate for African American males decreased by 50 percent while the graduation rate increased by 60 percent. Improving the academic trajectories of Black youth enhances the overall quality of educational equity for the entire school system.

The AAMA has received national recognition, with features in the *New York Times*, *USA Today*, *Diverse Issues in Higher Education*, and the *Huffington Post*. When former President Barack Obama launched *My Brother's Keeper*, AAMA was heralded as a beacon of promise. Subsequently David Johns, former executive director of the White House Initiative on Educational Excellence for African-Americans, frequently visited Oakland to garner best practices in the field. Chatmon received the prestigious recognition as a *Leader to Learn From* by *Education Week*. For many leaders in the school reform movement, these accolades could have constituted a standalone win.

AAMA stakeholders were not content with riding this wave of success. Although the office focused strategically on engaging, encouraging, and empowering African American male students, children do not develop in isolation. For AAMA to increase its impact, students' families and their neighborhoods needed to become an explicit part of the solution. Moreover, district demographics are ever changing; 41 percent of students are now Latino/a. Focusing on the needs of Black boys is a penultimate step toward racial justice, but it is not the entire journey. In 2016, the next iteration of the Office of African American Male Achievement was born.

Office of Equity

Building upon the successes of AAMA, in 2016, Chatmon launched the Office of Equity to pilot several programs and take to scale the work of racial equity and healing. Today, Chatmon is the deputy chief of equity and sits on the superintendent's cabinet, which brings together the top leaders of the district. He is poised to move the institution to implement the next stage of targeted universalism.

The Office of Equity is piloting several programs and scaling the work of AAMA to serve all African American students. First, Chatmon and his colleagues are broadening support beyond African American males to other racial/ethnic groups; this represents an important development within the strategy and also signals a successful evolution in programming. The second key shift is expanding the application of targeted universalism from individual schools to a network of schools within a specific regional area of extreme need.

By expanding into the Office of Equity this past year, AAMA has been able to bring to life an emerging area of work in Oakland: the focus on *African American Female Excellence* (AAFE). Long overdue, this area of support has been, in the words of Chatmon, "desperately needed." AAFE is being led by Nzingha Dugas, and began with a 100-day listening campaign and a community report out of findings. Similarly, Lailan Huen now serves as the inaugural director for the *Asian Pacific Islander Student Achievement* (APISA) initiative. She graduated from OUSD, is a long-time educator, and an active member of the API community. Raquel Jimenez has taken the helm as the *Director of Latino/a Student Achievement*. As she wrote in her first newsletter, "In full appreciation of those who have stepped up to preserve, defend, and lovingly teach our cultures, histories, knowledge and ways of life, it is my honor to serve as the inaugural Oakland Unified School District, Office of Equity, Director of Latino/a Student Achievement (LSA)." These new directors of their respective units are joining a ferocious and fearless community of equity warriors, such as Jerome Gourdine (who was promoted and now serves as the director of AAMA), Jahi Torman (program manager), Baayan Bakari (curriculum specialist), Lamar Hancock (literacy specialist) and others.

Altogether, the Office of Equity is joining together piecemeal movements that have been underway in Oakland for generations. Each director is tasked with organizing deep listening campaigns with key constituents and holding a community conversation around the findings. Similar to AAMA, programs are student-centered and asset-based. However, there are also differences. For instance, fights among African American girls were escalating so a plan was devised to organize restorative healing circles. By continuously elevating the children—in particular, children of color—who are furthest away from opportunity, OUSD is addressing and ameliorating structural inequities in schooling (Figure 13.1).

Chatmon once told me that he surrounds himself with eagles, and that being connected to great, enthusiastic change-makers puts the joy into justice. While

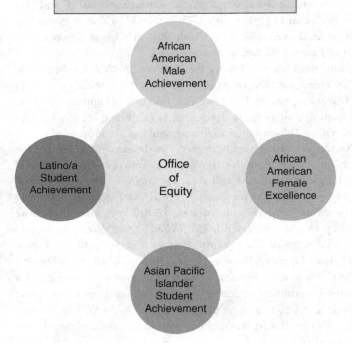

The Office of Equity *energizes, inspires, and empowers* students and staff at all levels of the district to actively disrupt inequities, examine biases, and create inclusive and just conditions. Towards this end, the Office of Equity:

1. Ensures improved (and continuously improving) outcomes for AA, LA, API students;

2. Develops new initiatives that address systemic inequities associated with race, gender, and class;

3. Supports improved outcomes for groups of students that have historically been underserved by the school system.

FIGURE 13.1 OUSD Office of Equity

people are the power, transformation is implemented through place-based strategies. Even eagles have to land. And this relates to Chatmon's next phase of implementation. Another key shift underway is the expansion of the AAMA theory of action. After several years of work with individual schools at more than twenty sites, there is an intentional move toward greater efficacy and deeper support for school communities using a regional approach in the city's most disparate pockets of West Oakland.

In partnership with OUSD's Office of Research, Assessment, and Data, the Office of Equity compiled information based upon neighborhood stress levels (1=least stressed to 6=most stressed) that took into account a normalized composite score for several indicators, such as crime, food security, socio-economics, and other environmental issues. The entire West Oakland Area received an overall score of 4.48 and from there two sites were selected.

On the ground this translates into a "network improvement science" approach. The Carnegie Foundation explains, "Improvement science is explicitly designed to accelerate learning-by-doing. It's a more user-centered and problem-centered approach to improving teaching and learning."[6] As part of this strategy, both AAMA and AAFE will now be housed directly in West Oakland. Taking a holistic approach and connecting multiple stakeholders to improve student outcomes within the community, Chatmon and his staff are wrapping around an elementary and middle school (in a feeder pattern) with the goal of creating an ecological change for African American students *and* families. With stronger, real-time relationships and the efficiency of co-location, AAMA/AAFE leaders will be able to develop rhythms with principals and cultural keepers at each site with greater traction and nuances. Table 13.1 summarizes the input points.

These strategies and programs have all been piloted independently at other Oakland school sites over the last eight years, but never before has there been a synergy of scope to align the best of these practices simultaneously within a feeder pattern. Ultimately, this prototype program will serve as a "proof point" to further accelerate the change necessary to utilize schools as beacons for community revitalization (Warren, 2005; 2014). The long-term vision is to shift the narrative by normalizing success, celebrating community assets, and reclaiming the legacy of African American power in West Oakland.

Again, Chatmon is excited by the possibilities: "Fall and spring *ManUp!* Conferences will engage hundreds of residents and bring in African American students and families from across the state to the West Oakland Region," he shares with me. "This will allow the community that has such a stigma to reclaim its historical prominence and show up as host." Chatmon takes a breath, "Sister Vajra;" the tone of his voice prompts me to put my pen and notepad down and look up. "Just with these celebrations," he says slowly, "we are going to normalize success and build off of our community assets and collective genius." I smile and nod; I too find a moment to take a deep breath and pause.

The last eight years spent building the AAMA have been tumultuous and triumphant. Chatmon has learned that school improvement is not based upon one person nor is it skin-deep. He expounds:

> The system is far stronger, a far more robust structure, far more technical and structural than any human being. It's not only the superintendent, but the executive cabinet … If you had a radical, revolutionary individual that had audacity along with the board to just reimagine a public school ecosystem that wasn't tethered to the historical, racist practices and policies, then I think we could reimagine something. But the system is far greater and stronger than any superintendent.

TABLE 13.1 Key strategies

Input	Impact
KHEPERA, curriculum*	AAMA's curriculum refocuses learning using African-centered approaches to knowledge
Adult Learning	Professional development on culturally responsive pedagogies
Case Management	Student wrap around supports in partnership with community-based organizations and the county office
Communities of Practice	Site/group specific workgroups disaggregating and analyzing "real-time" school data on an ongoing basis
Multi-tiered School Site Study Teams	Multiple stakeholder engagement for school culture change
Student Achievement Celebrations	Narrative shift that leverages hope and community power
Cascade Mentorship	Peer learning supports based upon culturally responsive critical literacy practices
Family Engagement	Holistic parent support and education
Strategic Communications and Marketing	Move the voices of the students into the center of the school redesign process
Restorative Circles	Addressing the ailments of intergenerational trauma with intentional personal and communal healing.

*Khepera is an ancient Kemetic word that means to come into being—*to transform*.

He harkens back to Superintendent Tony Smith who was intentional about "leveraging white privilege to call out structural racism," but even then, he was one leader who only lasted four years.

Systems-Change for Social Justice

District-wide reform cannot rely solely on one person or policy. In *Schooling for resilience: Improving the life trajectory of Black and Latino boys*, Fergus, Noguera, and Martin (2014) caution that good intentions and heroic efforts are not enough to statistically change student outcomes. Real reform takes time and cannot be beholden to quick-fix board mandates or political whim. Over a decade earlier, Stigler and Hiebert (1999) came to a similar conclusion:

> Policy makers adopt a program, then wait to see if student achievement scores will rise. If the scores do not go up—and this is most often what happens, especially in the short run—they begin hearing complaints that the policy is not working. Momentum builds, experts meet, and soon there is a new recommendation; then a change of course comes, and often in the opposite direction.
>
> *(p. 8)*

In order for the roots of improvement to gain credibility, they must be connected to a greater, sustainable cause. In Oakland, the ground was fertile for AAMA because of generations of activism. "We believe if the system does not change," John Smith of AAMA asserts, "then we need to change our perspective of the system and find our way through the system."

Building on this idea, a reporter from Newsweek questioned me about *The Black Sonrise.*[7] As we were going over the curriculum of the Manhood Development Program, he surmised that it was *just* reminiscent of Afrocentric freedom schools of the 1960s. If that was the case, I retorted, you probably would not have flown all the way from New York to interview us for your story. He grinned, "Well ... that is true." I nodded, and we discussed how AAMA is innovative precisely because of its transformative praxis within a large urban school district. This is not your mom-and-pop anti-establishment radicalism. It is more inclusive, perhaps even more co-opted. As AAMA gains in popularity, it must guard against becoming just another fad that is pursued half-heartedly by other districts but never fully realized.

AAMA is the by-product of the long-standing fight for education in the African American community. The Office was born out of struggle and was able to survive because "failure was not ever an option," shares Chatmon. He reiterates that AAMA is "not on one person" but rather "the timing was such that it was our season to bloom ... Our greatest success will not be the work we've done now, but the number of seeds now that are being harvested in Oakland; in Detroit, Michigan; Seattle, Washington; New Orleans; New York public schools; and Washington, D.C." alongside other "grassroots movements across the nation."

Root Solutions

The all-Black agricultural school that legendary Oakland activist, Oscar Wright attended on a plantation in Mississippi did not teach algebra or geometry, chemistry or biology. It was a set-up and, according to Wright, despite the rhetoric to the contrary, the same system that deliberately failed him more than seventy years ago remains in place today. So for Wright, the only solution imaginable is when African American elders and adults step-up, man-up, and step into the lives of the next generation. This is what he has spent his life doing.

Among the regular participants at AAMA gatherings is Oscar Wright. Over fifty years ago, he was a parent in Oakland and he embarked on a crusade for public education. He attended nearly every board meeting and chastised the district for allowing Black and Latina/o students to be tracked into remedial classes and suspended at disproportionately high rates.

The AAMA came to fruition because of the steadfast commitment by Wright and others. Today I watch him interact with students at the bi-annual *Man Up!* Conference at Oakland High; his face beams with pride and I almost detect a couple of tears. "To see what's happened here," Wright shares with me, "and how focused these kids are, really make me feel, at ninety-one years old, that maybe we are going to have a good chance to keep on moving forward."

★★★

Seed Solutions

It is our last official interview and the years have passed by. I am speeding down I-80 from my office at UC Davis to Chatmon's office in downtown Oakland. I am listening to Boosie's latest album. On the eighteenth track, with his song, *Hands Up*, he provides a painful first-person account of police brutality; he cries out that he is being preyed upon by a system that was built to enslave him. His words conjure my own despair. Oscar Grant. Trayvon Martin. Michael Brown. Eric Garner. Tamir Rice. Freddie Gray. Sandra Bland. Philando Castille. And too many more.

When I finally make it into the office to meet with *my brother*, Christopher Chatmon, I am distraught, impatient, and riled up. He gives me an assuring hug and I look right at him. As is customary, his outfit is still very spot-on; his hat always seems to match his shoes. This idiosyncrasy in his style makes me chuckle a little, too. Over the years, the only difference I notice is a few more grey hairs on his goatee beard. In the space between us, when it feels like the woes of the world are endless, Chatmon's sensibility is optimistic. His demeanor disarms me.

Nevertheless, once I am settled into his space and my notepad is out, I go right in, without hesitation. I bring up a quote and recite to Chatmon:

> In 1903, sociologist W. E. B. Du Bois posed that *the problem of the twentieth century is the problem of the color-line*, and now, here we are in 2017, and the blood of racial injustice continues to flow through the streets.[8]

I also share headlines about Castile and others whose killers were not convicted. The ailments can seem insurmountable—like we are bound to a poisonous tree. I plead for Brother Chatmon to tell me, "What is the solution?" Chatmon shakes his head and leans forward. He wants me to grasp, and really know that "It's solutions, Vajra. It's plural."

If there are root causes, then naturally, there are root solutions. Chatmon did not want AAMA to become a "window dressing on a broken house." To fix the house, Chatmon and the AAMA staff made a conscious decision to not just show up differently for students, but also show up differently for one another. They sought to create "sacred space" inside staff meetings and bring an unapologetic love for Black people into meetings, even when they were the only Black people present. The ethos, however, was not divisive or antagonistic. AAMA had the audacity and courage to love and celebrate Blackness powerfully, which in turn, created a healthier dynamic for them to authentically share and build community with others.

Moreover, Chatmon entered into school district meetings armed with the AAMA philosophy. To infuse the system with AAMA, he knew he needed to show up with the same power, self-determination, and courage he expected of the young kings at school. He embodied African American Male Achievement in word and work. When Chatmon was in an executive cabinet meeting, for instance, he called everyone brother and sister. Although it was not the norm, he probed into people's stories to discover unforeseen connections and common purposes. He strategically supported AAMA's growth by engaging a wide range of stakeholders from all across the district in an extended family model.

The pathways that AAMA has constructed over the last several years represent a transformative lifeline to the traditional schooling model. The knowledge base and brotherhood grounds students to their own greatness. From this seed of consciousness, the roots grow deep and the tree stands tall. College does not become yet another stepping stone in the assimilative white washing process wherein students of color—and African American males in particular—are made to feel misplaced and displaced. This does nothing to foster personal success and collective empowerment.

As AAMA proudly asserts in their media campaign: "The best way to predict the future is to create it." To grapple with the challenges and triumphs of inequity in schools, Oakland provides an important case-study for others interested in urban school reform, having taken a direct and unique approach to addressing the achievement gap and intergenerational patterns of inequity. Based on data from the Office of Civil Rights, they were forced to acknowledge that the school system was perpetually harming a particular demographic of its students: Black males. From this, AAMA was born. In naming Chris Chatmon as the first executive director and launching an AAMA Task Force under Chatmon's leadership, Superintendent Smith and OUSD were committing to interrupt the inequitable patterns. As is often the case, there's a big difference between an organization's rhetoric and the reality of the situation. But enough people took the mandate seriously. Leaders like Dr. Jean Wing joined the efforts because she saw it as a beacon that could guide and inspire everyone to "change systems and structures." She was right.

Once the AAMA door officially opened, the immediate flood of interest and collaboration from families was beautifully overwhelming. For the first time in generations, they had an office—*inside the district*—that was designed to be on their side. In actuality, Chatmon could have spent all of his time responding to individual needs, but he chose to create larger initiatives to address the underlying problems. He also could have remained in his office and kept busy with the bureaucracy. Again, he went a different route. His first major initiative was to mobilize listening campaigns at schools. He knew he had to be led by the voices of the African American male children—for they are the experts of their own lives.

"The greatest success of AAMA," explains Jerome Gourdine, "is sheer endurance." The organization has been growing non-stop since its inception. "Starting from a department of one with no budget to now a department of over thirty between facilitators, administrative, and office staff to engage, encourage, and empower our Kings has been a testament to following a vision to implementation to sustainability."

As previously mentioned, the north star for Chatmon and the AAMA team has been equity, but the roadmap to get there has been paved with three essential stepping stones: Engage, Encourage, and Empower. The three Es are not just an anthem for African American students and their teachers, but also an important call-to-action for school districts nationwide.

In our final moment, Chatmon remains tenacious, his enthusiasm still infectious. Chatmon imbues a celebration of sorts. It's in his eyes and in his step. He is not too old (mid-forties), but he reflects on his mortality. If I was to die tomorrow," he discloses, "I worked my ass off to uphold a legacy. I gave it my all!" He leans from around the desk: "All aspects of me that I didn't even know I had." When he passes, he wants the world to have received a "conspiracy of care," saw a Black man who "stood for something," and "worked hard." "I am truly blessed. I've been married for twenty years[9] and I'm like damn, just the love that I have for my wife. My sons. Wow. *Pinch me!*"

Three stickers adorn Chatmon's laptop that he takes everywhere he goes. They reveal the essence of his passion and purpose. One is an image of an Oak tree which reads: *Oaklandish.* The other is the popular quote from Ghandi: *be the change you want to see in the world.* And finally, a passage from Dr. Martin Luther King: *Darkness cannot drive out darkness; only light can do that. Hate cannot drive out hate; only love can do that.*

As we close the book on our journey together, he brings me back to our beginning. Yet now, his conviction is even stronger. He states, "Our young Black boys will excel. It is not a question of *if* but *when.*" Through "strategic partnerships" that "link up the right people," entire systems and cultures transform. I ask him, "What is it that you want for every young Black male in Oakland Unified School District?" He responds, "Wow." Then he tilts his head and looks me in the eye: "That whatever they dream, whatever they envision for themselves, that they know and hold that it can be true." This empowerment is courageous and contagious. It does not just occur in the classroom or with the students; it is embodied in the daily routine of the people connected to this work. While the seeds were planted through the AAMA, this is not about a particular office or position. It is a movement to work toward a justice that is greater than ourselves by reconfiguring systems of schooling as spaces that nurture the brilliance of Black children.

Notes

1 The term "gentrification" was coined by Sociologist Ruth Glass in 1964 to describe the process by which a neighborhood's "original working-class occupiers are displaced" by influx of higher-income newcomers.

2 Forced relocation impacts teachers as well. The teacher salaries across the district are less than the national average, which is strenuous on all educators. Brother Quinton explains, "I can no longer afford to live in my community" and may not be able to work for AAMA if he is forced to move out-of-state.

3 http://www.sfgate.com/bayarea/article/Gentrification-transforming-face-of-Oakland-5387273.php.

4 For an example of what can work, see Thompson, S. (2016). Core Practices: Fuel Superintendents' Equity Focus. *Journal of Staff Development, 37*(6), 32–36.

5 http://www.eastbaytimes.com/2017/05/10/oakland-school-board-names-new-superintendent/.

6 Carnegie Foundation for the Advancement of Teaching. (n.d.). *Using improvement science to accelerate learning and address problems of practice.* Retrieved from http://www.carnegie-foundation.org/our-ideas/.

7 *The Black Sonrise* is my evaluation of the Manhood Development Program: https://www.ousd.org/Page/12267

8 Although this proposition gained prominence in the Souls of Black Folk (1903), Du Bois had already introduced the concept in a lecture at the third annual meeting of the American Negro Academy in 1900 titled "The Present Outlook for the Dark Races of Mankind." His purpose, he states (1900b: 47), was to consider "the problem of the color line, not simply as a national and personal question but rather in its larger world aspect in time and space." He sought to critically examine the question of "what part is the color line destined to play in the 20th century?"

9 Chatmon's wife, LaShawn Route Chatmon, is a leader in the field of racial equity in her own right and is the founding executive director of *The National Equity Project* (http://nationalequityproject.org).

14

BOLD HORIZONS

When I began this examination into racial equity inside Oakland Unified School District, I did not realize it would meander into a journey that would demarcate the last five years of my life. But I have felt called and committed to use the research process in service of this larger struggle to reimagine schools. I have carried many of the lessons I learned from the Office of African American Male Achievement (AAMA) into my own work as the director of Research and Policy for Equity at UC Davis. Moreover, because of my work in Oakland, I am now evaluating the Umoja initiative,[1] which services 57 community colleges throughout California and has served over 10,000 students since their founding in 2006. Similar to AAMA, Umoja focuses on African American student success through culturally responsive instructional models and holistic services (see their philosophy below).

An excerpt from Umoja's Educational Philosophy:

- Informed by an ethic of love and its vital power, the Umoja Community will deliberately engage students as full participants in the construction of knowledge and critical thought.
- The Umoja Community seeks to help students experience themselves as valuable and worthy of an education.
- African American students are inextricably connected to global struggles for liberation throughout the African Diaspora. In light of this, the Umoja Community views education as a liberatory act designed to empower all students to critique, engage, and transform deleterious social and institutional practices locally and internationally.

> • The Umoja Community will instill in our students the knowledge and skills necessary to enable them to make positive differences in their lives and the lives of others.

When I went to the statewide Umoja Conference to begin data collection in the fall of 2016, I was pleasantly surprised to reconnect with so many students I had interviewed as children in Oakland through AAMA. These African American students are now young men at various community colleges. For these students, in particular, Umoja is not a new philosophy, but another part of their educational path that emphasizes racial pride and upliftment.

In *Just Mercy*, Stevenson (2014) makes the distinction that the opposite of poverty is not wealth; it is justice. According to my research, the opposite of racism is not equality; it is empowerment. Empowerment is an educational tool that releases us from the entrapment of the social reproduction of racism.

To date, empowerment has become an ill-defined catchphrase in educational reform. In the field of social work, however, scholars specify that empowerment means, "being committed to both individual growth and social action to achieve structural change (Reamer, 1991; Morrison Van Voorhis and Hostetter, 2006). Applying this framework to classroom practice, social justice education does not merely examine difference or diversity but pays careful attention to the systems of power and privilege that give rise to social inequality, and encourages students to critically examine oppression on institutional, cultural, and individual levels in search of opportunities for action in the service of transformation (Hackman, 2005; McLaren, 2016; Monchinski, 2010; Segarra & Dobles, 1999). For Freire, "Education worldwide is political in nature." Although this is true, it is also racial. This is because, as I stated in Chapter 2, the mythology of white supremacy is a global phenomenon and social system (Ladson-Billings & Tate, 1995; Welsing, 1991).

Discussions of racial achievement gaps are fairly common in school reform conversations, but they are rarely interrogated as a symptom of white supremacy. This is troubling and misleading. In the opening of this book, I shared pieces about my experiences in the Black and Xicana/o Studies Departments at Berkeley High School. In 10th grade I was enrolled in African American History I. During our final examination, the teacher, Mr. Davis, told us to turn over our tests and write for the next ninety minutes on the question posed. He encouraged us to use evidence from course readings to construct our arguments and personal experiences to strengthen our thesis statement. The question:

> *What are you doing to stop and/or curtail the spread of white supremacy in your self, community, and this world?*

This question was asked to a room full of African American students, and me. I remember it verbatim because it is engrained inside my quest for justice. I have carried it with me and posed it to mentors, professors, colleagues, and youth. It surfaces, yet again, like a festering wound when I consider the implications of transformative schooling.

For Freire, "Education worldwide is political in nature." Although this is true, it is also racial. This is because, as I stated in Chapter 2, the mythology of white supremacy is a global phenomenon and social system (Ladson-Billings & Tate, 1995; Welsing, 1991). Although schooling does not hold the monopoly on learning (Baldridge, 2014; Watson, 2012), it does hold the majority of our children. The law mandates education. And although it is our democratic right, it is complicated because we cannot extract the thread of mass schooling from the larger tapestry of racist American policies and practice. Furthermore, school is a—perhaps the— socializing force of the state (Bowles & Gintis, 1976; MacLeod, 1995; Rosenthal, 1994). As a sorting mechanism, school outcomes often reflect racialized divisions (Diamond, Randolph, & Spillane, 2004; Ferguson, 2001; Milner, 2013; Oakes, 1985).[2] This is more problematic then the outcomes of a racial achievement gap, for white supremacy is a learned ideology.

In my experience as a teacher, community organizer, and scholar, I know first-hand that the majority of people join the field of education for altruistic, beautiful reasons. People who desperately want social justice in their lifetimes see schools as a natural space for improving society. Though perhaps naive, maybe society will become fairer if we battle prejudice and ignorance one student at a time. If these are our ideals, then it can become uncomfortable to think about schools as oppressive institutions. Harkening back to the discussion in Chapter 3, a critical lens de-normalizes patterns of privilege and marginalization by focusing on the reasons schools have never been able to become "great equalizers."

Reproducing Racism

In an ecosystem of oppression, polarities are like interlocking realities. There are the owners and the owned; the innocent and the guilty; those that are taught they are bastards and those that are taught they are brilliant. Privilege is based upon marginalization. Wealth is based upon poverty. Whiteness is dependent upon racism for its survival. When we focus exclusively on one side of the spectrum, it limits our understanding of the intersections of injustice and the ways to disrupt it inside schools, inside communities, and inside ourselves.

Consider for a moment that a child's worldview and culture is the antithesis of schooling policies, practices, and procedures. Consider that the ways a teacher talks is foreign to the ways of being inside the family circle (Ballenger, 1997, 2003). What if advancing in school moves a person farther away from personal sovereignty, dignity, and a positive identity (Adams, 1995)? What if gaining in school means losing your soul? What happens when we ask students to inadvertently choose between who they are as people and who we expect them to be as scholars? As alluded to in the opening, these questions are like a loaded gun, especially in most low-income neighborhoods, where there is a vast disconnect between the teachers and administrators who are disproportionately white and the students who are overwhelmingly children of color. In many cases and through decades of research, scholars have concluded that the identity and cultural gaps between students and the schoolhouse can be detrimental, even dangerous (Dumas, 2014; Freire, 1970; Nasir, et. al., 2013; Woodson, 1933). To put it bluntly: If your education teaches you to internalize your own oppression, it is hazardous and harmful.

I closed Chapter 9 with some context and a quote from an intellectual trailblazer, Carter G. Woodson. Again, his work raises contemporary questions. In the dissertation study, *Culture, Curriculum, and Consciousness: Resurrecting the Educational Praxis of Dr. Carter G. Woodson, 1875–1950*, Givens (2016) explains that while studying at Harvard University, "white professors blatantly challenged Woodson on Black contributions to American history" (p. 47). Since Woodson was an African American historian in his own right, he began to critique and codify the ways the educational system is "reliant upon the sustained misrecognition of Black humanity" (ibid.). According to Givens' research, Woodson discovered that the ideology taught in schools was based upon anti-Black sentiments that deteriorated the self-perception of Black students, justified racial violence, and sustained their abject experience. Building on this notion, it is vital to acknowledge that the philosophies and texts that were used to teach African American children to hate themselves were also commonplace throughout compulsory schooling. Consequently, children of all races were systematically learning to demean and disregard the humanity of Black people and African contributions to civilization. Woodson (1933) teaches:

> To handicap a student by teaching him that his black face is a curse and that his struggle to change his condition is hopeless is the worst sort of lynching. It kills one's aspirations and dooms him to vagabondage and crime. It is strange, then, that the friends of truth and the promoters of freedom have not risen up against the present propaganda in the schools and crushed it. This crusade is much more important than the anti-lynching movement, because there would be no lynching if it did not start in the schoolroom.
>
> *(p. 3)*

This quote is powerful for a number of reasons, one of which is that Woodson underscores that schools reproduce racism. If, according to Woodson, we can learn to be divisive and hate ourselves as well as each other, then how do we learn to be more holistic and humane? My findings suggest that the problems and solutions are actually one and the same: education.

Learning—in its most liberating state—shifts our consciousness, stretches our ideas, and cultivates understanding. Patel (2016) eloquently shares, "Learning is fundamentally a fugitive, transformative act. It runs from what was previously known, to become something not yet known" (p. 6). As human beings, we have the incredible ability to change and be changed. But if the structures outlive us, does this impact our ability to transform them? When I first stepped foot onto the grounds of Harvard University another student warned me, "Change this institution as much as this institution will try to change you." It was a warning that woke me up, and nearly stopped me in my tracks.

Over the years, I wrestled with the intractable nature of institutions, yet I discovered solace in a particular sentiment: *interaction*. There is the interaction between ourselves and information in the ways both Woodson (1933) and Patel (2016) describe, but there is also interface, exchange, and symbiotic relationship in the reciprocity of sharing space that goes beyond personal agency. Although vested to asymmetries of power, existence itself is a form of resistance because we are remaking the world and ourselves anew with our encounters (Freire, 1970; Noguera; 2003).

This brings me to Oakland. At the theoretical level, I certainly understood that measurable shifts "against the system" can occur, but, to be quite honest, when I heard about AAMA, I pessimistically thought, on the practical level, here we go again: hire one Black man to deal with the crisis of racism for an entire school district. Impossible. Scapegoat. Predictable. But that is not what happened.

In actuality, an educator with a big heart and gregarious personality took charge to single-handedly build a brand new department within a sick school system. First, he recognized that any movement could not rest upon one person's shoulders. So he utilized his vast community networks and allies locally and nationally to develop strategic partners, rather quickly, that aided in the solution. Second, he began listening campaigns on the ground with students and families inside the schools who were experiencing the woes of a racist educational system. He asked them for the answers. Third, he responded with commitments and quickly developed actions plans. Fourth, he stumbled and fell and made mistakes. Not every program worked or was sustainable, but he took the lessons to heart, albeit wins or losses. Fifth, he remained optimistic and grounded by his own family and sought to reach, teach, and embody—through daily acts and decisions—African American Male Achievement.

As a model of racial equity, Chatmon and the leaders of this movement in OUSD have been able to draw critical connections between instructional practice and the transformation of educational infrastructures. To date, the Office of African American Male Achievement is integral to this larger and longer fight for equitable schools that dismantle racism and re-center our humanity. As demonstrated throughout my analysis, systems are not static. Christopher Chatmon's theory of change and the verified impact further demonstrates this point. Ecological and cultural shifts cascade out and cause a system ("the pond") to recover holistically (see the diagrams on pages 44–45).

I have mentioned AAMA's impact both theoretically and practically. I would be remiss if I did not take a moment to discuss its personal impact. While collecting and analyzing data over these last couple of years (2012–2017), I was forced to face my own cynicism. I fully and wholeheartedly experienced moments of an academic revolution. This is not to imply some kind of romanticization. The work is wrought with its own inadequacies and idiosyncrasies, and that still holds true.

But in reality as well as in research, it is not about the quest for perfection; I was in Oakland because I thirsted for answers. I wanted to know if, and how, we can move schools toward social justice. I am now convinced that systems born in white supremacy can transform to better serve Black children.

Racial justice unlocks human justice.

Domination is finite. Humanity's yearning for community is infinite. Love is an experience of the infinite. This directly connects to the kinds of educational opportunities created for/with children. We will not have the impetus to fully reimagine society if we do not first transform our schools. And even more than that, racial justice unlocks human justice. "Imagination," asserts the popular speaker and author Sir Ken Robinson, "is the source of every form of human achievement. And it's the one thing that I believe we are systematically jeopardizing in the way we educate our children and ourselves."

Racial Justice Framework

Which logic models are useful if the system itself is illogical? This rhetorical question helps break open the mythologies of white supremacy and injurious nature of coloniality. School systems are not innocent bystanders in the reproduction of racism. But education—whether in a classroom, community center, or at the kitchen table—can seed social change. As we critique the functions of schools, we cannot forego the liberatory nature of learning (Patel, 2016). Or as Shujaa (1994) asserts: there exists a fundamental paradox of "Black life in White societies" that causes "too much schooling and too little education."

Oppression constrains, confines, and suppresses the collective imagination. The roots of resistance, then, are nourished by care and commitment, hope and harmony. Here is where the work of equity warriors comes into full view.

The Office of Equity in Oakland Unified School District relies upon *rituals of resistance* that, when practiced consistently and methodically over time, create shifts in the culture of the institution. Meetings and community events honor the ancestors, respect the past, and acknowledge the land; distinctive histories and herstories nourish a collective appreciation for difference; and the present is celebrated through the lives of the children—for they embody the future.

In this movement, racial justice, radical healing, and educational equity are synergistic, harmonious instruments in the orchestra of this fight to decolonize schooling. A racial justice paradigm exposes systemic ills, asks the hard questions, and simultaneously incubates possible answers. Different kinds of solutions can, and should, exist simultaneously but they need to be pushing in the same direction—towards educational equity. A key attribute of an organic, grounded racial justice framework is that a "one size fits all" approach can become yet another Eurocentric entrapment of homogeneity.

District-wide reform cannot rely solely on one person or policy. Real reform takes time and cannot be beholden to quick-fix board mandates or political whim.

In order for the roots of improvement to gain credibility, they must be connected to a greater, sustainable cause. In Oakland, the land was fertile because of generations of activism within and beyond the borders of the school district.

Equity is not strictly policy-driven or compliance-based. It is a value system of service, humility, and love. It is about how individuals show up and work together, with purpose and integrity, to move the mountain of school reform. Essentially, we are striving to transform systems to become more soulful, more humane, and inevitably more democratic. As Horton and Freire (1990) teach us, *we make the road by walking it.*

Liberation from Miseducation

While the African American community is leading the movement for racial equity in Oakland, addressing and eliminating institutionalized racism is not their responsibility, and I do not want to leave anyone with this impression. Ross et al. (2016) came to a similar conclusion: "Black male teachers cannot be the only ones expected to engage in countering Black suffering and reimagining liberatory possibilities in schools" (p. 96). Even though the mythology of white supremacy impacts all people, it is fundamentally about us—*white people.* Racism is about whiteness. And as the dominant group within the educational workforce, we have particular responsibilities. In fact, while the mythology of white supremacy impacts all people, it is fundamentally about us—*white people.* As the dominant group within the educational workforce, I turn to June Jordan who proclaimed, "We are the ones we have been waiting for."

Let us pause and consider that we have mastered technology but have not mastered ourselves. Scientific advancements can take people into unknown galaxies and yet we are still missing critical pieces about how to put our humanity back together. Primordial misgivings about race keep us divided and often paralyzed by prejudice. Few have put the quandary of race into a more poignant analysis then Ta-Nehisi Coates (2015). In *Between The World and Me,* he posits,

> Americans believe in the reality of "race" as a defined, indubitable feature of the natural world. Racism—the need to ascribe bone-deep features to people and then humiliate, reduce, and destroy them—inevitably follows from this inalterable condition. In this way, racism is rendered as the innocent daughter of Mother Nature, and one is left to deplore the Middle Passage or the Trail of Tears the way one deplores an earthquake, a tornado, or any other phenomenon that can be cast as beyond the handiwork of men. But race is the child of racism, not the father... the belief in the preeminence of hue and hair, the notion that these factors can correctly organize a society and that they signify deeper attributes, which are indelible—this is the new idea at the heart of these new people who have been brought up hopelessly, tragically, deceitfully, to believe that they are white. These new people

are, like us, a modern invention. But unlike us, their new name has no real meaning divorced from the machinery of criminal power.

(p. 7)

Coates' timely examination of race breaks us away from solely focusing on the Black body, but frames the cage as a façade of whiteness and Americanization. We are all implicated.

Since racism exists in the milieu of social interactions and systems, it is experienced at birth and reified before children even formulate their first words. Without the language or historical context to deconstruct why certain people are perpetually disadvantaged, oppression gets operationalized intuitively and internalized. These patterns often become self-fulfilling prophecies of marginalization and privilege—the building blocks for westernized hierarchies and social systems.

While I do not want to re-center whiteness in this larger quest to understand equality, I also realize that school systems (like all state-sanctioned institutions in this country) are disproportionately white. It is important that white people unpack and understand this work in our own ways and with our own particular convictions (Frankenberg, 1996; Leonardo, 2009; McIntosh, 2004).

In Oakland, AAMA created an inoculation (vaccination) to protect students from the delusions and deleterious impact of internalized racism (Fanon, 1963; Hilliard, 1998; Nobles, 1998, 2006). White people need some immunization as well, but because of the *white—humanity* binary, our identity development and self-actualization will take a different form. To this end, here is a little something for *us* to ponder. Below are four prevailing myths that demarcate the backbone of white existence (and remember, race is a social construct):

1. White People are the Center of Civilization and Progress
2. White People Run the World
3. White People are the Majority and the Norm
4. Whiteness is Real

If we can accept the fallacies of our identities in their current form, I present eight, components of a *Critical white Consciousness* (CwC). These ideas are not exhaustive, but meant to be generative as we work, collectively and humbly, to build a transformative racial equity framework and ongoing movements to reimagine education as the praxis of empowerment.

1. Equity starts with autobiography. If we are to interact authentically with people who are often different from us, we must actively reflect on our own stories, biases, privileges, and assumptions. As much as we might not want to admit it, we are the embodiment of our ancestors; the blood on their hands in the name of Americanization, settler colonialism, and whiteness runs through our veins.

2. As genuine allies, we cannot scapegoat racism by denying or hiding from our identities. To consider even a slight possibility that we can be colorblind in a racialized society is like claiming a fish in an aquarium might not be wet. It is what it is—we are all wet—so let's deal with ourselves with integrity and empathy. And when these dynamics get intense or the information is too much to bear, try not to get defensive, for it is the surest way to miss the lesson.

3. Once you become critical and conscious of your skin, this is just the beginning of a lifelong journey. In meditation, for instance, there is a focus on the breath. And part of the goal is to become so aware of your breath that even when you are out grocery shopping or playing at the park you are still centered in a meditative state—you are fully present. *Critical white Consciousness* (CwC) involves us becoming acutely aware of the skin that we are in—people of color are forced to see themselves in this light because of the ways society *others* reality—but for us, we need to awaken and then re-awaken to our privileges. What does it mean to be white becomes a quotidian practice.

4. My nephew once asked me, "Do you wish that you were born Black?" I looked him eye-to-eye and stated definitively: "GOD does not make mistakes. I am who I am and I strive to love who I am, and so should you." Given the world we live in, when it seems everything is for sale, including racial identity, I see our confusion and maladjustment around racism getting more misconstrued. We cannot run away from ourselves, no matter how hard we try to conceal who we are or create deception about where we come from. Self-love and genuine self-esteem are still very important. Not being at home in/with ourselves is actually synonymous of our larger white sickness.

5. As a child of the myth of white supremacy, we are constantly perpetuating or dismantling the very system that created us. This is not about experiencing poverty so that we can feel oppressed or traveling abroad to a foreign place, like Guatemala or India, so we can feel like a minority; it is about using our skin to dismantle the master's house. If you were living in the days of slavery, who would you have been? If you were at that picnic when they lynched and castrated a Black man, what would you have been doing? Smiling for the camera, perhaps? *This is not about white guilt or white fragility, but human responsibility*. It is about actions, some of which privilege affords us. For instance, the leaders in the AAMA movement continuously applauded Superintendent Tony Smith for "calling out" racism; they are convinced that it "passed through" because he is white and male.

6. Toni Morrison aptly explains, "People who practice racism are bereft... If you can only be tall because somebody is on their knees, then you have a serious problem. And my feeling is white people have a very, very serious problem, and they should start thinking about what they are going to do about it."[3] Poverty traps, while racism tricks. White supremacy is a disease of the soul. It creates delusions of power that we are taught to internalize, perpetuate,

and defend. There is an unexplored psychological and pathological toll that racism takes on the oppressor. As such, it will take its own kind of radical healing and healing justice (Ginwright, 2010; 2015) to reconnect ourselves to humanity.

7. Perpetuating white supremacy knows no hue. People of color can—and do—perpetuate colonial mentalities, a point brought up by numerous AAMA staff and stakeholders. Being an equity warrior is more than skin deep, which is why I discussed the ontological fight for freedom in Chapter 4. It is not politics or positions that define us, but actions and ethics.

8. We, too, have to liberate ourselves from the misconceptions and miseducation. This is not about asking or expecting people of color to teach us about our ignorance because the burden of our awakening cannot fall on anyone else's shoulders. I urge us to read and "double-study" that which we know and that which we think we know about history. Take for instance the song "Amazing Grace," which we have likely heard throughout our lives. While it is closely associated with the African American community, it was written by a former slave trader, John Newton. The song describes his spiritual awakening (from a blind wretch to a person who, through grace, can now see). As he wrote in an abolitionist pamphlet in 1788: "It will always be a subject of humiliating reflection to me, that I was once an active instrument in a business at which my heart now shudders."[4] From John Brown to Elizabeth Margaret Chandler, from Howard Zinn to Noam Chomsky, from Amy Goodman to Erica Meiners, there are many white activists courageously working toward justice.[5]

There is no simple recipe to racial equity. It is a struggle that is real, but also really beautiful. There is a word in South Africa, *ubuntu*, that reflects the idea that humanity is bound together in ways that are invisible to the eye, yet gripping to the soul; a oneness that creates compassion and ignites innovation. Our interconnectedness exists, whether we like it or not, so the challenge is to find common ground. In Oakland, the common ground was an unapologetic radical Black love that inspired institutional shifts and saturated the ecosystem. Throughout this process, people of all ethnicities joined the call to engage, encourage, and empower.

District Dynamics

Engage, Encourage, Empower is not just an anthem for African American students and their teachers, but is an important call-to-action for school districts. Inside most bureaucracies, including OUSD, there are hierarchies that create animosity and contempt. Some adults try to control and manipulate situations. Often, children get caught in the crossfire of egos, politics and irrelevant policies. Cognizant of the unhealthy ecosystem, Brother Chatmon relied on systems-theory to think about "energy flow, balance, counter-balance" and institutional alignments that serve children in new, more powerful ways. "In these systems, they want you to act in a hierarchy" but "everyone is a leader," says Chatmon. To transform the institutional space, words like *love, king,* and *brother* became beacons in a larger shift toward racial justice. These *rituals of resistance* were connected from the treetops to the roots, enacted daily on the playground and in the classroom, inside the office and during the cabinet meeting. Connecting words and deeds joins our hearts to our feet. Such a commitment allows a necessary bridge to form between critical theories and humanizing practices. This is significant.

For improvements to take root and blossom, modalities need to become embodied as daily practice affectively and effectively. To reinforce this point, let's briefly consider restorative justice. In many school districts, it has been adopted as a strategy and approach to building community. It is toted as an alternative to the zero-tolerance punish and suspend method of discipline that disproportionately targets and criminalizes students of color. To repair the damage, teachers are encouraged to use restorative circles to foster authentic communication, resolution, and greater harmony. The irony to this approach is that the people who are making the policy are rarely practicing the very principles they are asking children to enact.

As demonstrated in Superintendent Wilson's portrait, school board meetings, for instance, are often contentious and can resemble a school playground gone awry with foul language, name-calling, bullying, and backstabbing. The same could be said for some staff meetings where contentions are high and resolution seems nonexistent. Fundamentally, policies are applied at a micro-level with pressure for results, but are rarely actualized or embodied system-wide. To put it another way, there is a gap between what we want for our children and what we want for ourselves. Until we, as adults, start to manifest our ideals, we cannot expect our children to fully follow our lead and heal.

★★★

In the struggle to improve the entire ecosystem, this study sought to contextualize and bring empirical evidence to bear on the pedagogies and educational philosophies of people at all tiers of the system who are striving for institutional transformation. Democratic ideals and varying personal convictions converge inside the portraits that shaped my investigation. In particular, the detailed narratives of Chris Chatmon, Matin Abdel-Qawi, Jahi Torman, Baayan Bakari, Kevin Jennings, Charles Wilson, Antwan Wilson, and Obasi Davis shed light on the macro-structural analysis. For each of these critical stakeholders, education is a premiere mechanism for empowerment. For Chris Chatmon and Charles Wilson, fostering authentic connections with individuals at all tiers of the system is fundamental to their approach to district-wide change. This approach is relatively *relationship-based*. With respect to Dr. Jean Wing and Antwan Wilson, their keen focus on the evidence serves as the basis for their decisions. This approach is relatively *issue-based.* Both modalities are important and, when taken together consistently over time, allow leaders to address and ameliorate the ills of inequity. For Charles Wilson and Anwan Wilson, education is a mechanism to combat poverty and school is the primary tool that can be used to break cycles of marginalization. While the others in the study would likely agree, they emphasized the cultural-political discourses that link agency and achievement. The youngest person featured, Obasi Davis, offered a unique perspective. He was the only person in the study to speak directly to the profound social wounds that result in a bequeathed rage for the system, including its schools. He is less concerned with building relationships or rallying around issues—he yearns for a type of radical healing that is grounded in history—that explains and reframes race in America for all people, not just African Americans.

Altogether, there is a balm in Oakland. In a quest for racial equity, a large urban school district wrought with inequities, financial problems, and political upheaval, took a bold and unique approach to address the achievement gap through a framework that did not villianize or victimize the children. The strategy was to treat the entire ecosystem through targeted universalism, by focusing explicitly on the demographic least served by the system: African American male students. The solution, then, was to facilitate various inoculations—from course development, to hiring Black male educators, to intensive media campaigns, to leveraging new resources and partnerships, to professional development—all of which focused on engaging, encouraging and empowering the school district to do right by all children.

The Soul of Social Change

While districts are designed to deliver bottom lines, we have to push, toil, and weed out those neoliberal market mentalities aimed at efficiency over education. We cannot allow the seeds of mass schooling sowed by white settlers during the industrial revolution to frame the parameters of opportunity. Inevitably, our academic revolution will be determined by how vast we dream and how well we work together to actualize new futures of educational possibility.

Although equity starts with autobiography, it is not as simple as one's own story and experiences. Equity demands, by its very definition, that we courageously name, challenge, and transform ourselves and the systems we are apart. This process represents our present being, future becoming, and historical belonging.

Along this journey for justice, the roadblocks and the magnitude of oppressive forces can seem paralyzing while at the same time the people, like those in this study, can be very inspiring. It is important to realize and hold to heart that our problems and solutions occur simultaneously, like a paradox of progress. Change agents of all kinds continue to push through and move beyond the borders, dedicating their lives to a "practice of freedom" (hooks, 1994; Giroux, 2010).

As scholars and practitioners who pontificate (and sometimes create) radical disruption, we must force ourselves into the spaces of discomfort that prompt us to expand, connect, and grow. Audre Lorde teaches that, "It is not our differences that divide us. It is our inability to recognize, accept, and celebrate those differences." I propose that this might be one of our only ways to get to/through our racial divides to collectively build transcendent, healthy ecosystems.

In other words, to actually move toward racial equity inside schools, we must move toward one another. Darder (2015) underscores that love is a powerful "decolonizing epistemology—a dialectical framework from which we could break through the oppressive structures and practices of hegemonic schooling and society." Part of having a transformative approach is discovering new ways to build power out of interdependence; schools are ripe for this kind of energetic exchange.

The soul of social change is learning.

★★★

I also want to take heed that empirical research will not get us where we need to go; at best, it will simply help pave the way. This is because social justice is not just meant to be studied, it is here to be lived. In this vein, I am cognizant that no single study can offer a panacea. There is just not enough time or space or singular wisdom to hold an issue of this magnitude within the pages of a book.

To embolden our horizons, I turn toward actions in our lifetimes. Seeds can turn into a forest; small steps can get us to a mountaintop. As points of possibility:

- Wangari Maathai from Kenya began to plant trees in 1977 as a means of reversing the severe crop damage wrought by deforestation. Ultimately, more than 45 million trees were planted as a result of this one woman's passion and perseverance. In her book, *Replenishing the Earth: Spiritual Values for Healing Ourselves and the World* (2010), she discusses her resolve to act: "It's fair to ask what spiritual resources could be used to gather the courage and strength to take a stand against what one sees as wrong. Perhaps it is attaining a level of consciousness that does not allow one to feel peace with oneself if something is being done that seems unjust. That same awareness can give you a resolve so that you are not overwhelmed. Instead, you feel empowered to take action and gradually it becomes possible to figure out what to do."

- Continents away, in a completely different context, two African American college students, Vanessa Garrison and Morgan Dixon, bonded over "2Pac, Nikki Giovanni and their inability to say no to smothered pork chops." They became lifelong friends and co-founded GirlTrek. To date, GirlTrek is the largest health nonprofit for Black women and girls. Inspired by Harriet Tubman, Ella Baker, and their own maternal lineages, their mission is profoundly simple:

- To lace up our sneakers and walk each day as a declaration of self-care!
- To heal our bodies, inspire our daughters, and reclaim the streets of our neighborhoods.
- To reestablish walking as a healing tradition in Black communities as tribute to those who walked before us.
- A health movement organized by volunteers across America to inspire one million by 2018.

- Inside the academy, yet another courageous act occurred. In 2016, the famous law professor and author of *The New Jim Crow*, Michelle Alexander, decided to "walk away from the law." In a heartfelt and shocking letter to the world released on her social media site, she explained that, "Solving the crises we face isn't simply a matter of having the right facts, graphs, policy analyses, or funding. And I no longer believe we can *win* justice simply by filing lawsuits, flexing our political muscles or boosting voter turnout. ... This is not simply a legal problem, or a political problem, or a policy problem. At its core, America's journey from slavery to Jim Crow to mass incarceration raises profound moral and spiritual questions about who we are, individually and collectively, who we aim to become, and what we are willing to do now." For these reasons, in the coming years, Professor Alexander will study at a seminary and journey to uncover the "spiritual dimensions of justice work."

Equity-driven work is not for the faint of heart. It demands the courage to love, not just personally, but collectively. Love that transcends and connects people across generations, geographies, and genealogies is not paternalistic or missionary—it is by its very nature, diverse and inclusive. Equity is the material manifestation of justice on earth.

Equity is the material manifestation of justice on earth.

Education is radical work. My research builds upon critical discourses and decolonizing methodologies (e.g., Patel, 2016; Tuck, & Yang, 2014). These studies problematize the reproduction of racist imperialistic hegemonies in both research and practice. However, there is not enough theoretical application into areas of possibility, like Oakland, that are striving and struggling to heal from and disrupt patterns of institutionalized racism. As Lawrence-Lightfoot writes, "social science portraiture may play a critical role in shaping educational practice and inspiring organizational change" (1983, p. 378).

As a formidable case study, the AAMA inside Oakland Unified School District embodies a liberatory epistemology in their interactions and transactions. This kind of transformation involves the co-creation of spaces, relationships, and practices that reimagine organizational ecosystems as spaces that humanize and harmonize. Together we learned that shifting the culture of school systems takes strategic planning, *rituals of resistance*, and patience. Toward this end, I relied on portraiture to take you inside the lives and inner-workings of equity warriors to unveil and connect radical theories with on-the-ground solutions. May their courage broaden our horizons, personal convictions, and system-wide solutions.

I close these pages with a sense of "critical hope" (Duncan-Andrade, 2009) and I draw final inspiration from Maxine Greene (2009) who explained that "of course we want to empower the young for meaningful work…but the world we inhabit is palpably deficient: there are unwarranted inequities, shattered communities, unfulfilled lives." So she asks, "How are we to move the young to break with the given, the taken-for-granted—to move toward what might be, what is not yet?" (p. 84). Her answer stretches into these final moments as she posits that poetry gives rise to our potential; the pallet of creativity can manifest an insurrection of the imagination.

In the case of the AAMA, the fallacies of underachievement and internalized racism dissipate as students in Oakland discover that prison or an untimely death is not their fate. These young people are redefining education as a precipice for lifelong learning and liberation—all through the lens of an academic revolution. To close, a middle school student in the Manhood Development Program stands and orates his personal affirmation:

> I am a Diamond in the Rough.
> I am a Miracle in Disguise.
> I am the Essence of Time.
> I am Unstoppable.
> I am the Victorious One.
> I am the Blood that Pumps your Main Artery.
> I am that Breath of Fresh Air.
> I am the Bullet in the Chamber.
> I am the Chosen One.
> I am the American Dream.

Notes

1 http://umojacommunity.net
2 This is not to imply that children of color are not in Advanced Placement courses, for instance, but that vast gaps in educational equality are intentional, cultural, and structural. We do not even have equal funding for equal schooling, let alone the same expectations for all students.
3 https://www.youtube.com/watch?v=6S7zGgL6Suw.
4 http://trisagionseraph.tripod.com/Texts/African.html.
5 See also, Warren (2010). *Fire in the heart: How white activists embrace racial justice.*

APPENDIX A

Community Writing Sprints Protocol

Opening and Intention:

Have your voice heard through your writing. The larger Office of African American Male Achievement (AAMA) report we envision needs to reflect the expertise of the leaders, like all of you, in your own words. To accurately document the larger story, we need you! You are fundamental to this process—your honesty, realness, and vulnerability is vital. Essentially, the story quilt will not be complete without your patch.

Create a collective writing pallet:

- *What words come to your mind when I say AAMA?*
- *AAMA in Oakland Unified School District?*
- *AAMA at the school sites?*
- *AAMA in the community?*
- *AAMA in your mind?*
- *AAMA in your feet?*
- *AAMA in your heart?*

Personal Writing Questions:

1. When did you first become involved in the movement for Black male achievement in Oakland? Where does your story begin? Take us into that time...
2. What is the greatest success of AAMA thus far? Why?
3. What is the greatest weakness of AAMA thus far? Why?

4. AAMA is now 5 years old. What will AAMA look like at 10 years old? Be specific.

5. Describe the Manhood Development program and curriculum to a young and eager white teacher in Oakland.

6. Explain AAMA to an African American elder who spent their life trying to improve schools for children of color.

7. What is your role within AAMA? What are you fighting for? What you are fighting against? Why are you fighting?

8. A district in Cleveland, Ohio is desperate to replicate AAMA. What do you suggest they do? Who do they need around the table to launch it? What is your advice?

9. A student is considering enrolling in the new Khepera Academy but they do not know what it is. Tell them about it. How did it start? What advice do you have for him? Why is it important?

10. What kind of student is *best* suited for AAMA? Share a particular success story/moment of impact. What kind of student is *least* suited for AAMA? Share a particular success story and moment of challenge.

11. Who is left out of this movement, and why?

12. At the end of the writing session...

If you would like to provide it, please put your personal contact information on the back of your page.

Sharing is Caring.
Thank you for your insights and participation.
Your presence is our power.
May these words move people to shape systems that improve lives.

APPENDIX B

Sample List of Texts Used in AAMA Classrooms

- *The African Origin of Civilization*—Cheik Anta Diop
- *African People in World History*—John Henrik Clarke
- *The Autobiography of Malcolm X*—Malcolm X
- *Before the Mayflower: A History of Black America*—Lerone Bennett Jr.
- *Black Boy*—Richard Wright
- *Can't Stop, Won't Stop*—Jeff Chang
- *Go Tell It to the Mountain*—James Baldwin
- *The Golden Age of The Moor*—Ivan Van Sertima
- *Introduction to African Civilizations*—John G. Jackson
- *Invisible Man*—Ralph Ellison
- *Manchild in the Promised Land*—Claude Brown
- *The Mis-education of the Negro*—Carter G. Woodson
- *Narrative of the Life of Frederick Douglass*—Frederick Douglass
- *Nile Valley Contributions to Civilization*—Anthony T. Browder
- *The Pact*—Sampson Davis, George Jenkins, and Rameck Hunt
- *Philosophy and Opinions of Marcus Garvey*—Amy Jacque Garvey
- *Roots*—Alex Haley
- *The Spook Who Sat by the Door*—Sam Greenlee
- *They Came before Columbus*—Ivan Van Sertima
- *The World's Great Men of Color*—J.A. Rogers
- *The Wretched of the Earth*—Frantz Fanon

APPENDIX C

Sample Lesson from the Manhood Development Program

In Brother Quinton's lesson plan, he uses Brother Jahi's three steps (I Do, We Do, You Do) to devise his activity. The theme for the month is self-mastery and the today's activity is "Where are you headed?"

On the board it clearly states that the standards are Comprehension and Collaboration (CCSS.ELA-Literacy 9-10.1) and Presentation of Knowledge and Ideas (CCSS.ELA-Literacy.SL 9-10.4).

Word of the Day: Reflect

Quote of the day: "I'm starting with the man in the mirror, I'm asking him to change his ways, and no message could be any clearer, if you want to make the world a better place, take a look at yourself and then make that change."
—Michael Jackson

ENGAGE Direct Instruction: "I DO"

1. My personal testimony of a time I made a poor decision.
2. Explain how I felt after examining the three steps of reflection which are to Think Again, Remember Feelings, and Learn Something New.

ENCOURAGE Guided Practice: "WE DO"

1. Ask if anybody would like to share a situation of their own in which they didn't use good judgment.
2. Talk through the situation together using the three steps of the reflection process.

EMPOWER Independent Practice: "YOU DO"

1. Students will be placed into groups of three to share stories, and to state something that they'd like to change about themselves or in their lives based upon the reflection process.
2. Use active listening skills to respond to what you hear and give feedback.
3. Repeat the process until each group member has shared.

Exit Slip Question of the Day: How can I use my reflection today to help me reach my goals tomorrow?

Homework Write-Up: When was the last time you helped someone? What did you do?

APPENDIX D

School Reform for Racial Justice (Institutional/Intergroup/Individual)

INSTITUTIONAL: Strategic Macro-Level Pressure Points

- **Purpose:** The North Star represents the long-term goal. A clear, defined purpose serves as a compass through the turbulent waters of school reform.
- **Power Base:** Stakeholders within and beyond the district hold the institution accountable. Continuous emphasis on building authentic, sustainable relationships. Celebrate and appreciate the people power.
- **Proof:** Decisions are based upon data that is disaggregated based upon race, gender, and SES. Qualitative and quantitative research supports and helps refine the daily praxis to improve lives. Findings are shared with the schools and communities to move the partnership forward.
- **Profit:** Diverse funding portfolio and savvy fundraising that do not rely on one entity, alone, for support. Intentional and creative ability to harness community resources that support economic self-determination and sustainability.
- **Perseverance:** Win, learn, and continue to move. Consistent commitment that serves students and families differently. Embodying the change you wish to create.

The abovementioned pieces "rain down" and constantly interact with the work on the ground, supporting growth, development, and goals.

INTERGROUP: Movement-Building within the Ecosystem

In Oakland, transformation was realized because of a collective, harmonious model for African American student success revolving around four domains of systems-change for social justice:

- **Visionary Leadership:** Jobs with a 50,000-foot view connect to the ground and is rooted in practice. Tenacious leaders are able to foster unity both vertically and horizontally to improve and move systems.
- **Committed Builders:** Educators, elders, young people, superintendents, scholars, policymakers, and parents must work together to interrupt patterns of underachievement in word and in work, at the intersection of agency and action.
- **Community of Caring Teachers:** Educators care deeply about student's social-emotional, cultural, and academic wellbeing. Because of the nature of this work, it demands patience, partnerships, a rigorous culturally responsive curriculum, and an unwavering belief in the brilliance of all children.
- **Black Achievement:** Learning environments foster positive racial identity development by invoking the power of the past and the legacies of resistance that pave the way for each generation. Schooling then becomes a liberatory tool that uplifts and empowers the next generation to use what they know to improve the world.

INDIVIDUAL: Personal accountability to the larger movement for racial justice (Figure 17.1)

1. What are your intentions?
2. What are your actions?
3. What is the impact?
4. What have you learned?
5. What are your points of pride as well as problems of practice?
6. How do these reflections shape your praxis as you begin again?
7. What are your intentions? …

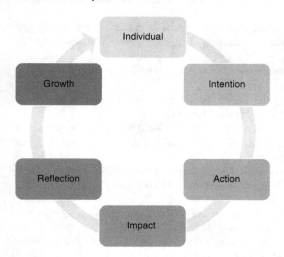

FIGURE 17.1 Personal accountability cycle

BIBLIOGRAPHY

Adams, D. W. (1995). *Education for Extinction: American Indians and the Boarding School Experience, 1875-1928*. St. Lawrence, KS: University Press of Kansas.

Anderson, J. D. (1988). *The Education of Blacks in the South, 1860–1935*. Chapel Hill, NC: University of North Carolina Press.

Andrade, J. D., & Morrell, E. (2008). *The Art of Critical Pedagogy: Possibilities of Moving from Theory to Practice in Urban Schools*. New York: Lang.

Anyon, J. (2005). *Radical Possibilities*. New York: Routledge.

Apple, M. (2013). *Can Education Change Society?* New York: Routledge.

Apple, M. W. (1995). *Education and Power*. London: Routledge.

Apple, M. W. (2004). *Ideology and Curriculum*. 3rd ed. New York: Routledge.

Apple, M. W., & Buras, K. L. (2006). *The Subaltern Speak: Curriculum, Power, and Educational Struggles*. New York: Routledge.

Artiles, A. J. (2011). Toward an Interdisciplinary Understanding of Educational Equity and Difference: The Case of the Racialization of Ability. *Educational Researcher, 40*(9), 431–445.

Asante, M. (2000). *The Egyptian Philosophers: Ancient African Voices from Imhotep to Akhenaten*. Chicago, IL: African American Images.

Baldridge, B. J. (2014). Relocating the Deficit: Reimagining Black Youth in Neoliberal Times. *American Educational Research Journal, 51*(3), 440–472.

Baldridge, B. J., Lamont Hill, M., & Davis, J. E. (2011). New Possibilities: (Re)engaging Black Male Youth within Community-Based Educational Spaces. *Race Ethnicity and Education, 14*(1), 121–136.

Ballenger, C. 2003. "Because You Like Us: The Language of Control." In *Education Policy and Practice: Bridging the Divide*. S. Plaut and N.S. Sharkey (eds.). Cambridge, MA: Harvard Educational Review.

Ballenger, C. (1997). Social Identities, Moral Narratives, Scientific Argumentation: Science Talk in a Bilingual Classroom. *Language and Education, 11*(1), 1–14.

Beckert, S. & Rockman, S. (eds.) (2016). *Slavery's Capitalism: A New History of American Economic Development*. Philadelphia: University of Pennsylvania Press.

Bolton, C. (2005). *The Hardest Deal of All: The Battle over School Integration in Mississippi, 1870–1980.* Jackson, MI: University Press of Mississippi.

Bonds, A., & Inwood, J. (2016). Beyond White Privilege: Geographies of White Supremacy and Settler Colonialism. *Progress in Human Geography, 40*(6), 715–733.

Bonilla-Silva, E. (2006). *Racism without Racists: Color-Blind Racism and the Persistence of Racial Inequality in America.* Lanham, MD: Rowman & Littlefield.

Boser, U. (2014). Teacher Diversity Revisited: A New State-by-State Analysis. Washington, DC: Center for American Progress.

Bowles, S., & Gintis, H. (1976). *Schooling in Capitalist America: Educational Reform and the Contradictions of Economic Life.* New York: Basic Books.

Bradley, M. (1978). *The Iceman Inheritance: Prehistoric Sources of Western Man's Racism, Sexism and Aggression.* Toronto: Dorset Pub.

Brofenbrenner, U. (1979). *The Ecology of Human Development.* Cambridge, MA: Harvard University Press.

Browder, A. T. (1992). *Nile Valley Contribution to Civilization.* Beltsville, MD: International Graphics.

Bryk, A. S., Sebring, P. B., Allensworth, E., Luppescu, S. & Easton, J. Q. (2010). *Organizing Schools for Improvement: Lessons from Chicago.* Chicago, IL: University of Chicago Press.

Burks, B. S., Jensen, D. W., & Terman, L. M. (1930). *Genetic Studies of Genius: Volume III. The Promise of Youth: Follow-Up Studies of a Thousand Gifted Children.* Stanford, CA: Stanford University Press.

Catone, K. (2017). *The Pedagogy of Teacher Activism: Portraits of Four Teachers for Justice.* New York: Peter Lang.

Cherng, H. Y. S., & Halpin, P. F. (2016). The Importance of Minority Teachers: Student Perceptions of Minority Versus White Teachers. *Educational Researcher, 45*(7), 407–420.

Clarke, J. H. (1993). *African People in World History.* Baltimore, MD: Black Classic Press.

Coates, T. (2015). *Between the World and Me.* New York: Spiegel and Grau.

Coleman, J. S. (1966). "Equality and educational opportunity: Summary report." *United States Office of Education & National Center for Education Statistics.* Washington, DC: U.S. Dept. of Health Education and Welfare Office of Education.

Crenshaw, K. (1995). *Critical Race Theory: The Key Writings that Formed the Movement.* New York: The New Press.

Dance, L. J. (2002). *Tough Fronts: The Impact of Street Culture on Schooling.* New York: Routledge.

Darder, A. (2002). *Reinventing Paulo Freire: A Pedagogy of Love.* Cambridge, MA: Westview Press.

Darder, A., Baltodano, M., & Torres, R. (eds.) (2003). *The Critical Pedagogy Reader.* New York: Routledge Falmer.

Dee, T. S., & Penner, E. K. (2017). The Causal Effects of Cultural Relevance: Evidence from an Ethnic Studies Curriculum. *American Educational Research Journal, 54*(1), 127–166.

Dei, G. J. (1994). Afrocentricity: A Cornerstone of Pedagogy. *Anthropology and Education Quarterly, 25*(1), 2–28.

Dei, G. J. (1996). The Role of Afrocentricity in the Inclusive Curriculum in Canadian Schools. *Canadian Journal of Education, 21*(2), 170–186.

Dei, G. J. S. (2012). *Teaching Africa: Towards a Transgressive Pedagogy.* Dordrecht, the Netherlands: Springer.

Delpit, L. (1988). The Silenced Dialogue: Power and Pedagogy in Educating other people's children. *Harvard Educational Review, 58*(3), 280–299.

Delpit, L. (2006). *Other People's Children: Cultural Conflict in the Classroom.* New York: The New Press.

Diamond, J. B., Randolph, A., & Spillane, J. P. (2004). Teachers' Expectations and Sense of Responsibility for Student Learning: The Importance of Race, Class, and Organizational Habitus. *Anthropology & Education Quarterly, 35*(1), 75–98.

Dickson, V. E. (1920). What First-Grade Children Can Do in School as Related to What Is Shown by Mental Tests. *The Journal of Educational Research, 2*(1), 475–480.

Diop, C. A. (1974). *The African Origin of Civilization: Myth or Reality.* Westport, CT: Lawrence Hill.

Diop, C. A. (1991). *Civilization or Barbarism.* New York: Lawrence Hill.

Dixson, A. D., & Rousseau, C. K. (eds.) (2006). *Critical Race Theory in Education: All God's Children got a Song.* New York: Taylor & Francis.

Dumas, M. J. (2014). 'Losing an Arm': Schooling as a Site of Black Suffering. *Race Ethnicity and Education, 17*(1), 1–29.

Duncan-Andrade, J. (2009). Note to Educators: Hope Required when Growing Roses in Concrete. *Harvard Education Review, 79*(2), 181–194.

Evans-Winters, V. & Bettina L. (eds.) (2016). *Black Feminism in Education: Black Women Speak Back, Up and Out.* New York and Bern: Peter Lang.

Fanon, F. (1963). *The Wretched of the Earth: Pref. by Jean-Paul Sartre. Transl. by Constance Farrington.* London: Grove Press.

Fergus, E., Noguera, P., & Martin, M. (2014). *Schooling for Resilience: Improving the Life Trajectory of Black and Latino Boys.* Cambridge, MA: Harvard Education Press.

Ferguson, A. (2000). *Bad Boys: Public School in the Making of Black Masculinity.* Ann Arbor, MI: University of Michigan Press.

Foucault, M. (1975/1977). *Discipline and Punish, The Birth of The Prison,* trans. Alan Sheridan. Harmondsworth, UK: Penguin.

Frankenberg, R. (1996). When We are Capable of Stopping, We Begin to See: Being White, Seeing Whiteness. *Names we call home: Autobiography on racial identity,* 3–17.

Freire, P. (1970). *Pedagogy of the Oppressed.* New York: Continuum Publishing.

Freire, P. (1998). *Teachers as Cultural Workers.* Boulder, CO: Westview.

Freire, P. (2000). *Pedagogy of Freedom.* Lanham, MD: Rowman & Litttlefield.

Freire, P. & Macedo, D. (1987). *Literacy: Reading the Word and the World.* Connecticut and London: Bergin and Garvey.

Ferguson, A. (2001). *Bad Boys: Public School in the Making of Black Masculinity.* Ann Arbor, MI: University of Michigan Press.

Gay, G. (2014). Culturally Responsive Teaching Principles, Practices, and Effects. *Handbook of Urban Education,* 353–372.

Gay, G., & Howard, T. C. (2000). Multicultural Teacher Education for the 21st Century. *The Teacher Educator, 36*(1), 1–16.

Garfinkel, I., McLanahan, S. S., & Wimer, C. (eds.) (2016). *Children of the Great Recession.* New York: Russell Sage Foundation.

Geertz, Clifford. (1973) "Thick Description: Toward an Interpretative Theory of Culture". In The Interpretation of Cultures. New York: Basic Books.

Ginwright, S. (2004). *Black in School: Afrocentric Reform, Urban Youth, and the Promise of Hip-hop Culture.* New York: Teachers College Press.

Ginwright, S. (2010). *Black Youth Rising: Activism and Radical Healing in Urban America.* New York: Teachers College Press.

Ginwright, S., Noguera, P., & Cammarota, J. (eds.) (2006). *Beyond Resistance! Youth Activism and Community Change.* New York: Routledge.

Ginwright, S. A. (2015). Radically Healing Black Lives: A Love Note to Justice. *New directions for student leadership, 2015*(148), 33–44.

Giroux, H. (2010). Rethinking Education as the Practice of Freedom: Paulo Freire and the Promise of Critical Pedagogy. *Policy Futures in Education, 8*(6), 715–721.

Givens, J. R. (2016). *Culture, Curriculum, and Consciousness: Resurrecting the Educational Praxis of Dr. Carter G. Woodson, 1875–1950.* Dissertation submitted in partial satisfaction of the requirements for the degree of Doctor of Philosophy in African American Studies, UC Berkeley.

Givens, J. R., Nasir, N. I., & de Royston, M. M. (2016). Modeling Manhood: Reimagining Black Male Identities in School. *Anthropology & Education Quarterly, 47*(2), 167–185.

Gordon, B. M. (1990). The Necessity of African-American Epistemology for Educational Theory and Practice. *The Journal of Education, 172*(3), 88–106.

Gordon, R., Della Piana, L., & Keleher, T. (2000). Facing the Consequences. Washington, DC: Expose Racism and Advanced School Excellence Initiative (ERASE).

Gramsci, A. (1973). *Letters from Prison: Selected, Transl. from the Italian, and Introduced by Lynne Lawner.* New York: Harper & Row.

Greene, M. (2009). "In Search of a Critical Pedagogy." In Darder, A., Baltodano, M., & Torres, R. D. (2009). *The Critical Pedagogy Reader.* 2nd Ed. New York: Routledge

Gregory, A., Skiba, R. J., & Noguera, P. A. (2010). The Achievement Gap and the Discipline Gap: Two Sides of the Same Coin?. *Educational Researcher, 39*(1), 59–68.

Guha, R. (1983). Subaltern Studies II. *Writings on South Asian History and Society, Delhi, 1982–1989; Partha Chatterjee y Gyan Pandey (comps.), Subaltern Studies VII: Writings on South Asian History and Society, Delhi, 1992; David Arnold.*

Guha, R. (1999). *Elementary Aspects of Peasant Insurgency in Colonial India.* Duke University Press.

Hackman, H. W. (2005). Five Essential Components for Social Justice Education. *Equity & Excellence in Education, 38*(2), 103–109.

Hancock, S. D. & Warren, C. A. (eds.) (2017). *White Women's Work: Examining the Intersectionality of Teaching, Identity, and Race.* Charlotte, NC: Information Age Publishing.

Harding, H. A. (2005). "City girl": A Portrait of a Successful White Urban Teacher. *Qualitative Inquiry, 11*(1), 52–80.

Hilliard, A. G. (1998). *SBA: The Reawakening of the African Mind.* Gainesville, FL: Makare Pub Co.

hooks, b. (1994). *Teaching to Transgress: Education as the Practice of Freedom.* New York & London: Routledge.

hooks, b. (2003). *Teaching Community: A Pedagogy of Hope* (Vol. 36). New York: Psychology Press.

hooks, b. (2013). *Writing beyond Race: Living Theory and Practice.* New York & London: Routledge.

Horton, M., Bell, B., Gaventa, J., & Peters, J. M. (1990). *We Make the Road by Walking: Conversations on Education and Social Change.* Philadelphia: Temple University Press.

Howard, G. R. (2016). *We Can't Teach What We Don't Know: White Teachers, Multiracial Schools.* New York: Teachers College Press.

Howard, T. C. (2016). Why Black Lives (and Minds) Matter: Race, Freedom Schools & the Quest for Educational Equity. *The Journal of Negro Education, 85*(2), 101–113.

Howard, T.C. (2014). *Black Male(D): Peril and Promise in the Education of African American Males.* New York: Teachers College Press.

Howard, T. C. (2013). How Does It Feel to Be a Problem? Black Male Students, Schools, and Learning in Enhancing the Knowledge Base to Disrupt Deficit Frameworks. *Review of Research in Education, 37*(1), 54–86.

Howard, T.C. (2010). *Why race and culture matters in schools: Closing the achievement gap in America's classrooms.* New York: Teachers College Press.

Jackson, J. G. (1985). *Ethiopia and the Origin of Civilization*. Baltimore, MD: Black Classic Press.

James, G. G. (1954). *Stolen Legacy* (Vol. 1). Library of Alexandria.

King, J. E. (2005). *Black Education: A Transformative Research and Action Agenda for the New Century*. Mahwah, NJ: Lawrence Erlbaum.

King, J. E., Swartz, E. E., Campbell, L., Lemons-Smith, S., & López, E. (2014). *Re-membering History in Student and Teacher Learning: An Afrocentric Culturally Informed Praxis*. New York: Routledge.

Kock, L.D. (1992) Interview with Gayatri Chakravorty Spivak: New nation writers conference in South Africa. *A Review of International English Literature, 23*(3), 29–47.

Kunjufu, J. (1982). *Countering the Conspiracy to Destroy Black Boys*. Chicago, IL: African American Images.

Ladson-Billings, G. (1994). *The Dreamkeepers: Successful Teachers of African American Children*. San Francisco, CA: Jossey-Bass.

Ladson-Billings, G. (1995). But That's Just Good Teaching! The Case for Culturally Relevant Pedagogy. *Theory into Practice, 34*(3), 195–202.

Ladson-Billings, G., & Tate, W. F. (1995). Toward a Critical Race Theory of Education. *Teachers College Record, 97*(1), 47.

Lawrence-Lightfoot, S. (1983). *The Good High School*. New York: Basic Books.

Lawrence-Lightfoot, S. (1999). *Respect: An Exploration*. New York: Perseus Books.

Lawrence-Lightfoot, S., & Davis, J. (1997). *The Art and Science of Portraiture*. San Francisco, CA: Jossey-Bass.

LeCompte, M. (1993). *Ethnography and Qualitative Design in Educational Research*. 2nd ed. New York: Academic Press.

Leonardo, Z. (2009). *Race, Whiteness, and Education*. New York: Routledge.

Lewis, A. E., & Diamond, J. B. (2015). *Despite the Best Intentions: How Racial Inequality Thrives in Good Schools*. Oxford: Oxford University Press.

Lipman, P. (2011). *The New Political Economy of Urban Education: Neoliberalism, Race, and the Right to the City*. New York: Routledge.

Loewen, J. W. (1995). *Lies my Teacher Told Me: Everything your American History Textbook Got Wrong*. New York: The New Press

Lopez, I. F., & Lopez, I. H. (1997). *White by Law: The Legal Construction of Race*. New York: NYU Press.

Lynch, K., Baker, J., & Lyons, M. (2009). *Affective Equality: Love, Care and Injustice*. London: Palgrave Macmillan.

McIntosh, P. (2004). White Privilege: Unpacking the Invisible Knapsack. *Race, Class, and Gender in the United States, 6*, 188–192.

McLaren, P. (2016). Critical Pedagogy. *This Fist Called My Heart: The Peter McLaren Reader, Volume I*, 27.

MacLeod, J. (1995). *Ain't No Makin' It: Leveled Aspirations in a Low-Income Neighborhood*. Boulder, CO: Westview Press.

Madhubuti, H. R. (1990). *Black Men, Obsolete, Single and Dangerous?: Afrika Family in Transition*. Chicago, IL: Third World Press.

Mahiri, J. (1998). *Shooting for Excellence: African American and Youth Culture in New Century Schools*. New York: Teachers College Press.

Maxwell, J. A. (1996). *Qualitative Research Design: An Interactive Approach*. Thousand Oaks, CA: Sage Publications.

Maxell, J. (1992). Understanding and Validity in Qualitative Research in *Harvard Educational Review;* Fall 1992; *62*, 3; Research Library Core pg. 279.

Maykut, P. and Morehouse, R. (1994). *Beginning Qualitative Research: A Philosophic and Practical Guide.* London: Routledge.

Meiners, E. R., & Winn, M.T. (eds.) (2014). *Education and Incarceration.* New York: Routledge.

Miles, M. B., & Huberman, A. M. (1994). *Qualitative Data Analysis.* Thousand Oaks, CA: Sage.

Miles, M. B., Huberman, A. M., & Saldaña, J. (2014). *Qualitative Data Analysis: A Methods Sourcebook.* 3rd ed. California: SAGE.

Milner, H. R. (2013). Analyzing Poverty, Learning, and Teaching through a Critical Race Theory Lens. *Review of Research in Education, 37,* 1–53.

Monchinski, T. (2010). *Education in Hope: Critical Pedagogies and the Ethic of Care* (Vol. 382). New York: Peter Lang.

Monroe, C. R. (2005). Understanding the Discipline Gap through a Cultural Lens: Implications for the Education of African American Students. *Intercultural Education, 16,* 317–330. doi:10.1080/14675980500303795

Nasir, N. (2012). *Racialized Identitites: Race and Achievement Among African American Youth.* Stanford, CA: Stanford University Press.

Nasir, N. I. S., Ross, K. M., Mckinney de Royston, M., Givens, J., & Bryant, J. (2013). Dirt on My Record: Rethinking Disciplinary pPactices in an All-Black, All-male Alternative Class. *Harvard Educational Review, 83*(3), 489–512.

Nieto, S. (2013). *Finding Joy in Teaching Students of Diverse Backgrounds: Culturally Responsive and Socially Just Practices in U.S. Classrooms.* Portsmouth, NH: Heinemann.

Nobles, W.W. (1998). To be African or not to be: The question of identity or authenticity—Some preliminary thoughts. *African American identity development,* 185–205.

Nobles, W. (2006). *Seeking the Sakhu: Foundational Writings for an African Psychology.* Chicago, IL: Third World Press.

Noguera, P. (1995). Preventing and Producing Violence: A Critical Analysis of Responses to School Violence. *Harvard Educational Review, 65*(2), 189–213.

Noguera, P. (2003). *City Schools and the American Dream.* New York & London: Teachers College Press.

Noguera, P. (2008). *The Trouble with Black Boys:... And Other Reflections on Race, Equity, and the Future Of Public Education.* San Francisco, CA: Jossey-Bass.

Noguera, P. & Wells, L. (2011). The Politics of School Reform: A Broader and Bolder Approach for Newark. *Berkeley Review of Education, 2*(1).

Noguera, P. A. (2012). Saving Black and Latino Boys. *Education Week,* 693–703.

Oakes, J. (1985). *Keeping Track: How Schools Structure Inequality.* New Haven: Yale University Press.

Oakes, J., Lipton, M., Anderson, L., & Stillman, J. (2015). *Teaching to Change the World.* New York: Routledge.

Ogbu, J. U. (1991). Immigrant and involuntary minorities in comparative perspective. *Minority Status and Schooling: A Comparative Study of Immigrant and Involuntary Minorities,* 3–33.

Patel, L. (2016). *Decolonizing Educational Research: From Ownership to Answerability.* New York and London: Routledge.

Peller, G. (2012). *Critical Race Consciousness: Reconsidering American Ideologies of Racial Justice.* Boulder, CO: Paradigm Publishers.

Perry, T., Steele, C., & Hilliard, A. G. (2003). *Young, Gifted, and Black: Promoting High Achievement Among African-American Students.* Boston, MA: Beacon Press.

Picower, B., & Kohli, R. (eds.) (2017). *Confronting Racism in Teacher Education: Counternarratives of Critical Practice.* New York: Routledge

Pollard, D., & Ajirotutu, C. (2000). *African-Centered Schooling in Theory and Practice.* Westport, CT: Bergin & Garvey.

Pollock, M. (2004). *Colormute: Race Talk Dilemmas in an American School.* Princeton, NJ: Princeton University Press.

Powell, J. (2008). Post-Racialism or Targeted Universalism, *Denv. U. L. Rev., 86*, 785

Powell, J. (2010). Postracialism or Targeted Universalism. *Clearinghouse Rev., 44*, 62.

Powell, J. & Watt, C. (2009). Negotiating the New Political and Racial Environment. *JL Soc'y, 11*, 31.

Rodríguez, L. F. (2015). *Intentional Excellence: The Pedagogy, Power, and Politics of Excellence in Latina/o Schools and Communities.* Lang, Peter New York.

Rogers, J.A. (1972). *World's Great Men of Color.* New York: Macmillan Publishing Company.

Rosenthal, R. (1994). Interpersonal Expectancy Effects: A 30-Year Perspective. *Current Directions in Psychological Science, 3*(6), 176–179.

Rosenthal, R., & Jacobson, L. (1968). Pygmalion in the Classroom. *The Urban Review, 3*(1), 16–20.

Ross, K. M., Nasir, N. I. S., Givens, J. R., de Royston, M. M., Vakil, S., Madkins, T. C., & Philoxene, D. (2016). "I Do This for All of the Reasons America Doesn't Want Me To": The Organic Pedagogies of Black Male Instructors. *Equity & Excellence in Education, 49*(1), 85–99.

Rowe, A. C., & Tuck, E. (2017). Settler Colonialism and Cultural Studies: Ongoing Settlement, Cultural Production, and Resistance. *Cultural Studies↔Critical Methodologies, 17*(1), 3–13.

Scott, J. C. (1985). *Weapons of the Weak: Everyday Forms of Peasant Resistance.* New Haven, CT: Yale University Press.

Scott, J. C. (1990). *Domination and the Arts of Resistance: Hidden Transcripts.* New Haven, CT: Yale University Press.

Secada, W. G. (1989). Agenda Setting, Enlightened Self-interest, and Equity in Mathematics Education. *Peabody Journal of Education, 66*(2), 22–56.

Segarra, J. & Dobles, R. *Learning as a Political Act: Struggles for Learning and Learning from Struggles.* Cambridge, MA: Harvard Education Press.

Sertima, I.V. (1976). *They Came Before Columbus.* New York: Random House.

Sertima, I.V. (1992). *Golden Age of the Moor.* New Brunswick, NJ: Transaction Publishers.

Shor, I. (1992). *Empowering Education: Critical Teaching for Social Change.* Chicago, IL: University of Chicago Press.

Shor, I. & Freire, P. (1987). *A Pedagogy for Liberation: Dialogues on Transforming Education.* Westport, CT: Bergin & Garvey.

Shujaa, M. J. (1994). *Too Much Schooling, Too Little Education: A Paradox of Black Life in White Societies.* Trenton, NJ: Africa World Press.

Skiba, R., & Peterson, R. (2003). Teaching the Social Curriculum: School Discipline as Instruction. *Preventing School Failure: Alternative Education for Children and Youth, 47*(2), 66–73.

Solorzano, D., Ceja, M., & Yosso, T. (2000). Critical Race Theory, Racial Microaggressions, and Campus Racial Climate: The Experiences of African American College Students. *Journal of Negro Education*, 60–73.

Spivak, G. C. (1988). "Can the Subaltern Speak?" In *Marxism and the Interpretation of Culture.* Cary Nelson & Lawrence Grossberg (eds.). Pp. 271–313. Urbana, IL: University of Illinois Press.

Spivak, G. C. (2005). Scattered Speculations on the Subaltern and the Popular. *Postcolonial studies, 8*(4), 475–486.

Stigler, J., & Hiebert, J. (1999). *The Teaching Gap: Best Ideas from the World's Teachers for Improving Education in the Classroom.* New York: Free Press.

Strauss, A., & Corbin, J. (1998). *Basics of Qualitative Research: Techniques and Procedures for Developing Grounded Theory.* New York: Basic Books.

Terman, L. M. (1913). Psychological Principles Underlying the Binet-Simon Scale and Some Practical Considerations for Its Correct Use. *Journal of Psycho-Asthenics, 18,* 93–104.

Terman, L. M. (1915). The Mental Hygiene of Exceptional Children. *Pedagogical Seminary, 22,* 529–537.

Terman, L. M. (1919). *The Intelligence of School Children.* Boston, MA: Houghton Mifflin.

Terman, L. M. (1920). The Use of Intelligence Tests in the Grading Of School Children. *The Journal of Educational Research, 1*(1), 20–32.

Terman, L. M. (1924a). The Conservation of Talent. *School and Society, 19,* 359–364.

Terman, L. M. (1924b). Tests and Measurements Of Gifted Children. *Washington Education Journal, 3,* 172–190.

Terman, L. M. (1925). *Genetic Studies of Genius: Volume I. Mental and Physical Traits of a Thousand Gifted Children.* Palo Alto, CA: Stanford University Press.

Terman, L. (1959). The Gifted Group at Mid-Life: Thirty-Five Years Follow-Up of the Superior Child. Stanford, CA: Stanford University Press.

Terman, L. M., Dickson, V. E., Sutherland, A. H., Franzen, R. H., Tupper, C. R., & Fernald, G. M. (1922). *Intelligence Tests and School Reorganization.* World Book Company.

Thompson, S. (2016). Core Practices: Fuel Superintendents' Equity Focus. *Journal of Staff Development, 37*(6), 32–36.

Tillman, L. C. (2004). (Un) intended Consequences? The Impact of the Brown v. Board of Education Decision on the Employment Status of Black Educators. *Education and Urban Society, 36*(3), 280–303.

Tuck, E. (2009). Suspending Damage: A Letter to Communities. *Harvard Educational Review, 79*(3), 409–427.

Tuck, E., & Yang, K. W. (2014). R-words: Refusing Research. *Humanizing Research: Decolonizing Qualitative Inquiry with Youth and Communities,* 223–248.

Tuckman, B. (1999). *Conducting Educational Research,* 5th ed. Philadelphia: Harcourt Brace College.

Villegas, Ana María, and Irvine, Jacqueline Jordan. (2010) "Diversifying the Teaching Force: An Examination of Major Arguments." *The Urban Review, 42*(3), 175–192.

Warren, C. A. (2017). Empathy, Teacher Dispositions, and Preparation for Culturally Responsive Pedagogy. *Journal of Teacher Education,* doi: 0022487117712487.

Warren, M. (2005). Communities and Schools: A New View of Urban Education Reform. *Harvard Educational Review, 75*(2), 133–173.

Warren, M. R. (2010). *Fire in the Heart: How White Activists Embrace Racial Justice.* Oxford: Oxford University Press.

Warren, M. R. (2014). Transforming Public Education: The Need for an Educational Justice Movement. *New England Journal of Public Policy, 26*(1), 11.

Watson, V. (2012). *Learning to Liberate: Community-Based Solutions to the Crisis in Urban Education.* New York: Routledge.

Watson, V. (2013). Censoring Freedom: Community-Based Professional Development and the Politics of Profanity, *Equity & Excellence in Education, 46*:3, 387–410.

Watson, V. (2014). *The Black Sonrise: Oakland Unified School District's Commitment to Address and Eliminate Institutionalized Racism.* Final evaluation report submitted to Oakland

Unified School District's Office of African American Male Achievement. Retrieved from http://www.ousd.org/Page/12267

Watson, V. (2016). Literacy Is A Civil Write: The Art, Science And Soul of Transformative Classrooms. In *Social Justice Instruction: Empowerment on the Chalkboard*. Precis, Springer International Publishing For Book Series on Education, Equity and the Economy.

Watson, M. J., & Wiggan, G. (2016). Sankofa Healing and Restoration: A Case Study of African American Excellence and Achievement in an Urban School. *Journal of Pan African Studies, 9*(1), 113–141.

Welsing, F. C. (1991). *The Isis Papers*. Chicago, IL: Third World Press.

Williams, H. A. (2005). *Self-taught: African American Education in Slavery and Freedom*. Chapel Hill, NC: The University of North Carolina Press.

Willis, P. (1977). *Learning to Labor: How Working Class Kids get Working Class Jobs*. New York: Columbia University Press.

Windsor, R. R. (1969). *From Babylon to Timbuktu*. New York Exposition Press.

Woodson, C. G. (1933, 2006). *The Mis-Education of the Negro*. Eritrea, East Africa: The Associated Publishers.

Zinn, H. (1995). *A People's History of the United States 1492–Present*. New York: Harper Perennial.

INDEX

Note that numbers in bold refer to tables.